Germany's War and the Holocaust

D1564473

Germany's War and the Holocaust

DISPUTED HISTORIES

■

Omer Bartov

CORNELL
UNIVERSITY PRESS
Ithaca and
London

First published 2003 by Cornell University Press
First printing, Cornell Paperbacks, 2003

Printed in the United States of America

Library of Congress Cataloging-in-Publication Data

Bartov, Omer.
    Germany's war and the Holocaust : disputed histories /
Omer Bartov.
        p. cm.
    Includes bibliographical references and index.
    ISBN 978-0-8014-8681-4 (pbk. : alk. paper)
    1. Holocaust, Jewish (1939–1945)   2. World War, 1939–1945
—Germany.   3. Germany—Armed Forces—History—World
War, 1939–1945.   4. World War, 1939–1945—Campaigns—
Eastern Front—Atrocities.   5. National socialism—Historiog-
raphy.   6. War crimes.   7. World War, 1939–1945—Atroci-
ties.   I. Title.
    D804.3.B362 2003
    940.53'18—dc21

2002014121

Cornell University Press strives to use environmentally
responsible suppliers and materials to the fullest extent possible in the publishing of its books. Such materials include veg-
etable-based, low-VOC inks and acid-free papers that are
recycled, totally chlorine-free, or partly composed of non-
wood fibers. For further information, visit our website at
www.cornellpress.cornell.edu.

Paperback printing   10 9 8 7 6 5 4 3 2

For Shira and Rom

Contents

Introduction

In the last few years, three issues have been at the forefront of historical scholarship on modern Germany, and especially the Third Reich. First, the study of the Holocaust and other aspects of Nazi Germany's policies of mass murder has expanded enormously. Second, the relationship between the German military and the regime's policies of occupation, subjugation, "ethnic cleansing," and genocide has received increasing attention. And third, a growing volume of literature has focused on the impact of World War II and genocide on the formation of postwar identity and the politics of memory, especially in Germany, but also in many other European countries, the United States, and Israel.

Several events can serve to illustrate the new focus in research and writing on, as well as public interest in, the criminal nature of Germany's war between 1939 and 1945, the genocidal policies pursued by the Nazi regime, and the links between the two. One prominent example is the publication of and subsequent debate on Daniel Jonah Goldhagen's book, *Hitler's Willing Executioners.*[1] Based on the study of several reserve police units involved in the murder of thousands of Jews, an examination of a number of Nazi labor camps, and a reconstruction of some of the death marches during the last months of the war, the book argues that the Holocaust was the direct outcome of a uniquely German type of exterminationist antisemitism. Goldhagen insists on erasing the distinction between Nazis and Germans and asserts that by the time of the Third Reich, following a long process of an evolving culture of antisemitism, the vast majority of Germans would have been glad to participate in, and certainly supported, the elimination of the Jews of Europe.

This book unleashed a major scholarly and public debate in the

[1] D. J. Goldhagen, *Hitler's Willing Executioners: Ordinary Germans and the Holocaust* (New York, 1996).

United States and Britain and, even before its appearance in a German translation, dominated the academic and media scene in Germany for many months. Obviously, Goldhagen's thesis came very close to leveling a charge of collective guilt at the German people during the Hitler dictatorship, an argument that had been rejected by the majority of Germans and most foreign scholars for many years. At the same time, the book insisted on the centrality of antisemitism to the genocidal policies of the regime. This assertion refocused the debate on the nature of Nazism, which for the previous couple of decades had veered away from ideology and prejudice and insisted on structural factors as the main causes of Nazi policy.[2] Finally, the book insisted on observing the individual perpetrators (and, to a somewhat lesser extent, individual victims), and thereby reversed a trend that emphasized the bureaucratic and mechanical aspects of the killing process and greatly underplayed the individual identity and motivation of the killers.

The second and more or less simultaneous event had to do with the publication of the diaries of the philologist Victor Klemperer, a converted Jew married to an "Aryan" woman who spent the entire period of the Nazi dictatorship in Dresden, writing a highly detailed and perceptive account of these years in his diary.[3] This massive two-volume work competed with Goldhagen's book as one of the sensational best sellers of the 1990s in Germany. In some ways, Klemperer's diary presented precisely the opposite view, since it demonstrated both the stubborn patriotism of a man who was being persecuted by the regime for what it perceived as his alien nature, and at the same time provided numerous examples of German individuals who expressed sympathy for their Jewish neighbors and at times even came to their help. In another sense, however, Klemperer's diary offered the German public a new view of the reality of the Third Reich, since it was written by a highly articulate member of the German academic elite who simultaneously had been pushed to the margins of society and reported on its progressive deformation from within the belly of the beast. Rather than being either an account by an insider—which would have normally contained a great deal of conscious and unconscious apologetics—or by an outsider—who could not be expected to provide much insight into German society—this was an extraordi-

[2] For a review of these historiographical developments, see O. Bartov, ed., *The Holocaust: Origins, Implementation, Aftermath* (London, 2000), 1–18.

[3] V. Klemperer, *I Will Bear Witness*, 2 vols. (1995; New York, 1998–1999).

narily acute analysis of the day-to-day workings of German life under Hitler by the epitome of the insider transformed into the paradigmatic outsider.

Thus Klemperer's book refocused scholarly and public attention on the plight of German Jewry and the process whereby a small but significant segment of German society had been marginalized, ostracized, deported, and finally murdered in full view of their German co-citizens. Precisely Klemperer's patriotism and insistence on his Germanness compelled readers of this text to ponder how those who had contributed so much to German culture could have been stripped of their identity and handed over to the killers. In other words, Klemperer made the victim into a recognizable fellow German and thereby erased the barrier that had kept the victims of the regime more conveniently as alien foreigners and Jews.

The third event that marked the changing focus of scholarly research and public interest was the exhibition "War of Extermination: Crimes of the Wehrmacht, 1941–1944," which toured Germany and Austria throughout the second part of the 1990s and was viewed by close to a million visitors.[4] What made this exhibition into a major event was both the exhibit itself, which contained many hundreds of photographs, mostly taken by the perpetrators, of atrocities committed or facilitated by regular army soldiers, and the public debate that was unleashed repeatedly thanks to the fact that the exhibition moved from one town to the next. What many Germans found hard to take was that the exhibition demonstrated in the most graphic manner the complicity of Wehrmacht soldiers in the Holocaust and other crimes of the regime, especially in the occupied parts of the Soviet Union and Yugoslavia.

The army had long managed to protect itself from the charges of complicity with the Nazi regime that had been leveled at other agencies of the dictatorship. Although scholarship had begun exposing military involvement in Nazi policies as early as the 1960s, and with increasing momentum since the 1980s, the public at large often either

[4] For the exhibition catalogue, see *The German Army and Genocide: Crimes Against War Prisoners, Jews, and Other Civilians, 1939–1944*, ed. Hamburg Institute for Social Research (New York, 1999). For the accompanying volume of essays, see H. Heer and K. Naumann, eds., *War of Extermination: The German Military in World War II, 1941–1944* (1995; New York, 2000). For the debate over the exhibition and the larger context of war crimes, see O. Bartov, A. Grossmann, and M. Nolan, eds., *Crimes of War: Guilt and Denial in the Twentieth Century* (New York, 2002).

did not know about these specialized studies or preferred to ignore their implications.[5] The most obvious ramification of such revelations was—not unlike the somewhat less well documented charges made by Goldhagen—that the majority of Germans knew about the mass killing perpetrated by the regime and that large numbers of them actually took part in or directly facilitated the implementation of genocidal policies. Close to 20 million soldiers passed through the ranks of the Wehrmacht, that is, a vast proportion of men of military age out of a total population of some 80 million. These men either participated in numerous massacres or witnessed them at close quarters, and many of them are known to have reported such events, whether with fascination, glee, or horror, to their families in the rear. The implication of this was not only that Germans knew much more than they wanted to concede after the war, but that the young men who rebuilt both Germanys had shortly before been closely associated with genocide during their long years of service in uniform.

The exhibition was closed in November 1999 due to growing public pressure following the revelation that some—and as it turned out, very few—photographs had been mislabeled by the organizers. In particular, what helped the critics of the exhibition was that some photos were in fact not of the victims of the Wehrmacht but of men and women murdered by the NKVD, the Soviet secret police. This was quickly linked by some conservative critics to the more general assertion that rather than being a criminal organization, the Wehrmacht had merely reacted to and striven to protect Germany from the crimes of the Red Army and other Soviet agencies. This kind of logic had already been employed by German propaganda during World War II, arguing that it was necessary to invade and destroy the Soviet Union because otherwise the USSR would do the same to the German Reich.

In a sense, the debate over the Wehrmacht exhibition was indicative not only of the opening up of research and public interest, but also of its reverse, a conservative nationalist backlash that perceived scholarly endeavors to uncover the still hidden truths of Germany's war and its close links to genocide, and especially the public airing of such scholarly findings, as a threat to German identity, pride, and national reassertion following reunification. From this perspective, this was probably

[5] O. Bartov, "German Soldiers and the Holocaust: Historiography, Research, and Implications," in Bartov, *Holocaust*, 162–84.

the most important event of the three outlined above and, I might add, one that ended on an ambivalent note. The commission of experts appointed by the Hamburg Institute for Social Research that had organized the exhibition found that apart from very few errors, both the contents of the exhibition and its fundamental thesis regarding the complicity of the Wehrmacht in genocide were accurate and supported by a mass of scholarship.[6]

Nevertheless, the original exhibition was scrapped. Instead, a newly designed and differently titled exhibition opened in Berlin on November 28, 2001.[7] Thus, one can say that the conservative section of German academe and the media won a tactical victory. The shadow it cast over the veracity of the assertion of Wehrmacht complicity in genocide will suffice to keep the public uncertain as to who is right and to what extent current politics led to a manipulation of historical sources. That said, it is just as true that once aired in public, this issue will not go away. The sheer volume of publications these days indicates that the Holocaust, military crimes, and the links between them, are now at the center of scholarly work and will gradually seep into the public mind by means of a constant media interest in these issues.[8]

The exhibition "Crimes of the Wehrmacht" was very much a German affair. Indeed, although the exhibition was expected to come to the United States in late 1999, its visit was canceled due to the scandal about the labeling of its photographs. The Klemperer diaries were also primarily a German affair, although their publication in an English translation aroused a fair amount of interest. Conversely, Goldhagen's book was one of those periodic interventions of foreign scholarship and other forms of representation, especially where Nazism and the Holocaust are concerned, that have shaped German debates and public perception. In this sense, *Hitler's Willing Executioners* may be compared to the television mini-series *Holocaust* of the late 1970s and the film *Schindler's List* of the early 1990s.

---

[6] O. Bartov, C. Brink, G. Hirschfeld, F. P. Kahlenberg, M. Messerschmidt, R. Rürup, C. Streit, H.-U. Thamer, *Bericht der Kommission zur Überprüfung der Ausstellung "Vernichtungskrieg. Verbrechen der Wehrmacht 1941 bis 1944"* (Hamburg Institute for Social Research, November 15, 2000).

[7] See the new exhibition catalogue, *Verbrechen der Wehrmacht: Dimensionen des Vernichtungskrieges 1941–1944*, ed. Hamburg Institut für Sozialforschung (Hamburg, 2002).

[8] See R.-D. Müller and H-.E. Volkmann, eds., *Die Wehrmacht: Mythos und Realität* (Munich, 1999).

Other influential and widely-read works of scholarship that indicate a constant interest in Nazism and the shift toward themes of genocide and its links to Germany's war in the East were also written by non-German scholars. These include the massive new biography of Hitler written by the British historian Ian Kershaw, the first volume by the Israeli-American scholar Saul Friedländer of his study on Nazi Germany and the Jews, and the similarly bulky general history of the Third Reich by Michael Burleigh.[9] Despite the many differences between these new studies, what distinguishes them from previous scholarship—and in some ways links them to much earlier works that stressed the role of the Führer, ideological intention, and the pseudo-religious nature of both Nazism and antisemitism[10]—is their focus both on the Holocaust and on the war.

Thus Kershaw's biography of Hitler devotes much greater space to the Führer's role as supreme warlord of Germany in the latter phases of World War II than earlier works; Friedländer's study not only focuses on the beginning of Nazi anti-Jewish policies in the 1930s but also locates these policies at the center of the Nazi state and insists on the importance of the relationship between the regime and the Jews; and Burleigh's history of the Third Reich heavily stresses the regime's criminality quite apart from asserting that Nazism served as a kind of ersatz religion, a political faith whose core was extreme violence and destructiveness.[11] We can thus conclude that the general drift of scholarly and public interest has been to refocus attention on the links between Germany's war and the Holocaust.

Finally, it is necessary to point out the tremendous expansion of interest we have recently witnessed in the impact of Germany's war and the Holocaust on subsequent generations and on reformulations of collective and individual identity. The debates mentioned above all contained elements of this politics of memory even as they simultaneously played a major role in enhancing our understanding of the past. Indeed, they demonstrated the close relationship between views of the

[9] I. Kershaw, *Hitler,* 2 vols. (New York, 1999–2000); S. Friedländer, *Nazi Germany and the Jews,* vol. 1 (New York, 1997); M. Burleigh, *The Third Reich: A New History* (New York, 2000).

[10] K. Heiden, *Der Fuehrer: Hitler's Rise to Power* (Boston, 1944); L. Poliakov, *Harvest of Hate: The Nazi Program for the Destruction of the Jews of Europe* (Philadelphia, 1954); J. P. Stern, *Hitler: The Führer and the People* (Glasgow, 1975).

[11] See also O. Bartov, "A Man Without Qualities," *TNR* (March 12, 2001): 34–40; Bartov, "Hitler's Willing Believers," *TNR* (November 20, 2000): 29–38.

past and the perceptions, ideologies, and politics of the present. Historical interpretations are always dependent on present circumstances, just as contemporary perceptions rely on views of the past.

Several major events in recent years indicate the centrality of the past for the politics of the present and the major role played by the politics of memory in molding current national identities. These include the on-going debate over the memorial to the Jews murdered in the Holocaust and over the Jewish museum, both in Berlin; a string of controversies over memory, commemoration, and complicity in France; and, most recently, the revelations of Polish civilian complicity in the genocide of the Jews and its implications for Poland's suppression of its role as an active participant in the persecution of its Jewish population and the need to reforge the nation's memory of German occupation which, until now, presented it exclusively as a victim of Nazism.[12] To this might be added a series of debates during the last few years in Israel about the manner in which the Holocaust was exploited in earlier political rhetoric, education, fiction, and scholarly literature in order to legitimize Zionism; the extent to which the *Yishuv*—the pre-state Jewish community in Palestine—came to the rescue of Jews during the Holocaust; and the terms under which the survivors of the Holocaust were absorbed into Israeli society, which required the erasure or suppression of memory as a precondition to rapid transformation into newborn Israelis.[13] All these issues, which can only be hinted at here, demonstrate the centrality of the Holocaust and the war conducted by Germany to a vast and varied number of individuals and communities, including, as has recently been argued, the United States and especially its Jewish population.[14]

The present volume offers a critical analysis of this recent literature on and interpretations of the links between Germany's war of destruction, the genocidal policies of the Nazi regime, and the reconstruction of German and Jewish identities in the wake of the catastrophe. Based on

[12] C. Wiedmer, *The Claims of Memory: Representations of the Holocaust in Contemporary Germany and France* (Ithaca, 1999); N. Wood, *Vectors of Memory: Legacies of Trauma in Postwar Europe* (Oxford, 1999); J. T. Gross, *Neighbors: The Destruction of the Jewish Community in Jedwabne, Poland* (Princeton, 2001).

[13] T. Segev, *The Seventh Million: The Israelis and the Holocaust* (New York, 1993); Y. Gutman, ed., *Major Changes Within the Jewish People in the Wake of the Holocaust* (Jerusalem, 1996); in Hebrew.

[14] P. Novick, *The Holocaust in American Life* (Boston, 1999).

previously published but substantially revised and in part consolidated articles and essays, this collection will guide readers through the
myriad scholarship and debates on a crucial period in the twentieth
century whose repercussions are still very much present today.

The complex connections between modern military confrontations
and a wide array of policies toward civilian populations should be self-
evident to anyone who surveys the last century. Such state-organized
actions range from so-called "population policies" and "ethnic cleansing" to systematic incarceration in concentration camps, from the
forced recruitment or enslavement of labor to mass murder. Policies of
exploitation, subjugation, and genocide tend to take place under the
cover of war; modern warfare, in turn, often produces and motivates
widespread violence against civilian populations as a means to annihilate the enemy totally and destroy his ability to wage war again.[15]
Moreover, while attempts to come to terms with past catastrophe, to
explain it to later generations, and to derive from it some meaning and
lessons for the future, can help prevent its recurrence, they may also
provide arguments for similar actions against the real or imagined perpetrators of previous disasters. In other words, the confrontation with
man-made catastrophe can help us understand the roots and nature of
this century's destructive urges as well as humanity's extraordinary
recuperative capacities; but it can also legitimize the perpetuation of
violence and aggression.[16]

This book attempts to view this complex historical development
from three distinct but closely related perspectives. Part 1 probes the
nature of German warfare in World War II, the extent to which it exemplified the evolution of modern war and its links to genocide, and
the predilection of both its contemporary and subsequent representations to create an image of war combining romantic recollections and
technological prowess that masked the realities of mass destruction.
Chapter 1 thus examines German warfare in the East as an inherent element in mass murder, and considers the relationship between the
complicity of the Wehrmacht in genocide and the postwar myth of

[15] N. M. Naimark, *Fires of Hatred: Ethnic Cleansing in Twentieth-Century Europe*
(Cambridge, Mass., 2001); A. Weiner, *Landscaping the Human Garden* (Stanford, 2002);
J. Kotek and P. Rigoulot, *Le siècle des camps: Détention, concentration, extermination* (Paris,
2000).

[16] O. Bartov, *Mirrors of Destruction: War, Genocide, and Modern Identity* (New York,
2000).

army resistance to Hitler. Chapter 2 investigates the image of Blitzkrieg as a means to glorify war, debilitate the enemy, and evade the realities of exterminatory warfare both during and after the event. By way of illustration, this chapter then evaluates the successes and failures of German historiography to confront the links between the Wehrmacht and the crimes of the Nazi regime.

Part 2 turns to several new attempts to analyze the roots and nature of Nazi Germany's extermination policies. Chapter 3 examines the suggestion that the Holocaust was closely linked to the Nazi regime's plan to radically transform the demographic structure of Eastern Europe and Western Russia. This thesis, asserted most forcefully by the German historian Götz Aly, presents the "final solution of the Jewish question" as merely an element in a much grander scheme, the so-called *Generalplan Ost*, intended to depopulate Germany's new "living space" (*Lebensraum*) of its Slav and Jewish inhabitants and to colonize it with "Aryans" from the Reich and ethnic Germans from beyond its rapidly expanding borders. This project failed because, contrary to German expectations, the Red Army did not collapse; hence only one component of the plan was carried out, namely, the mass extermination of the Jews.[17] This chapter scrutinizes the merits and limitations of such a contextualization of the Holocaust. It welcomes the recognition of the links between Germany's war, its "population policies," and the Final Solution, but it also questions the extent to which Nazi demographic schemes can be viewed as the primary cause of the genocide of the Jews.

Chapter 4 addresses another set of arguments about the nature of Nazi extermination policies, this time concerning the concentration camp system. Here I juxtapose two recent interpretive paradigms that offer a revision of conventional views about the structure, functioning, and goals of the Nazi "concentrationary universe." For the German sociologist Wolfgang Sofsky, the concentration camp was a site in which absolute power gained total autonomy from its original ideological legitimization and contemporary political context.[18] Predicated on an "ideal type" of the concentration camp, this sociological analysis is highly informative regarding the basic dynamics of camp society, whereby utter brutality and violence toward the inmates was com-

---

[17] G. Aly, *"Final Solution": Nazi Population Policy and the Murder of the European Jews* (1995; New York, 1999).

[18] W. Sofsky, *The Order of Terror: The Concentration Camp* (1993; Princeton, 1997).

bined with an effort to gain the collaboration of certain categories of prisoners by offering them positions of power over their fellow inmates. Nevertheless, this chapter criticizes Sofsky's view of the camps as distinct and separate from the rest of society; such a view, I argue, misses the crucial originating and motivating factors without which we cannot understand the establishment, evolution, and subsequent representation of the system as a whole. Moreover, this focus on a view from within of a certain type of camp as representative of the whole leads to a failure on Sofsky's part to integrate the genocide of the Jews into this sociological model of isolated sites of "absolute power." The second part of this chapter levels a similar critique at a massive new collection of articles on the concentration camps, which can be seen as representative of recent German historical research on and interpretations of the Nazi system.[19] Many essays in these volumes are based on rich documentation culled from newly opened archival holdings in Eastern Europe and Russia. By carefully reconstructing the historical record of the camps, the authors seek to demonstrate that earlier conventions about the nature of the system, as well as such sociological models as that developed by Sofsky, can no longer be accepted without major modifications. However, as this chapter shows, most of these historians also fail to integrate their local analyses of concentration camps into the larger picture of Nazi Germany's racial and genocidal policies. Furthermore, while they acknowledge the unique role allotted to the Jews by the regime as its primary target, their choice of camps and perspective of analysis implicitly or explicitly diverts our attention to other sites and protagonists.

Chapter 5 looks at the recent attempt by Daniel Jonah Goldhagen to offer a monocausal interpretation of the Holocaust.[20] As noted above, while most scholars believe that the genocide of the Jews must be traced back to the highly complex dynamics and mechanisms of a modern bureaucratic state, Goldhagen's argument aroused a great deal of attention precisely because it proposed a simple and all-encompassing explanation both for the origins of the Holocaust and for the willingness of its perpetrators to carry it out. By asserting that the Holocaust was the direct consequence of long-term German "eliminationist" antisemitism, transformed under the Nazi regime into an "ex-

---

[19] U. Herbert, K. Orth, and C. Dieckmann, eds., *Die nationalsozialistischen Konzentrationslager: Entwicklung und Struktur*, 2 vols. (Göttingen, 1998).
[20] Goldhagen, *Willing Executioners*.

terminationist" mode, Goldhagen suggested that all Germans were, at least potentially, willing perpetrators. To be sure, such arguments were made already in the immediate aftermath of the war.[21] But as I argue in this chapter, these explanations miss the crucial historical context within which genocide occurs, just as much as they tend to ignore the specificity of the Holocaust's features as an unprecedented case of modern industrialized mass killing.

The question whether we can think of most Germans as having been (potentially) Nazis has exercised the minds of scholars, politicians, and laymen alike ever since the heyday of Hitler's rule. Part 3 of the book is therefore devoted to several paradigmatic interpretations of the Nazi period, its aftermath, and its implications for postwar self-perceptions and national identities. Chapter 6 offers a comprehensive analysis of the reception of Goldhagen's book in several countries. Precisely thanks to its radical assertions, the reception of *Hitler's Willing Executioners* can serve as a prism through which we may gauge the perception of the Nazi period and the manner in which it has been interpreted by and integrated into a variety of national contexts. Here I am not interested in the author's arguments per se, but rather in how the public discourse on the book reflected differing views and prejudices about the effects—or lack thereof—of Nazi rule and genocide on the reconstruction of postwar existence. I show that while both Americans and Germans were intensely interested in the book, the former saw it as *confirming* their negative opinions about Germans and their positive view of themselves, whereas the latter largely perceived it as *undermining* long-held prejudices and as releasing deeply repressed emotions. Conversely, I argue that while both in France and in Israel the public remained relatively indifferent to the book, despite the media hype that surrounded it, the reasons for this indifference were strikingly different. The French were far too involved in their own debate on Vichy to become interested in a text that merely repeated their anti-German prejudices, whereas many Israelis were irritated by a young American presenting as new an assertion they had heard *ad nauseam* from local scholars and survivors. Moreover, Israeli intellectuals feared that this international best seller on Jewish victimhood under Nazi rule would be used as yet another instrument to justify what they saw as objectionable policies of occupation by their government.

---

[21] I. Kershaw, *The Nazi Dictatorship*, 3ᵈ ed. (London, 1993), chap. 5.

Hence by examining the reception of Goldhagen's book we can learn a great deal about the extent to which World War II, Nazism, and the Holocaust play a role in the self-perception and identity of Europeans, Israelis, and Americans. This chapter concludes with an analysis of Stanley Milgram's well-known behaviorist theories, which were repeatedly cited during the Goldhagen debate. Here I point out that while Milgram was said to provide an ideologically neutral explanation of human conduct in extreme situations, his findings were in fact seriously skewed by the prejudices that guided the manner in which he evaluated the subjects of his experiment.

A very different view of Germany under the Nazi regime can be found in the recently published diaries of the German-Jewish scholar Victor Klemperer, to which I have already referred. Many commentators have described this massive and meticulous record of daily life in the Third Reich as the ultimate proof that Goldhagen's assertions about the intensity of German antisemitism are false. Yet, as I argue in chapter 7, while Klemperer was deeply attached to Germany and to what he termed his own "Germanness," and did indeed record various instances of sympathy by non-Jews, his diaries are nevertheless a singular chronicle of German society's progressive Nazification, partly through gradual adoption of the regime's ideology, sometimes for the most petty or opportunistic reasons, with disastrous consequences ultimately for Germany and, even more drastically, its victims. Moreover, I aver that at the core of Klemperer's diaries is not only a statement on the Germans but also on the intense patriotism, loyalty, and subsequent deep sense of betrayal felt by so many German Jews. For Klemperer, who exemplified most dramatically this tragic condition, it was his "Aryan" neighbors, colleagues, and friends who finally appeared as far less German than himself, since they adopted or at least accommodated themselves to Nazism, seen by him as inherently "un-German."

German Jews such as Klemperer could think of themselves as the last Germans in a land whose population had shed all attributes of "Germanness." Conversely, as I assert in the closing chapter, postwar Germans who perceived themselves as the unacknowledged victims of a catastrophe visited upon them through no fault of their own, constructed their model of victimhood by allusion to the fate of the Jews. In the first decades of their existence, both Germanys were reluctant to dwell on the actual mass murder of European Jewry; there was, in that sense, an acute absence of representation of prewar Jewish presence and wartime Jewish "removal" in much of German historiography, film, and literature. And yet, when Germans searched for a way to represent their own pain, loss, and suffering (often allegedly denied them because of their victimization of others), they could not but refer indirectly to what gradually came to be seen as the ultimate example of the victim, namely, the Jews. This is what I call the representation of absence: the predilection of German historians, filmmakers, novelists, to construct their own fate in the image of Germany's most notable victims. While this tendency was diminishing since the 1980s, there is increasing evidence that following reunification it is once more on the rise. From this perspective, therefore, the manner in which Germans are still trying to come to terms with (or to make use of) the "disappearance" of the Jews from their midst without directly referring to it, may serve us as yet another key to understanding German self-perceptions at the turn of the century.

PART ONE

War of Destruction

[1]

Savage War

GERMAN WARFARE AND MORAL CHOICES IN WORLD WAR II

THE REALITIES OF WARFARE

Between 1941 and 1945 the Third Reich conducted the most savage military campaign in modern history. The invasion of the Soviet Union, code-named "Operation Barbarossa," cost the lives of some 24 million Soviet citizens,[1] well over half of whom were civilians, and devastated vast areas of western Russia from Leningrad in the north to Stalingrad in the south. Over three million Red Army prisoners of war, or 60 percent of the overall number of Soviet soldiers captured, died in German captivity. Although the Soviet Union emerged from the war as a military superpower, it took decades to recover from the human tragedy and economic disaster of the German occupation.[2]

The German war in Russia raises a number of important questions, relevant both to the history of the Third Reich as a whole and to the history of modern warfare. First, why was "Barbarossa" conducted in such a savage manner, and what ends was this policy expected to serve? Second, to what degree did the units fighting at the front participate in the murderous actions of the regime? Third, was the war in the East indeed a unique and unprecedented phenomenon in modern history by comparison to other instances of brutal warfare?

Conception

War played a central role in Nazi ideology. It was no coincidence that Hitler called his book *Mein Kampf*, that is, "my battle." According to

[1] R. Overy, *Russia's War* (New York, 1998), 287–89.

[2] O. Bartov, *Hitler's Army: Soldiers, Nazis, and War in the Third Reich* (New York, 1991); G. Hirschfeld, ed., *The Policies of Genocide: Jews and Soviet Prisoners of War in Nazi Germany* (London, 1986).

the Nazi world-view, life consisted of a constant struggle for survival, in which the best would win, or rather, in which the very fact of victory and survival would show the inherent physical and spiritual superiority of the winner, on the one hand, and the inferiority and moral depravity of the vanquished, on the other. Traditional norms of behavior, ethical conventions, and legal restrictions had nothing to do with this eternal battle; all that mattered was survival through victory and total annihilation of the enemy. Conversely, battle did have a profound ennobling effect, for in it the best qualities of the individual were called forth and the nation was purged of all slackness and degeneration. Thus war was not merely an inevitable condition, but also a necessary and welcome one. War forged a community of battle, a *Kampfgemeinschaft,* which in turn would produce the community of the people, the *Volksgemeinschaft,* that Nazi ideal of a racially pure, militarized, fanatically determined society, where affinities of blood and endless conquest would compensate for class inequality and lack of political freedom.

The ideal war, according to Hitler, was one of conquest, subjugation, and extermination, and the ideal area in which to conduct such a war was in the East, where the German people would win for itself the living space, or *Lebensraum,* necessary for its moral and racial purity, as well as for its ultimate emergence as the master race (*Herrenvolk*) of Europe and Asia, if not indeed the whole world.[3] However, due to political and military constraints, this ideal could not be immediately realized. Before turning to the East, the Third Reich first had to make certain that its western flank was secure. Germany had experienced a two-front war between 1914 and 1918, and Hitler was determined to prevent a recurrence of such a hopeless strategic situation. Also, while the western powers were quite willing to let Germany fight it out with Bolshevik Russia, Stalin was unwilling to take the main brunt of Nazi military might and concluded a pact with Hitler which enabled the Third Reich first to smash Poland and divide its territory with the USSR, and then to turn against France.

The fighting in the West was inherently different from what was soon to be seen in the East. This had to do both with ideological determinants and with political calculation. Nazi racial theory placed the Jews at the very bottom of the biological ladder: they were to be sim-

---

[3] E. Jäckel, *Hitler's World View: A Blueprint for Power* (Cambridge, Mass., 1981).

ply done away with, whether by exclusion and expulsion (as was done in the early years of the regime) or by extermination, which began to be practiced on a mass scale simultaneously with the attack on the Soviet Union. Only slightly higher were the Slavs, who were considered as subhumans (*Untermenschen*), to be murdered, worked, and starved to death, or used as slave labor for the German colonizers of their lands.[4] As for the French, and even more so the English, Nazi racial "experts" remained rather vague, whether because of what they perceived as racial affinities with the German "Aryans," or because of the "higher" culture of Western Europe. Thus, while France was seen as a "degenerate" or "decadent" civilization, it was not marked for subjugation, but rather for a secondary role in the Nazi scheme of a German-dominated Europe. Politically, Hitler was always keen on reaching some settlement with the British, both because of his ambiguous view of the "Anglo-Saxon race," and because of his fear of a two-front war. Consequently, the German army fighting in the West was given strict orders to conduct itself according to the rules of war. This was easier also because the average German soldier had far fewer prejudices about the French and the English than about the Russians, and because Western Europe seemed to him more similar to his homeland than the Russia he was soon to invade.[5]

Once France was defeated, and following Hitler's realization that he would be able neither to persuade the British to reach an agreement with Germany nor to destroy British military strength whether from the air or by a landing from the sea, the German army was given orders to prepare for an invasion of the Soviet Union. Now at last Hitler could have the war of destruction (*Vernichtungskrieg*) and ideologies (*Weltanschauungskrieg*) he had always wanted to fight. In this he was far from alone, for his generals were in full agreement with the need to conduct a wholly different kind of war against what they called "Judeo-Bolshevism" and the "Asiatic hordes" of the East.

The "Barbarossa Decree" was composed of the operational orders for the attack on the Soviet Union, as well as of what have come to be called the "criminal orders," a set of instructions regarding the manner in which the army was to conduct itself during the campaign.

[4] For a more complex analysis of Nazi attitudes to Slavs, see J. Connelly, "Nazis and Slavs: From Racial Theory to Racist Practice," *CEH* 32, no.1 (1999): 1–33.

[5] On Hitler's wartime policies see I. Kershaw, *Hitler*, 2 vols. (New York, 1999–2000). On discipline in the Wehrmacht, see Bartov, *Hitler's Army*, 59–105.

These included the infamous "commissar order," calling for the immediate execution of all Red Army political officers captured by frontline units; the curtailment of military jurisdiction, which stipulated that soldiers could not be tried for offenses committed against enemy soldiers and civilians as long as they did not thereby impinge on combat discipline; regulations regarding the behavior of soldiers in the occupied territories, which called for ruthless punitive action against guerrillas and anyone assisting them, as well as against members of the Communist Party and Jews; and orders for the army closely to collaborate with, and furnish military and logistical assistance to, the *Einsatzgruppen* (death squads) of the SS, whose task was the mass murder of Jews and all other Soviet citizens belonging to "biological" and political categories deemed unworthy of life by the authorities of the Third Reich.[6]

To these orders the army added a series of logistical instructions, based on the assumption that in order to conduct a rapid campaign deep into Russia the units should not be hampered by a cumbersome supply apparatus, whose maintenance was expected to confront numerous difficulties because of the Soviet Union's primitive transportation infrastructure and a serious shortage of vehicles in the Wehrmacht. The conclusion was that, as far as possible, the army should sustain itself from the resources of the (often wretchedly poor) occupied population, with scant regard for the obvious repercussions this policy would have on the civilians' chances of survival. Moreover, the cold utilitarian calculation of operational efficiency was allied with the determination of the Nazi leadership not to allow any undue hardship among the German population in the rear as a result of the war, thereby preventing the outbreak of protests and demoralization of the kind that had swept Germany during the latter phases of World War I. Consequently, the army and the civilian administrative authorities that followed it into the Soviet Union, were ordered to exploit the agricultural, industrial, and demographic resources of the occupied territories to the benefit of Germany. It was estimated that this would cause the death by deprivation of tens of millions of Russians; this was greeted with satisfaction in view of the perceived need to "depopulate" the eastern *Lebensraum* so as to make it ripe for German colonization.[7]

6 C. Streit, *Keine Kameraden*, 2d ed. (Bonn, 1991), 28–61.
7 R.–D. Müller, "From Economic Alliance to a War of Colonial Exploitation," in *The*

Closely tied to the military aspects of the operation was the decision to use this opportunity to "eliminate" European Jewry once and for all, a policy given official sanction during the Wannsee Conference of January 20, 1942, during which the work of the various agencies involved in the "Final Solution" was brought under the overall control of the SS six months after the attack on Russia was launched.[8] The so-called "Final Solution of the Jewish Question" by mass, industrial murder of the Jewish population of Europe, could hardly have taken the form which characterized it between 1941 and 1945 had the Wehrmacht not created the necessary military, logistical, demographic, and psychological preconditions for its implementation by its invasion of the Soviet Union and the vicious war it conducted there.

Thus it is clear that "Barbarossa" was conceived as an ideological war of extermination and enslavement; its goal was to wipe out the Soviet state, to enslave the Russian people after debilitating them by famine and all other forms of deprivation, systematically to murder all "biological" and political enemies of Nazism, such as the Jews, the Gypsies, members of the Communist Party, intellectuals, and so forth, and finally to turn western Russia into a German paradise of "Aryan" colonizers served by hordes of Slav helots.

Implementation

For many years after World War II it was commonly assumed that although the Nazi regime was obviously criminal and had made use of murderous organizations such as the SS to carry out its policies of extermination, the army was not involved in such actions and in many ways resisted them, or at least kept itself in a position of critical isolation from the more unsavory aspects of Nazi rule. More recent scholarship, however, has shown this to be an entirely erroneous view, based mainly on apologetic postwar literature by German veterans and its indiscriminate acceptance by Western military historians who remained quite ignorant of the realities of the Eastern Front and tried

Attack on the Soviet Union, vol. 4 of *Germany and the Second World War (GSWW)*, ed. Militärgeschichtliches Forschungsamt (Oxford, 1998), 118–224. C. Gerlach, *Kalkulierte Morde: Die deutsche Wirtschafts- und Vernichtungspolitik in Weißrußland 1941 bis 1944* (Hamburg, 1999).

[8] See now C. Gerlach, "The Wannsee Conference, the Fate of German Jews, and Hitler's Decision in Principle to Exterminate All European Jews," in *The Holocaust: Origins, Implementation, Aftermath*, ed. O. Bartov (London, 2000), 106–61; M. Roseman, *The Wannsee Conference and the Final Solution* (New York, 2002).

to apply their experience in the West to the totally different conditions that reigned in Russia between 1941 and 1945.

The fact of the matter is that once "Barbarossa" was launched on June 22, 1941, the German combat troops on the ground showed little reluctance, indeed often demonstrated much enthusiasm, in carrying out the "criminal orders" issued by the regime and the high command of the army. Nor did the field commanders do much to restrain the troops; quite to the contrary, in many cases formation commanders exhorted their soldiers to act with even greater ferocity and determination against the "racial" and political enemies of the Reich. Such generals as Walther von Reichenau, Erich von Manstein, and Hermann Hoth appealed to their troops in October and November 1941 to remember that the "Jewish-Bolshevik system must be eradicated once and for all," that the German soldier is "a carrier of an inexorable racial conception and the avenger of all the bestialities which have been committed against the Germans and related races," and that he must therefore have *"complete* understanding for the necessity of the harsh, but just atonement of Jewish subhumanity."[9]

The enormous death toll among the Russian prisoners of war and civilian population was thus a direct result not merely of the heavy fighting but to a large extent of the implementation of Nazi policies in the occupied regions of the Soviet Union. Hitler had stated unambiguously before the campaign that German troops should not recognize their Soviet enemies as "comrades in arms"; there were to be, in his words, *keine Kameraden*. Consequently, in the first few months of fighting, the Wehrmacht shot out of hand thousands of commissars and handed over to the SD (the security service of the SS) for execution at least 140,000 Soviet political officers, and most likely a far larger number. By the end of the first winter in Russia some two million Soviet prisoners were already dead, mostly due to starvation and exposure. Unlike the Western campaign, the Wehrmacht had made no provisions for the large number of prisoners it expected to capture thanks to its tactics of encirclement. Instead, captured Red Army troops were marched hundreds of miles to the rear or transported in open freight trains in midwinter. Those who survived were then herded into empty fields surrounded by barbed wire and armed guards and allowed to starve to death. The troops became so used to

[9] Bartov, *Hitler's Army*, 129–31.

this treatment of Soviet soldiers as *Untermenschen* that even when the orders were changed due to the decision to conscript prisoners for forced labor in the Reich, they refused to relent and kept shooting them out of hand against the express orders of their direct superiors.[10]

As the logistical situation of the Wehrmacht deteriorated during autumn and winter 1941, the troops were ordered to resort to extensive requisitions, which stripped the population of its last reserves of food and caused widespread famine and death. Intensified guerrilla activity against the Wehrmacht, caused not least by desperation occasioned by the horrifying conditions in occupied Russia, brought brutal retaliatory measures which included not merely the hanging of anyone suspected of partisan activity, but also the destruction of thousands of villages and the murder of their inhabitants as part of a policy of collective punishment. Following the Red Army's counter-offensive of December 1941, and thereafter whenever the Wehrmacht was forced to retreat, German combat units resorted to a policy of "scorched earth" which devastated vast regions of abandoned territory and led to the death by deprivation of whoever was not killed right away by the withdrawing troops or sent back to the Reich as slave labor.[11]

Uniqueness

This brings us to the question of comparability and uniqueness, a key element in what has come to be known as the process of "coming to terms with the past" (or as the Germans call it, *Vergangenheitsbewälti- gung*, roughly translated as "overcoming the past").[12] This somewhat ambiguous term stands for the complex confrontation between personal and collective national memory (and its repression), on the one hand, and the memory (or amnesia) of individuals and groups be-

[10] Streit, *Keine Kameraden*, 105, 136; C. Streit, "Soviet Prisoners of War in the Hands of the Wehrmacht," in H. Heer and K. Naumann, eds., *War of Extermination: The German Military in World War II, 1941–1944* (1995; New York, 2000), 80–91; O. Bartov, *The Eastern Front, 1941–45: German Troops and the Barbarisation of Warfare*, 2d ed. (New York, 2001), 107–19; R. Otto, *Wehrmacht, Gestapo und sowjetischen Kriegsgefangenen in deutschen Reichsgebiet 1941/42* (Munich, 1998).

[11] H. Heer, "The Logic of the War of Extermination: The Wehrmacht and the Anti-Partisan War," in Heer and Naumann, eds., *War of Extermination*, 92–126; Bartov, *Eastern Front*, 129–40.

[12] Recent studies include N. Frei, *Vergangenheitspolitik: Die Anfänge der Bundesrepublik und die NS-Vergangenheit* (Munich, 1996); R. G. Moeller, *War Stories: The Search for a Usable Past in the Federal Republic of Germany* (Berkeley, 2001); J. Herf, *Divided Memory: The Nazi Past in the Two Germanys* (Cambridge, Mass., 1997).

longing to other national entities, along with historical documentary evidence, on the other; it also refers to the use and abuse of the past by individuals and groups with the view of legitimizing either past actions or current opinions and aspirations. While the past is constantly interacting with the present (both forming it and being informed by it in return), some past events and periods are of greater impact and significance than others.

There is little doubt that the Nazi regime still plays a major role in the political consciousness and individual psychology of many Germans today. This was witnessed in the 1980s in a number of public debates in the Federal Republic and, particularly, in the German historians' controversy, or the *Historikerstreit*. The controversy, which began in 1986, has remained in the background of much recent scholarship and public debates despite (or perhaps precisely because of) the upheaval of reunification, thereby reflecting the growing political relevance of the Nazi past to a Germany searching for a new definition of national identity.

The *Historikerstreit*, as the subtitle of one German publication on the issue had it, concerned "the controversy over the uniqueness of the National Socialist extermination of the Jews."[13] However, in an even wider sense, the debate was over the uniqueness of everything and anything that took place under the Third Reich, indeed over the meaning of uniqueness in history. From the purely scholarly point of view, the argument against uniqueness raised a valid point; namely, that if uniqueness implies incomparability, then it introduces an ahistorical terminology, that is, it decontextualizes the event by wrenching it out of the course of history and thereby rendering it inexplicable, even mythical. In other words, the historian cannot accept that any event in the past is wholly unique, since that would mean that this event would defy any rational historical analysis and understanding. More specifically, however, the argument regarding the uniqueness of the Holocaust does not necessarily mean that it is incomparable. Comparison

---

[13] *"Historikerstreit": Die Dokumentation der Kontroverse um die Einzigartigkeit der nationalsozialistischen Judenvernichtung* (Munich, 1987). English translation as *Forever in the Shadow of Hitler? Original Documents of the Historikerstreit, the Controversy Concerning the Singularity of the Holocaust* (Atlantic Highlands, N.J., 1993). Major studies include C. S. Maier, *The Unmasterable Past: History, Holocaust, and German National Identity* (Cambridge, Mass., 1988); R. J. Evans, *In Hitler's Shadow: West German Historians and the Attempt to Escape from the Nazi Past* (London, 1989); P. Baldwin, ed., *Reworking the Past: Hitler, the Holocaust, and the Historians' Debate* (Boston, 1990).

does not aim to show that two things or events are the same, but rather to shed light on two or more objects or phenomena by demonstrating both their similarities and their differences.

Yet the "revisionists," that is, the German scholars who called for a revision of the history of the Third Reich by means of "contextualizing" it through comparison and "demystifying" it through "detached" analysis, had a different aim in mind when they objected to the presentation of Nazism as unique. As their opponents claimed, the "revisionists," or at least their more extreme representatives, were interested in "relativizing" the history of Nazism, that is, in demonstrating that although the Nazi regime was indeed evil and criminal, there were many others like it, and therefore the Germans had no reason to feel more guilty about their past than any other people, and could calmly go about re-establishing a proud national identity based on a history of great political and cultural achievements.

While these arguments met with fierce opposition in Germany and abroad in so far as they concerned the murder of the Jews, they were received with far more sympathy when applied to the German army's conduct of the war. When the "revisionist" Ernst Nolte claimed that the only difference between the Holocaust and the Soviet gulags was the use of gas for killing, and that in any case the gulags were the begetters of Auschwitz because Hitler behaved as he did out of fear of the Bolsheviks, both the ethical import and the documentary evidence for his assertion were forcefully challenged by many of his colleagues.[14]

But when Andreas Hillgruber, another highly respected "revisionist," argued for the need of the historian to identify with the German soldiers' "heroic" defense of the Reich from the "orgy of revenge" with which the Red Army threatened the German civilian population, he touched on a sensitive point for the Germans.[15] The murder of the Jews could be ascribed to a relatively small circle of criminals, that is, it could be isolated from the main bulk of the German population (and, as some would have it, from the main current of German history). This

---

[14] E. Nolte, "Between Historical Legend and Revisionism? The Third Reich in the Perspective of 1980," and "The Past That Will Not Pass: A Speech That Could Be Written but Not Delivered," both in *Forever in the Shadow of Hitler?* (Atlantic Highlands, 1993) 13–14, 21–22, respectively.

[15] A. Hillgruber, *Zweierlei Untergang: Die Zerschlagung des Deutschen Reiches und das Ende des europäischen Judentums* (Berlin, 1986); O. Bartov, *Murder in Our Midst: The Holocaust, Industrial Killing, and Representation* (New York, 1996), 71–88.

was not so in the case of the Wehrmacht, based as it was on mass conscription and therefore highly representative of German society as a whole.

Moreover, the powerful sense of abhorrence of war in postwar Germany, following the destruction visited upon it during the closing phases of World War II, has made many Germans view war, any war, as hell. Paradoxically, this view has in turn legitimized the actions of German soldiers in the war as being in no way essentially different from those of all other soldiers. Thus, one finds a combination of antiwar sentiment, apologetics, and a sentimental admiration for the men who "saved" Germany, indeed the whole of Europe, from the "Bolshevik-Asiatic hordes," along with a powerful rejection of the notion that the Wehrmacht had served as Hitler's main instrument in implementing his policies of conquest and genocide.

The view of the Wehrmacht as an army like any other has long been shared by many non-German scholars, especially in the West, reflecting a wider trend in public opinion.[16] This was given expression in former President Reagan's assertion that the soldiers of the Wehrmacht and the Waffen-SS buried in the military cemetery of Bitburg were also victims of the Nazi regime.[17] It is therefore of some importance to point out in what respects the German army's conduct in the war was essentially different from that of any other army in modern history.

War is a highly brutal affair, and there is little doubt that individual soldiers can and do become brutalized in the course of fighting.[18] On the individual level, there is no difference between, for instance, the killing of civilians by a Wehrmacht soldier in Russia, by an American soldier in Vietnam, or by a Soviet soldier in Prussia. Once we shift a little from the individual level, however, we begin to see the differences. German soldiers fighting in Russia were allowed, indeed were or-

---

[16] O. Bartov, "Germany's Unforgettable War: The Twisted Road from Berlin to Moscow and Back," *DH* 25, no.3 (2001): 405–23. On the impact of the exhibition "Crimes of the Wehrmacht," mentioned above, see O. Bartov, "The Wehrmacht Exhibition Controversy: The Politics of Evidence," in *The Crimes of War: Guilt and Denial in the Twentieth Century*, ed. O. Bartov, A. Grossmann, and M. Nolan (New York, 2002), 41–60.

[17] For the debate, see G. Hartman, ed., *Bitburg in Moral and Political Perspective* (Bloomington, 1986).

[18] Compare the different views in S. Haynes, *The Soldiers' Tale: Bearing Witness to Modern War* (New York, 1997); J. Bourke, *An Intimate History of Killing: Face-to-Face Killing in Twentieth-Century Warfare* (New York, 1999).

dered, to commit mass killings of people who were clearly of no direct military threat to them. This was not the case of American GIs in Vietnam, or of Red Army troops in occupied Germany, even if many such instances did occur. And because this was not the policy, but rather an unauthorized action, the scale of the killing was smaller.

The Red Army in Germany had no policy of decimating the German population and turning Germany into a wasteland fit for Russian colonization. Had this been the case, we would not have seen the recent reunification of Germany, for there would have been nothing to reunite with. The German army in Russia, on the other hand, followed a clear policy of subjugation and extermination. Had Germany won the war, Russia would have disappeared as a political entity, and millions more Russians would have been murdered, with the rest being enslaved by their German colonizers. Nor did the U.S. Army have a policy of genocide in Vietnam, even if it did cause the deaths of hundreds of thousands of innocent civilians. If the Soviet Union installed brutal dictatorships in the East European countries it conquered, these were nevertheless not genocidal regimes, just as an American victory in Vietnam would not have meant the destruction of the Vietnamese people (whose existence under the victorious communists has not been particularly cheerful either). The strategic bombing of Germany, another example often used by German apologists, had no intention of wiping out the German people, even if it was of questionable military value and morally dubious.[19] Moreover, one cannot forget that the English and the Americans, as well as the Russians, were fighting against Nazi aggression: it was the Third Reich that had striven to conquer Europe, not Great Britain, America, or even the Soviet Union.

The Wehrmacht did not behave in the same manner everywhere. As has been seen, it was on the Eastern Front that the German army conducted a uniquely savage war. This was possible because of the overall agreement between the regime and its soldiers regarding the need to wipe out the Soviet Union, its political system, and much of its population. Shared racist sentiments acted as a powerful motivation in the conduct of war in the East. Doubtless, many other armies have known the effects of racism: the U.S. army, both in the Pacific War and in Viet-

---

[19] Compare conflicting views in E. Markusen and D. Kopf, *The Holocaust and Strategic Bombing: Genocide and Total War in the Twentieth Century* (Boulder, 1995), and R. Overy, *Why the Allies Won* (New York, 1996), chap. 4. Noteworthy is J. Glover, *Humanity: A Moral History of the Twentieth Century* (New Haven, 1999).

nam, and the Japanese army in Asia, have acted brutally, not least due to a racially oriented perception of the enemy.[20] Yet racism was not the official policy of the U.S. government, nor was the education of American youths as deeply grounded in racism as that of the Germans of the 1930s. When Japan was occupied by the U.S. Army it was not enslaved, even if many American GIs had clearly developed strongly racist views of the Japanese.[21] The Japanese, for their part, carried out highly brutal policies of occupation motivated by a mixture of imperialist goals and a sense of racial superiority propagated by the regime. Indeed, the Japanese army's conduct in China comes close to that of the Wehrmacht in Russia, just as its treatment of prisoners of war was abominable. Yet even here one must make the qualification that the Japanese did not adopt a policy of genocide.[22] Hence, for instance, the rate of survival of prisoners of war in Japanese hands was twice as high as that of Soviet soldiers in German hands.[23]

It is, indeed, on the issue of genocide that the German military surely comes out worse than any other modern army. This is both because the army itself actively pursued a policy of mass killing of Russians, and because it was an essential instrument in the realization of the "Final Solution." The attempt to differentiate between the Wehrmacht and the SS, between the fighting at the front and the death camps in the rear, presents a wholly false picture of the historical reality. As a number of highly detailed and thorough works have shown, the army was involved in the implementation of the "Final Solution" on every conceivable level, beginning with the conquest of the areas which contained the highest concentrations of Jewish population, through rendering logistical and manpower support to the *Einsatzgruppen* and the death camp administrations, to the bitter determination with which it resisted the final and inevitable defeat of the Third Reich at a time when the rate of the industrial killing of millions of human beings reached its peak.[24] The Wehrmacht was thus a crucial factor in the most horrendous crime perpetrated by any nation in modern history.

[20] J. W. Dower, *War Without Mercy: Race and Power in the Pacific War* (New York, 1986).

[21] J. W. Dower, *Embracing Defeat: Japan in the Wake of World War II* (New York, 1999).

[22] K. Honda, *The Nanjing Massacre* (New York, 1999).

[23] Bartov, *Eastern Front*, 153–56.

[24] See essays by Herbert, Manoschek, Gerlach, and Dieckmann in *National Socialist Extermination Policies: Contemporary German Perspectives and Controversies*, ed. U. Herbert (New York, 2000).

MORAL CHOICES

The most conspicuous instance of resistance to the regime in the Third Reich was arguably the July 1944 *Putsch* attempt. This act of rebellion by a number of officers has been the focus of a rich literature concerned with the technical, personal, political, and moral implications of a coup d'état against a criminal regime at a time of grave military crisis.[25] Conversely, one of the most striking features of the Nazi dictatorship is the remarkable loyalty to the regime manifested by the Wehrmacht's rank and file and junior officer corps throughout the war.[26] The following discussion will attempt to sketch out the range of moral choices available in the German army by exploring three separate but related spheres of the soldiers' existence at the front: the formal sphere of military discipline and martial law; the personal sphere of survival, fear, comradeship, and family; and the ideological sphere, molded by preconscription and army indoctrination.

Discipline

A seemingly obvious and clear-cut boundary to opposition and resistance is military discipline. Under the Third Reich, and increasingly during the war, the Wehrmacht resorted to extremely harsh, indeed brutal combat discipline, legitimized by the politicization of martial law, whereby offenses that harmed fighting effectiveness and morale were labeled as subversion and punished with great severity. This resulted in more than 20,000 executions of soldiers charged with desertion, cowardice, and self-inflicted wounds. Moreover, thousands of German soldiers were shot out of hand while trying to cross over to the enemy, fleeing in panic, or simply for failing to carry out orders on the battlefield.[27] Both the absence of any serious mutinies in the

[25] See T. S. Hamerow, *On the Road to Wolf's Lair: German Resistance to Hitler* (Cambridge, Mass., 1997); J. Fest, *Plotting Hitler's Death: The Story of the German Resistance* (New York, 1996); P. Hoffmann, *The History of the German Resistance, 1933–1945*, 3d ed. (Montreal, 1996).

[26] I. Kershaw, *The "Hitler Myth": Image and Reality in the Third Reich* (Oxford, 1987), 209, 217–18; M. G. Steinert, *Hitler's War and the Germans* (Athens, Ohio, 1977), 196, 264–73, 282–83, 289, 298–302.

[27] J. Thomas, "'Nur das ist für die Truppe Recht, was ihr nützt . . .' Die Wehrmachtjustiz im Zweiten Weltkrieg," in *Die anderen Soldaten: Wehrkraftzersetzung, Gehorsamsverweigerung und Fahnenflucht im Zweiten Weltkrieg*, ed. N. Haase and G. Paul (Frankfurt/M., 1995), 48; M. Messerschmidt and F. Wüllner, *Die Wehrmachtjustiz im Dienste des Nationalsozialismus* (Baden-Baden, 1987), 63–89; Bartov, *Hitler's Army*, 59–105.

Wehrmacht throughout the war and the outstanding determination with which the German army kept fighting until almost the very end, thus testify in part to the fact that the troops were terrified of their own commanders' wrath.

Discipline alone, however, rarely suffices to explain conformity; on the contrary, when administered in disproportionate doses, and especially in conscript armies, it may well cause, rather than prevent mutiny.[28] But in the Wehrmacht, and especially in the *Ostheer*, or Eastern Army, which comprised the lion's share of the German armed forces throughout most of the war, there were other important aspects to the transformation of martial law which both encouraged compliance with combat discipline, and enhanced the troops' sense of a common destiny, purpose; and guilt. Thanks to a combination of policy with unforeseen circumstances, the Wehrmacht created a mechanism that allowed the increasingly brutalized troops to direct their anger and frustration at targets other than their superiors and then tied them to each other with terror of the enemy's vengeance in case of defeat. Consequently, when we speak of the individual choosing between collaboration and resistance, we must take into account not only his superiors' brutal response to insubordination but also the dread of retribution by the enemy. This dilemma was at the core of the soldiers' existence at the front and remained a central motif in their subsequent rationalizations of the war experience.

If we are to understand indiscipline as a possible indication of resistance, then it is worthwhile to examine its changing manifestations among the troops and the means employed to curb it by the Wehrmacht. During the invasion of Poland, German senior officers complained about the high incidence of disciplinary problems, which was especially disturbing considering the swiftness of the campaign and the relatively low number of casualties.[29] This was probably caused both by the lack of enthusiasm with which war was greeted in Germany as a whole, and by the fact that the newly founded Wehrmacht still experienced numerous organizational, technical, and disciplinary

[28] See G. Pedrocini, *Les mutineries de 1917*, 2d ed. (Paris, 1983); L. V. Smith, *Between Mutiny and Obedience: The Case of the French Fifth Infantry Division during World War I* (Princeton, 1994).

[29] See BA-MA, RH26–12/252, 25.10.39, 20.11.39, 18.12.39; RH26–12/279, 29.9.39; 1.10.39; RH26–12/99, 25.10.40; RH26–12/236, 8.11.39.

hitches.[30] Moreover, officers complaining about soldiers' acts of brutality toward civilians attributed them to the example set by the SS.[31] Thus, as early as the Polish campaign, the army experienced two distinct though, of course, not unrelated forms of indiscipline: one which might be construed as constituting explicit or implicit, conscious or unconscious resistance to the regime and its policies of expansion, and another which actually conformed with the underlying ideological assumptions and goals of the regime.

During the campaign of May and June 1940, the lingering effects of fighting and occupation in Poland could clearly be observed. While combat units recorded an alarming rise in acts of brutality such as rape, armed robbery, and indiscriminate shooting, senior commanders insisted on draconian punishment, including the death penalty, in order to nip such occurrences in the bud.[32] Here was another curious example of the ambivalent relationship between military discipline and ideological penetration. The soldiers behaved as they did because in Poland they had become used to treating the enemy as inferior, a notion they had in fact acquired long before their conscription; in the West, however, due to political and ideological considerations, their superiors refused to tolerate unauthorized brutalities vis-à-vis the occupied population. But in their efforts to enforce discipline, the generals established the practice of executing their own troops on a scale vastly different from that of the *Kaiserheer* of World War I. In this the senior officer corps manifested the spirit of ruthlessness and contempt for life that characterized the Third Reich as a whole.

As detailed above, and unlike previous campaigns, the Wehrmacht marched into the Soviet Union equipped with a set of orders that translated Hitler's notion of a war of extermination and subjugation into the practical terminology of the military. In the present context it is most important to note the effects of the curtailment of martial law vis-à-vis the occupied population and Soviet prisoners of war. Here the close tie

[30] W. Wette, "Ideology, Propaganda, and Internal Politics as Preconditions of the War Policy of the Third Reich," in *The Build-up of German Aggression*, vol. 1 of *Germany and the Second World War* (GSWW) (Oxford, 1990), 11, 119–24.

[31] E. Klee, W. Dressen, and V. Riess, eds., *"The Good Old Days": The Holocaust as Seen by Its Perpetrators and Bystanders* (New York, 1991), 4–5.

[32] BA-MA, RH26–12/183, 21.5.40; RH26–12/274, 27.6.40; RH26–12/235, 2.10.40, 3.10.40; RH26–12/99, 25.10.40; RH26–12/108, 9.4.41; RH26–12/21, 6.5.41, 7.5.41, 8.5.41.

between the two aspects of law and discipline was most clearly revealed. For on the one hand, the troops dutifully obeyed orders to shoot political and "biological" enemies, to collectively punish entire communities, and to ruthlessly "live off the land." On the other hand, the otherwise rigidly disciplinarian Wehrmacht allowed the troops to go unpunished for unauthorized acts of brutality, indiscriminate shootings of prisoners of war and civilians, looting, and wanton destruction, though commanders repeatedly pleaded with their soldiers to desist from such "unsoldierly" conduct.[33] Indeed, it was difficult to punish the men for acts that merely emulated similar and far more destructive official actions. And, considering the almost complete immunity provided by the "Barbarossa Decree," it was exceedingly problematic and politically unwise to press charges even against soldiers who had maltreated the most helpless and obviously innocent civilians.

Wehrmacht commanders were initially anxious lest the progressive brutalization of their troops lead to widespread demoralization. In fact, rather that causing a general disintegration of discipline, these conditions enhanced unit cohesion, fighting morale, and motivation. Faced with the grim realities of an extraordinarily brutal and costly war, on the one hand, and with the prospects of harsh punishment for any attempt to evade it, on the other, the soldiers were now given an outlet for their accumulated fear and anger, especially when officers turned a blind eye to ostensibly forbidden actions. As long as they fought well, the soldiers were allowed to "let off steam" both by transgressing accepted civilian norms of behavior and by acting illegally even according to the far from "normal" standards of the front. Legalizing these actions would have deprived them of their value as a unifying element that bound the troops together by creating a keen awareness of their shared responsibility for horrific crimes.

Commanders may well have neglected to punish their soldiers for unauthorized actions because in Russia they had their hands full just keeping combat discipline intact, were hampered by the "Barbarossa Decree," were reluctant to imprison soldiers in view of the manpower crisis, and were at least in part themselves imbued with the same anti-Bolshevik, anti-Slav, and antisemitic sentiments proclaimed by the

---

[33] Bartov, *Eastern Front*, 106–41.

regime.[34] But by acting as they did, they enhanced the military cohesion of the army by making submission to brutal combat discipline more acceptable in view of the license given to the soldiers to act with similar brutality toward their real and imaginary enemies. They also made the idea of resistance to military superiors (and thereby to the regime) extremely difficult to contemplate, particularly on moral grounds, for the vast majority of their soldiers became implicated themselves in precisely the kind of crimes that might have otherwise caused moral revulsion, demoralization, perhaps even revolt.

Comradeship

Although draconian disciplinary measures proved effective in preventing mass desertions and disintegration, soldiers who did try to dodge the fighting appear to have rarely been morally, politically, or ideologically motivated.[35] Soviet interrogation files of Wehrmacht deserters, for instance, reveal that these soldiers tended to refrain from voicing opposition to the Nazi regime, though they could have expected to reap some benefits from such pronouncements.[36] Nor did Wehrmacht courts-martial, trying soldiers for cowardice, desertion, or self-inflicted wounds, normally accuse them of having had any overt ideological or moral motivation.[37] Indeed, most soldiers tried for self-inflicted wounds, for example, seem to have been young, often poorly educated men from the lower classes, who either could not face the prospect of returning from leave to the front, or broke down shortly after rejoining their units.[38] To be sure, martial law defined such offenses a priori as political, thereby legitimizing the severity of the sentences; but even the military judges themselves did not claim that the prosecuted had any conscious political intentions. Thus the impression one gains is that deserters, cowards, and all other kinds of shirkers were often men who had been unable to integrate socially into their units

---

[34] J. Förster, "Operation Barbarossa as a War of Conquest and Annihilation," in *GSWW*, vol. 4, 513–21.

[35] See BA-MA, RH26–12/131, 25.12.41; RH26–12/45, 5.10.41; RH26–12/139, 4.5.43; RH26–12/151, 24.9.43.

[36] See BA-MA, RH26–12/85, 24.10.42.

[37] BA-MA, RH26–12/45, 5.10.41; RH26–12/262, 27.12.41; RH26–12/267, 7.5.42; RH27–18/28, 18.8.41; RH27–18/63, 10.12.41; RH27–18/76, 19.3.42.

[38] F. Seidler, *Prostitution, Homosexualität, Selbstverstümmelung: Probleme der deutsche Sanitätsführung 1939–45* (Neckargemünd, 1977), 233–317.

and to adapt to combat conditions, rather than enemies of the regime; that is, they were psychologically and socially, not ideologically or morally, exceptional.

Comradeship was indeed an extraordinarily important element in the social and military cohesion of the Wehrmacht. As long as the rate of casualties permitted the existence of "primary groups" in the army, what kept the units together was to a large extent the carefully fostered social ties between their members. But even when the fighting in the East destroyed such socially cohesive groups, the sense of responsibility for one's comrades, even if one no longer knew them so well, remained extremely strong.

At the core of this loyalty to other members of the unit was a sentiment of moral obligation, though of course not unaffected by the expectation that individual altruism would eventually be repaid in kind by the group as a whole or by any one of its constituent members. Thus the cohesiveness of the original "primary group," which had derived its strength from long-term familiarity and shared experience as well as from premilitary affinities resulting from regional conscription, was replaced by the widespread sense of existential dependence among those who happened to be together on the line at any given moment, seen as the only means to confront that very same danger which had already destroyed the old, more traditional groups.[39]

It is interesting that participants and contemporary observers were themselves struck by the outstanding fighting performance and combat cohesion of the troops in the face of not only extremely unfavorable military odds but also of the increasing disintegration of those social ties previously considered essential for morale. The explanation was repeatedly sought in the individual's will to survive as the most important factor in keeping the men together and fighting, and it should come as no surprise to find echoes of the nihilistic social Darwinism of National Socialist rhetoric in almost every contemporary account, memoir, or oral reminiscence.[40]

[39] See further in Bartov, *Hitler's Army*, 29–58, and O. Bartov, "Daily Life and Motivation in War: The Wehrmacht in the Soviet Union," *JSS* 12 (1989): 200–214.

[40] See H. Spaeter and W. Ritter von Schramm, *Die Geschichte des Panzerkorps Grossdeutschland* (Bielefeld, 1958), 1:365–66, 2:251–270; L. Niethammer, "Heimat und Front: Versuch, zehn Kriegserinnerungen aus der Arbeiterklasse des Ruhrgebietes zu verstehen," in *"Die Jahre weiß man nicht, wo man die heute hinsetzen soll": Faschismuserfahrungen im Ruhrgebiet*, ed. L. Niethammer (Bonn, 1983), 191–92.

Yet once out of the realm of the "primary group," the new sense of existential comradeship extended also far beyond the purely military circle to encompass first the soldier's family and friends in the rear, and ultimately the Reich as a whole, if not, indeed, what the propagandists of the period referred to as "German culture" and "European civilization." Both the worsening situation at the front and the growing impact of the war on the rear convinced increasing numbers of soldiers that they were in fact fighting for the bare existence of everything they knew and cherished.[41] Numerous reports speak of how troops on leave became demoralized by the devastation the Allied strategic bombing offensive had wrought on German cities, and of the rapid revival of their spirits once they could avenge themselves on the enemy through fighting.[42] By now evasion of action was perceived not only as betrayal of one's comrades but also of one's family, friends and relations, nation and culture. Thus going into action became both a means of protecting the rear and of venting one's frustration at the sight or knowledge of the suffering and destruction in the Reich which one could not directly alleviate.

The other pole of the troops' conformity to combat discipline was their immense dread of the enemy, particularly in the Soviet Union. The soldiers had been exposed quite early in the war to scenes of brutalities by Soviet troops, and these blended well with the images of the enemy provided them by the Wehrmacht's propaganda. From the available evidence it is clear that the sense of terror from the enemy in the East was so powerful that it must be seen as a major element in motivating the soldiers to go on fighting until almost the very end.[43] Thus, for example, in mid-July 1941 Private Fred Fallnbigl wrote from the front that now he understood why "we had been forced into the war against the Soviet Union," since "God have mercy on us, had we waited, or had these beasts come to us. For them even the most horrible death is still too good. I am glad that I can be here to put an end to this genocidal system." Another soldier, writing from Russia in late August 1941, repeated the view that "precisely now one recognizes

---

[41] See H.-U. Rudel, *Stuka Pilot*, 2d ed. (Maidstone, 1973), 189; O. Buchbender and R. Stertz, eds., *Das andere Gesicht des Krieges* (Munich, 1982), 146, 158–59, 161, 167; W. and H. W. Bähr, eds., *Kriegsbriefe gefallener Studenten, 1939–1945* (Tübingen, 1952), 403, 410, 421–24, 449–50.

[42] See, BA-MA, RH26–12/89, 26.6.43.

[43] See, Buchbender and Stertz, 71, 78, 85, 112, 117–18, 166–67.

perfectly what would have happened to our wives and children had these Russian hordes . . . succeeded in penetrating into our Fatherland . . . Thank God," he concluded, that "these uncultivated, multi-raced men . . . have been thwarted from plundering and pillaging our homeland." Lance-Corporal O. Rentzsch concurred on September 1, 1941, that if "those hordes had invaded our land, that would have . . . made for great bloodshed." He was thus ready "to shoulder . . . all endeavors, in order to eradicate this universal plague." This cleansing operation, according to an NCO's letter, sent in July 1942, entailed "the destruction of eternal Jewry," for "What sorrows would have come to our homeland, had this beast of a man had the upper hand?"[44]

To be sure, such fear alone might have produced the opposite effect by inducing men to escape to the rear, even if it effectively prevented mass desertions to the Soviet enemy up to and including the last weeks of the war, when whole divisions marched rapidly westward in a desperate attempt to be taken prisoner by the "Anglo-Americans" rather than by the "Bolsheviks."[45] But the realities and images of the East also greatly tempered the natural tendency to escape by deserting to the rear. As courts-martial reports indicate, the rate of desertion in Russia remained for a long time actually lower than in the West. The reasons are not hard to find: having penetrated so deeply into enemy territory, the *Ostheer* became bogged down in a front that was turned to an enemy who refused to give up the struggle and whose rear was exposed to vast stretches of insecure areas in which an increasingly hostile population was willy-nilly coming over to the side of the Soviet partisans. To this was added the prevalent feeling, derived partly from fact and partly from prejudice, that the Russians were much more foreign than any previously occupied peoples in the West.[46] In this sense, the individual soldier was physically and mentally trapped, able neither to advance and conquer nor to run away; he was totally dependent on his comrades for survival in an alien, harsh, and dangerous country whose language he did not speak and to whose climate, geography, and ways

[44] Ibid., 155–56, 162. W. Manoschek, ed., *"Es gibt nur eines für das Judentum: Vernichtung." Das Judenbild in deutschen Soldatenbriefen 1939–1944* (Hamburg, 1995). A less harsh interpretation can be found in K. Latzel, *Deutsche Soldaten—nationalsozialistischer Krieg? Kriegserlebnis—Kriegserfahrung 1939–1945* (Paderborn, 1998).

[45] See C. Wagner, *Heeresgruppe Süd: Der Kampf im Süden der Ostfront, 1941–1945* (Bad Nauheim, n.d.), 340–41.

[46] See BA-MA, RH26–12/131, 25.12.41; RH26–12/139, 4.5.43; RH26–12/151, 24.9.43.

of life he could not adapt, its armed forces becoming more menacing by the month.

While crossing over to the enemy presented the prospect of being shot either by one's own comrades (which in fact often happened) or by the Russians (which contrary to expectations appears to have actually been less common), escaping to the rear involved not only the danger of being caught and sentenced to death by the military authorities, but also of falling into Soviet partisan hands, or even simply of losing one's way and perishing in the vast territories between the front and the homeland.[47] The choice made by most soldiers was thus clear and simple: it was safer to stay and fight than run and be killed—which happened to be precisely what their commanders repeatedly and successfully urged them to believe.

There is, however, a completely different dimension to the soldiers' conformity with army discipline. In the case of unauthorized plunder and brutality, officers complained a great deal, though they refrained from taking disciplinary action. But commanders seem to have confronted no such difficulties regarding the army's official policies of exploitation, destruction, and murder, for not only were no charges pressed, one is also hard put to find any other evidence to show that soldiers tried to evade these activities. This is all the more striking because there are indications that even SS and police units occasionally presented their men with the choice of not taking part in murder "operations" they felt unable to withstand.[48] To be sure, while for the SS mass killing of civilians was its raison d'être, the army considered this merely one and not the most important aspect of fighting in the East.[49] Moreover, the Wehrmacht authorities themselves objected to shootings of women and children by the troops (though not to executing thousands of male hostages nor to killing suspected partisans and agents of all ages and both sexes), fearing that this would undermine military discipline and demoralize the men.[50] Instead, either the SD

[47] See BA-MA, RH26–12/267, 7.5.42; RH26–12/85, 27.5.42.

[48] C. R. Browning, "German Memory, Judicial Interrogation, and Historical Reconstruction: Writing Perpetrator History from Post-War Testimony," in *Probing the Limits of Representation: Nazism and the "Final Solution,"* ed. S. Friedländer (Cambridge, Mass, 1992), 22–36; D. Goldhagen, "The 'Cowardly' Executioner: On Disobedience in the SS," *PP* 19 (1985): 19–32; Klee, 60–74.

[49] A more radical interpretation in H. Heer, *Tote Zonen: Die deutsche Wehrmacht an der Ostfront* (Hamburg, 1999).

[50] But see also H. Heer, ed., *"Stets zu erschießen sind Frauen, die in der Roten Armee*

was called in, or these "undesirable elements" were ejected from their villages in circumstances that ensured death by starvation and exposure. Nevertheless, it is interesting that, while some SS "professionals" relented from the killings, the army, which had its fair share of gruesome actions, recorded no such instances.[51]

It should also be added that those SS and police unit members who chose not to take part in such operations—and were not punished in any obvious way for their choice—stated both at the time and in subsequent postwar interrogations that they had simply become physically and mentally incapable of going ahead with the murders; that is to say, at no point did they imply that their choice had been caused by or had itself influenced their general attitude toward the regime. In other words, they saw themselves as too weak to perform what they fundamentally believed ought to be done, rather than strong enough to resist taking part in an atrocity.[52]

The way in which soldiers coped with these criminal aspects of the war adds much to our understanding of the real and perceived parameters of collaboration and resistance. There is little doubt that soldiers were powerfully motivated by moral outrage during the war, but they appear to have directed it against the enemy rather than against the regime and the army. The troops came to view their own actions as an essential part of an ideological war that by definition demanded extraordinary measures, just as Nazi propaganda had claimed all along. Moreover, the soldiers, who constantly experienced the practical implications of Hitler's "ideas," went one step further. Their very conviction of the need to act in a manner that they would have considered criminal under any other circumstances depended on the assumption, or rather the belief, that the enemy was inherently worse. No matter the scale of the Wehrmacht's atrocities, the enemy's, by definition, were greater. Thus as long as the morality of one's actions was gauged in relation to the enemy's, there could not be any absolute moral limit. Personal moral outrage, instead of tempering one's con-

---

dienen." *Geständnisse deutscher Kriegsgefangener über ihren Einsatz an der Ostfront* (Hamburg, 1995).

[51] New research in Germany, however, seems to have uncovered some instances of soldiers refusing to carry out criminal orders.

[52] C. R. Browning, *Fateful Months: Essays on the Emergence of the Final Solution* (New York, 1985), 39–56, 68–85; Bartov, *Eastern Front*, 119–29; H. Krausnick and H.-H. Wilhelm, *Die Truppe des Weltanschauungskrieges* (Stuttgart, 1981), 243–49.

duct, rather enhanced it by being directed at those perceived as the cause of all enormities. This was the mechanism whereby the soldiers came to terms with an unprecedented and, in many ways, unbearable psychological, moral, and physical situation. Indeed, what is the meaning of morally opposing one's own regime when even those who see through its propaganda simultaneously feel that they are fighting against a similarly, if not more, evil political system? This reasoning liberated the individual from responsibility for his own actions, for the root of the evil was to be found on the other side of the hill.[53]

Ideology

The parameters of collaboration and resistance, the tension between what soldiers considered inadmissible and unavoidable, forbidden and necessary, therefore had to do not merely with their rational analysis of the objective situation but at least as much with their perception of reality. In turn, the views and beliefs prevalent among frontline troops reflected the efficacy of Nazi propaganda and indoctrination, which, of course, owed much of its own success to popular prejudices and half-baked ideologies predating the Nazi "seizure of power."[54] The unresisting participation of the troops in actions that seem to us obviously criminal was thus not merely the result of harsh discipline, but also of the successful dissemination of a dehumanized image of the enemy that excluded him from the norms of behavior and morals of human society.

This does not mean that a few years of Nazi rule had managed completely to erase the moral sensibilities of the troops. There is evidence to show that many were indeed shocked by what they and their comrades were doing and even more so by the mass murders carried out by the *Einsatzgruppen* and witnessed by substantial numbers of soldiers.[55] But as a rule, the soldiers justified themselves by referring to the inhumanity of the victims. Their reaction was derived both from the savage fighting which had blunted the troops' emotions, and from the maltreatment of the enemy, which physically reduced indi-

---

[53] For a recent apologetic argument in this vein, see R.-D. Müller, "Die Wehrmacht—Historische Last und Verantwortung," in Müller and Volkmann, 3–35, and my response in *CEH* 34, no.4 (2000): 583–88.

[54] See, G. L. Mosse, *Fallen Soldiers: Reshaping the Memory of the World Wars* (New York, 1990).

[55] Klee, 24–33; but see also, 88–135.

viduals to such a wretched condition that they came to resemble the image of the *Untermenschen* propagated by the regime.[56]

When speaking of the moral dilemmas faced by the Wehrmacht's frontline troops, we should remember that they were mostly recently conscripted young men who had spent the formative years of their youth in an increasingly Nazified school system and, crucially, in the militarized atmosphere of the Hitler Youth (HJ) and *Arbeitsdienst* (compulsory Labor Service), which exposed them to relentless indoctrination. Many of these youngsters were attracted both to the regime's rhetoric of rebellion against old norms and traditions, and to the heroic image of a conquering, invincible Germany, charged with the mission of cleansing the whole world from the plague of communism and plutocracy, increasingly identified with "world Jewry." The HJ insisted on rigid regimentation, "blind" obedience, and unquestioning faith in the supreme value of action, while teaching profound contempt and distrust for contemplation and discussion; it worshipped the united strength of the group and the "iron" will of the individual, and it despised any manifestation of physical or psychological weakness. In many ways the HJ resembled a youth gang, longing to smash all the symbols and representatives of the existing social order, be they parental and school authority, the church and bourgeois values, or just as much the socialist and communist loyalties of the working class; it was as violent as any gang, and just as much centered around an admired, tyrannical leader.[57] But by becoming a vast national organization, and through being associated with and a cult of the Führer, it simultaneously satisfied the youthful desire for conformity and became the most important forerunner or school of what was rapidly becoming Hitler's army. This powerful combination of total revolt and total submission, of destructiveness and obedience, this fascination with smashing the present in the name of an ideal, ill-defined future somehow linked to a mythical past had far reaching consequences for the mentality of the Wehrmacht's troops.[58]

To be sure, it did not make them all into committed Nazis; but it pro-

---

[56] See, Buchbender and Stertz, 78–80, 84–87, 170.

[57] See, Niethammer, *Heimat und Front*, 210.

[58] See, H. Scholtz, *Erziehung und Unterricht unterm Hakenkreuz* (Göttingen, 1985); A. Heck, *A Child of Hitler*, 3d ed. (New York, 1986); R. Schörken, "Jugendalltag im Dritten Reich," in *Geschichte im Alltag—Alltag in der Geschichte*, ed. K. Bergmann and R. Schörken (Düsseldorf, 1982), 236–46.

vided them with an outlook which profoundly influenced their manner of both physically and mentally coping with and reacting to the realities of the war they were soon to find themselves fighting, whether or not they happened to be enamored of the regime. In other words, it drastically narrowed their perceived alternatives for action on the battlefield. Equipped with an apocalyptic view of history, a social Darwinian division of humanity into those who must survive and those who must be exterminated, and a vocabulary that celebrated the abolishment of all previous norms of behavior, values, morals, and beliefs, the troops were necessarily left with precious little choice. Having gaily rid themselves of the present, the young soldiers of the Reich had no notion of the kind of future they would like to forge for themselves. Attachment to the nihilistic rhetoric of the regime supplied the best escape from the absence of a positive prospect. The clearer it became that the war would not lead to the promised victory, the more powerful became the faith in the mythical *Endsieg*, or final victory, whose essence was a belief in the need to keep on destroying the present until eventually the ideal future emerged from the debris.[59]

Against this picture of conformity, we may want to remind ourselves that as recently as the 1980s, most social historians of the Third Reich insisted that the Nazi ideal of creating a *Volksgemeinschaft*, where class tensions and inequality would be replaced by national and racial unity under a benign Führer, was never achieved in practice.[60] Instead, these scholars argued, German workers retained a strong class-consciousness and kept up the struggle to improve their material conditions and, by implication, to gain political recognition. Evidence of strikes and intentional lower productivity, as well as political organization, seemed to indicate fairly widespread opposition to the regime among the working class, quite apart from active resistance, which was ruthlessly suppressed in the first years of Nazi rule.[61] Nevertheless, such alleged tensions between the working class and the regime found very little expression once the younger workers were conscripted into the Wehrmacht. Indeed, it seems that, contrary to expectations, from the mo-

---

[59] See, G. Sajer, *The Forgotten Soldier*, 2d ed. (London, 1977), 263–67.

[60] For criticism of this interpretation, see R. Gellately, *The Gestapo and German Society: Enforcing Racial Policy, 1933–1945* (Oxford, 1990); G. Diewald-Kerkmann, *Politische Denunziation im NS-Regime, oder Die kleine Macht der "Volksgenossen"* (Bonn, 1995).

[61] T. Mason, *Social Policy in the Third Reich: The Working Class and the "National Community"* (Providence, 1993).

ment such workers became soldiers they no longer presented the regime or their military superiors with any problems of discipline or motivation. We have no evidence of mutinies of soldiers stemming from class-consciousness and lingering opposition to a dictatorship that had obviously not fulfilled its promises of at least partial equality.[62] Conversely, some work on attitudes among workers in the Ruhr industrial region, based on interviews conducted in the 1980s, seems to indicate that many workers were in fact quite pleased with the economic achievements of the Nazis, which meant that unemployment was drastically reduced (thanks to a vast program of rearmament), leading to a significant improvement in the standard of living.[63] Moreover, it now seems that Nazi ideology was also much more successful in penetrating the strongholds of the working class than had been previously thought, particularly among the young. Men interviewed forty years later stated that they had joined the HJ with a great deal of enthusiasm, and did not view it as contradicting their identity as workers.

Thus, for example, Gustav Köppke, son of communist workers in the Ruhr industrial region, remembered in 1981 that while watching the *Kristallnacht* pogrom in 1938 at the age of nine, he found it "terribly impressive, when the SA marched . . . I was on the side of the strong guys; the Jews, they were the others." He further claimed that "Our workers' suburb and the Hitler Youth were in no way contradictory," because "whoever wanted to become something belonged to it." Indeed, "the Hitler Youth uniform was something positive in our childhood." For Köppke, who served as a volunteer in the SS Hitler Youth Division toward the end of the war, the defeat of Germany came as a shock: "I was raised then," he recalled thirty-five years later, "in the National Socialist time and had seen the world just as they had shown it to us. . . . And suddenly nothing made sense any more." Similarly, Gisberg Pohl, another son of a working class family interviewed in 1981, explained his participation in the suppression of the Warsaw

[62] O. Bartov, "The Missing Years: German Workers, German Soldiers," and A. Lüdtke, "The 'Honor of Labor': Industrial Workers and the Power of Symbols under National Socialism," in *Nazism and German Society, 1933–1945*, ed. D. F. Crew (New York, 1994), 41–66, 67–109, respectively.

[63] U. Herbert, "'Die guten und die schlechten Zeiten.' Überlegungen zur diachronen Analyse lebensgeschichtlicher Interviews," in Niethammer, *"Die Jahre,"* 67–96; Herbert, "'The Real Mystery in Germany': The German Working Class during the Nazi Dictatorship," in *Confronting the Nazi Past: New Debates on Modern German History*, ed. M. Burleigh (London, 1996), 23–36.

Ghetto uprising as a member of an SS Division by noting that "being a young man one easily made too much of it. We had after all gone to Russia, we wanted there [to destroy] subhumanity—that is, I was strongly convinced of my task, that I was right."[64]

These findings, taken together with the general high motivation of German troops, seem to indicate that even if the *Volksgemeinschaft* remained largely a myth (albeit a highly potent one), its military counterpart, the *Kampfgemeinschaft*, or the community of battle, served not only as a powerful ideal but was very much seen by many soldiers as a true reflection of reality. It is also clear that the Hitler Youth's rebellious conformism played a major role in the profound transformation of the Wehrmacht, flooding it with hundreds of thousands of fresh recruits within an extremely short span of time. The generals were quick to note the changing character of the army, both when they claimed (some with satisfaction, others apologetically, and yet others with sorrow), that the lower ranks would not support a *Putsch* against Hitler, and when they appealed (some cynically, some with much conviction) to the troops' Nazi loyalties in times of military crisis.[65] Thus the average combat soldier and junior officer, in his profound sense of a complete lack of choice, drilled into him through years of ideological indoctrination and social-organizational pressures, in his inability to conceive of any other alternative to the values propagated by the regime, and in his dependence on the polarized images of a deified Führer and a demonized enemy as his motivating engine, was probably closer to the National Socialist model of the fanatic, politically committed *Kämpfer* than the generals whose notorious orders—cited above—have come to symbolize the Nazification of the senior officer corps. Not surprisingly, soldiers' diaries, letters, and memoirs are strikingly devoid of references to opposition, be it active or passive.

Aftermath

It is interesting that especially in the first few postwar decades many of West Germany's more prominent novelists and filmmakers seemed to imply the same lack of moral choice under the Nazi regime. In Edgar Reitz's sixteen-hour film *Heimat* (1984) the one brief episode concerned with soldiers exposes them to an incident which might be construed

---

[64] Bartov, *Hitler's Army*, 111–12.
[65] See J. von Herwarth, *Against Two Evils* (London, 1981), 255.

either as a (distasteful but perhaps justified) execution of partisans or as an atrocity, that is, the killing of innocent civilians. The soldiers cannot change that reality; they can only act within it, either shoot, watch, or record it, as one of them, a member of a film crew in a propaganda company, actually does. The director provides his protagonists with no moral choices; they are the victims of a possibly immoral situation that they cannot escape. Similarly, in Helma Sanders-Brahms' film *Germany, Pale Mother* (1980), the soldiers go off to war, leaving the women to fend for themselves, and then return years later, drained and brutalized, to the debris of their homes and families. Here everyone is perceived as a victim of some savage, barbaric, yet strangely amorphous and faceless force; the only choices to be made concern one's own physical and mental survival, followed by a struggle for reconstruction. Defeat in these films is usually presented in the form of (often black) American GIs, who descend on the prostrate homeland. In Rainer Werner Fassbinder's *The Marriage of Maria Braun* (1979), which sets out to expose the perversity and hypocrisy of the *Wirtschaftswunder*, or "economic miracle" of the 1950s, the returning soldier is once more a victim of circumstances beyond his control, as is ultimately the woman who had tried to master fate and coolly control the chaos that surrounds her. To survive the occupation while waiting for her husband to return from captivity, she must take a black GI as a lover; but then she kills the lover to defend the husband. To survive the reconstruction while waiting her husband's return from prison (he takes the murder upon himself) she must take another lover, this time an elderly industrialist and emigrant (Jew?), who betrays her by paying the husband to stay away; finally she and her husband are blown up in a gas explosion in her modern villa, forever wretched and helpless victims of circumstances dating back to the Nazi regime and the war.[66]

The sense of helplessness and lack of choice is especially evident in many of the literary attempts to deal with the war. In Heinrich Böll's early story, *The Train was on Time*, Andreas returns to the front filled with immense fear of what awaits him, yet he sees no other choice. In Poland he meets a Polish prostitute, who is simultaneously also a pianist and an agent working for the Polish resistance. They fall in love,

---

[66] See the excellent analysis of these films in A. Kaes, *From Hitler to Heimat: The Return of History as Film* (Cambridge, Mass., 1989), 73–103, 137–92. German soldiers remain victims both in Frank Wisbar's Stalingrad epic, *Hunde, wollt ihr ewig leben?* (1959), and in Joseph Vilsmaier's *Stalingrad* (1993). See Moeller, *War Stories*, 149, 194–95.

but there is no way out, no choice but liberation through death, which she finally arranges for the two of them at the hand of the partisans. Thus Andreas, who is one of the "innocents" Olina herself believes she is killing, encounters his own nemesis in a situation filled with the Nazi images of the period. Although unintended by the author, this story reveals the extent to which he had himself become permeated with the regime's presentation of reality during his years of education in the Third Reich and of service in the Wehrmacht.[67] For Andreas is ultimately killed by a woman who powerfully displays the qualities of the perfidious enemy agent, attractive, intelligent, yet murderous, using her intellectual talents and physical qualities to emasculate and annihilate him, even if here the act is performed in the name of love and includes her own sacrifice. The soldier is humanized, is indeed "innocent," but is trapped in a situation that leaves him only the choice of collaboration or death.[68] The other alternative, desertion, is similarly portrayed as hopeless, meaningless, and inconsequential, more an inner process than a concrete step, performed by rare and exceptional types (or clowns) as in Günter Grass's *Cat and Mouse*, or as an act both secondary to the novel and of no possible significance to the course of the war, as in Siegfried Lenz's *The German Lesson*.[69]

Insofar as these authors concern themselves with the moral choices of the troops, it is clear that they were available only to individuals who were totally different from the vast majority of their contemporaries. The act of resistance, if it appears at all, is due to the personal uniqueness of the individual; if it involves a moral stand (which is not always the case), this too is a private, intimate position not shared by the multitude. Indeed, precisely because the evasion of or resistance to collaboration is reserved in these works to the insanely suicidal acts of extraordinary characters, one gains the impression of a consensus regarding the complete absence of viable avenues of resistance, at least as perceived by contemporaries; though even this consensus is implied by its opposite rather than actually discussed. The more extreme one's uniqueness is, the more one is a complete outsider, an alien, the more one is likely to manifest resistance and refuse to go along with the rest.

---

[67] This despite his refusal to join the HJ. See H. Böll, *What's to Become of the Boy? Or, Something to Do with Books* (1981; New York, 1984).

[68] H. Böll, *The Train Was on Time* (1949; London, 1973).

[69] G. Grass, *Cat and Mouse* (1961; New York, 1963); S. Lenz, *The German Lesson* (1968; New York, 1971).

But this also implies that we are no longer dealing with questions of moral choice but simply with a stroke of (mis)fortune that makes nonconformity inevitable due to pronounced physical and mental deformity, as is most vividly portrayed in Günter Grass's *The Tin Drum* (where the beautiful eternal Aryan child who drums and shrieks his way through the Third Reich significantly turns into a morose dwarf in the new Federal Republic).[70]

To conclude, contemporary personal documentation, postwar memoirs, and fictional treatments of the war all provide one with a stark impression of a grim, determined, and increasingly hopeless commitment to professional and national duty. As the war became ever more painful and disillusioning, these documents reflect a sense of powerful conviction in the necessity to go on fighting for a good cause against a demonic enemy; hence the perceived lack of alternative is in no way merely the function of a ruthless penal system. Moreover, in fighting the devil, the end must surely justify the means, and nothing can be more immoral than giving in to his camp. Only the conspirators, mostly high-ranking officers, seem to have discussed the moral aspects of their actions at length, some of them indeed reaching such moral elevation as to doubt the morality of killing even Hitler.[71] For the majority, however, the choice remained between continued collaboration justified by an increasingly irrational faith, and suicidal resistance triggered by hopelessness and dejection. Both alternatives might lead to death, but the former provided one at least with hope, comradeship, trust, and belief. It was this course that most of the Wehrmacht's soldiers chose to follow.

[70] G. Grass, *The Tin Drum* (1959; New York, 1964). Compare to the case of Oskar Schindler, as analyzed in O. Bartov, "Spielberg's Oskar: Hollywood Tries Evil," in *Spielberg's Holocaust: Critical Perspectives on Schindler's List*, ed. Y. Loshitzky (Bloomington, 1997), 41–60.

[71] E. Wolf, "Political and Moral Motives behind the Resistance," in *The German Resistance to Hitler*, ed. H. Graml et al. (London, 1970), 193–234.

From Blitzkrieg to Total War
IMAGE AND HISTORIOGRAPHY

THE POWER OF MYTH

The German Wehrmacht conducted two distinct, though not unrelated and at times overlapping types of warfare between 1939 and 1945. One was based on massive, concentrated, and well-coordinated attacks along narrow fronts, leading to encirclements of large enemy forces and aimed at achieving a rapid military and political disintegration of the opponent by undermining both his logistical apparatus and psychological determination at a minimum cost to the attacking force. The other constituted a stubborn and costly defense, along huge, static, or gradually retreating fronts, normally launching only local attacks and counter-attacks with relatively limited elements of the armed forces, and relying increasingly on fortifications and doggedness rather than on speed and daring. The first type, which came to be known as Blitzkrieg, or lightning war, since it assumed a brief, though intense military confrontation, called for the preparation of limited stocks of armaments (without any major, long-term changes in the economy) needed for the implementation of such shock tactics, namely tanks, armored personnel carriers, motorized artillery, and anti-aircraft guns, as well as fighter planes and tactical support light and medium bombers. The second type, generally called total war, and closely related to the experience of 1914–1918 (whose repetition so many European countries, and especially Germany, had hoped to avoid), necessitated a much more profound restructuring of the economy and the industrial organization of the nation, as well as a greater participation of, and a heavier burden on, the population, so as to be able to produce the endless quantities of matériel, to use most efficiently the existing material resources, and to mobilize the largest possible numbers of men and women in order to satisfy the voracious appetite of total industrial warfare.[1]

As long as Germany pursued political and military goals that could be achieved by resorting to a series of brief, albeit highly brutal, Blitzkrieg campaigns, it remained victorious. Once it moved beyond these relatively limited goals (by continuing the war with Britain and attacking the Soviet Union), Germany found itself increasingly embroiled in a total world war that it had no hope of winning, because of the much greater industrial and manpower capacities of its opponents. Hence we can say that the transition from Blitzkrieg to total war spelled the end of German military and political hegemony in Europe, even though at the time there were those in Germany (including such rational technocrats as Albert Speer) who argued that only a truly total mobilization of the nation would save it from defeat.[2] There is, however, controversy over the *nature, degree,* and *implications* of German military preparation. Whereas one school claims that the Nazi regime launched a Blitzkrieg campaign due to the domestic economic, social, and political cul-de-sac into which it had maneuvered itself, the opposing thesis holds that the regime was motivated by foreign political and expansionist ambitions, showed no signs of anxiety over any alleged domestic crisis, did not seem unduly worried about its popularity, and was all along preparing for total war rather than Blitzkrieg, a war it finally launched not because of any feeling of constraint, but because it seized upon what seemed to be its best opportunity.[3]

Debates over the nature and meaning of Blitzkrieg, not only as a mil-

[1] T. Mason, "Some Origins of the Second World War," and "Internal Crisis and War of Aggression, 1938–1939," in *Nazism, Fascism and the Working Class*, ed. J. Caplan (Cambridge, 1995), 33–52 and 104–30, respectively; A. S. Milward, *The German Economy at War* (London, 1965), and Milward, *War, Economy, and Society, 1939–1945* (Berkeley, 1977); *Germany and the Second World War* (GSWW), vol. 1, pts. 2–4, ed. Militärgeschichtliches Forschungsamt (Oxford, 1998); W. Deist, *The Wehrmacht and German Rearmament* (London, 1981); B. R. Posen, *The Sources of Military Doctrine* (Ithaca, 1984), chaps. 3 and 6.

[2] A. Speer, *Inside the Third Reich*, 5th ed. (London, 1979), 269–367, esp., 299–314, 351–56; *Organization and Mobilization of the German Sphere of Power*, vol. 5, bk.1, pts. 2–3 of *GSWW* (Oxford, 2000); R. Overy, *Why the Allies Won* (New York, 1996); Overy, *Russia's War* (New York 1998).

[3] R. J. Overy, "Germany, 'Domestic Crisis' and War in 1939," and "Hitler's War and the German Economy: A Reinterpretation," in Overy, *War and Economy in the Third Reich* (Oxford, 1994), 205–32 and 233–56, respectively; D. Kaiser, T. W. Mason, and R. J. Overy, "Debate: Germany, 'Domestic Crisis' and War in 1939," *P&P* 122 (1989): 200–240; D. Kaiser, *Politics and War* (Cambridge, Mass., 1990), 370–92, esp. 375–84.

itary tactic, but also as a type of war favored by certain kinds of regimes, and hence a strategic concept to be understood only as a combination of political, economic, and military factors, have to a large extent been molded by the images it has produced ever since its inception. Images, in the case of Blitzkrieg, have been especially important, since the very success of this type of war has depended to a large extent on the image it projected, just as much as on its reality. Indeed, it would be more accurate to say that the image of Blitzkrieg was *part* of its reality, though precisely for that reason it is, nevertheless, important to distinguish between the more quantifiable facts of specific Blitzkrieg campaigns and their perception by contemporaries and later generations.[4] Such an analysis may tell us more about the relationship between the material aspects of war, on the one hand, and the power of myth and psychological suggestion, on the other.

In what follows I will discuss several aspects of this issue. First, I will point out some of the implications of the disparities between the facts of Blitzkrieg as it was conducted by the Wehrmacht in the initial phases of World War II, and the impression it made not only on those subjected to its violence but also on its practitioners. Second, I will present some of the main controversies over the nature and meaning of Blitzkrieg and note their wider implications for the historiography of the Third Reich. Finally, I will briefly examine the images of Blitzkrieg both during the war and following the collapse of the Nazi regime, and remark on some of the more problematic and disturbing manifestations of the representation of the German war machine.

Realities and Impressions

The concept of Blitzkrieg was developed as an attempt to avoid the recurrence of a static, costly, and, especially for Germany, unwinnable war such as the Western Front of 1914–1918. In order to prevent a similar stalemate along well-defended lines of trenches and fortifications, new types of weaponry and tactics were needed. Such ideas were already emerging during the latter part of the Great War, and during the interwar period they were widely discussed and in some cases put into practice. All European nations were intrigued by the new technologies

---

[4] For contemporary accounts, see M. Bloch, *Strange Defeat: A Statement of Evidence Written in 1940* (New York, 1968), 25–125; H. Habe, *A Thousand Shall Fall* (London, 1942). For a recent analysis, see E. R. May, *Strange Victory: Hitler's Conquest of France* (New York, 2000).

developed during the period and the manner in which they could be put to military use. But their conclusions as to organizing their armed forces and rethinking their strategic and tactical concepts differed greatly. There is no doubt that the major European powers—the Soviet Union, Germany, France, and Britain—recognized the importance of using modern tanks and aircraft in any future war. But for a variety of reasons that had to do both with their different experiences during the war and with the domestic and foreign conditions in each country, it was only the newly established Wehrmacht that ultimately practiced the new form of Blitzkrieg in the initial phases of World War II.[5]

From the very beginning, it was clear to all those involved in conceptualizing and planning Blitzkrieg that this type of warfare depended to a large extent on the impression it made on the opponent, since it was aimed just as much at demoralizing the enemy as at destroying him. And, while the enemy was to be given the coup de grâce after being debilitated by a combination of deep thrusts from behind, thereby severing the contact between combat elements and logistics, as well as by bombing of control centers and civilian targets, one's own troops were expected to be greatly energized by the constant, if ultimately exhausting, momentum of the fighting. Hence Blitzkrieg was intended to create the impression of an invincible army both among its enemies and among its own soldiers.[6]

In this the Germans were highly, perhaps even dangerously successful. While the campaign in the West culminated in one of the greatest, and cheapest, victories in modern warfare, it created a new and vastly more confident perception of the German capacities for war among those Wehrmacht generals who had previously been somewhat reluctant to accept the risks of Blitzkrieg. The result was that the Western campaign was not analyzed clearly enough, and those aspects of the fighting which might have turned a great German victory into a disastrous defeat were neglected or ignored. Nor did the failure of the

---

[5] The prophets of armored warfare included J. F. C. Fuller and B. H. Liddell Hart in Britain, Charles de Gaulle in France, Heinz Guderian in Germany, and Mikhail Tukhachevsky in the Soviet Union. See also C. de Gaulle, *The Army of the Future* (1934; London, 1940); H. Guderian, *Achtung-Panzer* (1937; Reading, UK, 1999).

[6] German war newsreels (*Wochenschauen*) of the period, and such films as *Feuertaufe* (Baptism of Fire, 1940) and *Sieg im Westen* (Victory in the West, 1941), screened throughout occupied Europe, provide a vivid picture of both the reality and the image of Blitzkrieg. See D. Welch, *Propaganda and the German Cinema, 1933–1945* (Oxford, 1983), 191–221.

Battle of Britain deter German military leaders from planning an even vaster, and much riskier campaign in the Soviet Union, where precisely those elements which had formed the potential Achilles' heel of the German army's Western campaign were greatly accentuated. To make matters worse, the industrial output of military wares remained far below the rate needed for such an unprecedented operation, so that in terms of the ratio between space and material, the German Eastern Army was actually weaker than its Western counterpart of the previous year.[7]

The irony of this turn of events is obvious. While the Germans drew the correct military conclusions from the Great War, and prepared themselves better than anyone else for the fighting in the first part of World War II, it was their victories during those early campaigns that blinded them to the limitations of their own strategy. Hence their final and greatest Blitzkrieg ended in catastrophe, and had to be followed by a reversion to total war strategies highly reminiscent of 1914–1918, with the unavoidable conclusion of a complete and total German defeat. The impression created by the swift victories and tremendous energies unleashed by Blitzkrieg therefore debilitated not only the enemy, but also the minds of those who had launched it. From being a means to preventing total war, it came to be seen as a magic formula for German victory and found its own nemesis in bringing about precisely what it had been intended to thwart. The concentration of forces at a given point, which formed the essence of Blitzkrieg, appeared to both sides as reflecting total strength, rather than relative power limited to a specific time and space.[8]

The fact that Germany chose Blitzkrieg in the first place was, of course, related to its severe industrial and manpower constraints, which were not fully appreciated abroad and forgotten in the flush of early victory by the Germans themselves. We will have occasion to discuss the debates on this issue in the next section, but for now let us examine the relative strengths of the armies and armaments industries of the major powers involved in World War II.

It is now generally accepted that contrary to the image disseminated (for different reasons) both by the Germans and their foes at the time, and indeed popularly accepted for a long time after the end of the war,

[7] *GSWW*, vol. 4, 199–224.
[8] Further on the planning of "Barbarossa," see *GSWW*, vol. 4, chaps. 1 and 4.

the Wehrmacht's armored forces during its most successful Blitzkrieg operation were in fact numerically, and in some respects also qualitatively, inferior to those of its opponents. Germany attacked in the West with some 2,500 tanks, while the combined forces of the Allies had about 3,400 machines. Moreover, only 700 German tanks had the speed, armor, and caliber of guns to be effective against the heavier types of enemy machines.

However, whereas most French tanks were subjugated to the infantry and the few existing tank formations were lacking both training and support, the Germans concentrated their tanks in large and well-integrated Panzer divisions. These divisions were then organized in powerful Panzer groups, which could be used to punch through the enemy's front and drive deep into the rear, dislocating and isolating its forces from their logistical support. Hence it was thanks to a combination of innovative (but not entirely unknown) organizational and tactical concepts that the Wehrmacht overwhelmed its enemy. Nevertheless, the impression created was of overall numerical preponderance and technological superiority.[9]

This impression was enhanced by the much more highly developed air doctrine of the Luftwaffe, which in this case also enjoyed a numerical and technological advantage, as well as being able to deploy types of aircraft best suited for its strategy (but not for later phases of the war such as the Battle of Britain and the strategic bombing of Germany). Facing the Luftwaffe's 4,000 operational airplanes were about 3,000 Allied machines, including those aircraft stationed in Britain. And, compared to the Luftwaffe's crucially important 1,500 bombers, the Allies had only 700 mostly obsolete machines. Nevertheless, in this case too it was largely the use made of air power that decided the issue, rather than its numbers and quality. The fact that by the end of the campaign the French air force had more aircraft on the ground than it had at the beginning of the fighting testifies to the timidity and incompetence with which existing airplanes were employed at a time when their proper use could have made a crucial difference. The Luftwaffe, on the other hand, used its aircraft as "flying artillery," and due to good planning, training, and cooperation with the ground units, achieved its goal of unhinging the enemy's front, disorienting its command, sow-

---

[9] *Germany's Initial Conquests in Europe*, vol. 2 of *GSWW*, pt. 4 (Oxford, 1991), see esp. 263, 290 for figures; Posen, *Military Doctrine*, chap. 3.

ing chaos in its logistical system, and demoralizing both the front and the rear, thus greatly contributing to its rapid military and political collapse. The much-hailed Maginot Line, where a high proportion of the numerically superior Allied artillery was to be found, played no role in the fighting, apart from tying down large numbers of inactive French troops.[10]

In spite of the initial impression created by the swiftness and decisiveness of the German victory, it would be a mistake to view it as inevitable. First we should note that only some 7 percent of the German force was truly modernized (ten Panzer out of a total of 141 mostly infantry divisions). Second, and as a consequence of the previous observation, the kind of breakthrough demanded by Blitzkrieg tactics necessitated the concentration of almost all tank formations along a very narrow front, and the exploitation of the initial penetration further called for a growing gap between the armored thrust and its infantry and logistical support. Hence, while the Germans did manage to drive a wedge into the Allied force, the Allies were in a position to do the same to the Germans by driving a wedge between the nine Panzer divisions rushing to the Channel and the mass of the German army trudging far behind. To a large extent, then, the success of the German Blitzkrieg in the West depended both on its novelty and on the incompetence of the other side's command. Had the Allies understood the essence of Blitzkrieg tactics (an example of which had been already given them in Poland), had they organized their existing manpower and matériel appropriately, and, had they shown a slightly greater degree of cooperation and tactical skill, the Wehrmacht would have had a much harder time confronting their forces.[11]

Because the Germans were taken in by their representation of their own successes in the West as inevitable, and due to their prejudices about the nature of both the Russians in general and the Bolsheviks in particular, they had little doubt that a Blitzkrieg against the Soviet Union would lead to an even greater victory than the campaign just

---

[10] *GSWW*, vol. 2, 238–53, 278–304 (279 for figures). Posen, chaps. 4 and 6 (citing the commander of the French Air Force, General Joseph Vuillemin, on the number of aircraft at the Armistice, 133).

[11] As suggested in M. Howard, *War in European History*, 2d ed. (Oxford, 1977), 132. German divisional structure in May 1940 in *GSWW*, vol. 2, 249. German view in Guderian, *Panzer Leader*, 89–117; a French officer's perspective in A. Goutard, *The Battle of France, 1940* (London, 1958).

won in the West. This hope proved to be an illusion. Indeed, within a few weeks of fighting it became clear that the Wehrmacht could not conduct a war on the mammoth scale demanded by the Soviet Union using the same tactics and equipment of the Western campaign. Here both the ratio between manpower and machines, on the one hand, and space, on the other, as well as between the German and Soviet armed forces, was much less favorable than in the West. The tremendous victories achieved nevertheless by the Wehrmacht in the initial phases of "Barbarossa" were thus not only a tribute to the tactical ability of the German officers and the fighting skills of their soldiers, but could also be attributed to the incompetence of the Soviet commanders and the lack of training (but not of determination) among their troops. It should be noted that while the Wehrmacht attacked Russia with 3,600 tanks (of which only 450 could confront modern Soviet armor), the Red Army in the West had 15,000 tanks (of which close to 2,000 were excellent modern machines). The Luftwaffe deployed only 2,500 aircraft in the East, significantly fewer than during the Western campaign, while the Red Army deployed 9,000 admittedly mostly inferior aircraft. It is interesting to point out that in fact the Red Army had a better ratio between men and machines than the Wehrmacht, that is, it was more modern, since it had only 2.9 million soldiers along the Western front of the Soviet Union as opposed to the 3.6 million attacking German (and allied) troops.[12]

The attempt to repeat its Blitzkrieg tactics over a vastly larger space than in the West compelled the Wehrmacht to split its relatively limited forces into even smaller groupings, and to allot its modern elements to each of these separate bodies with the result of further weakening its punch. Worse still, in the central sector of the front, the huge tracts of land to be covered meant that the Wehrmacht's armor had to be split once again in order to encircle the large Soviet forces in Belorussia. Meanwhile, as the Germans drove ever deeper into Russia, the front tended to extend, so that by late fall 1941 it had doubled in length, from 800 to 1,500 miles, while supply lines stretched 1,000 miles to the rear. Insufficient motorization of the Wehrmacht's logistical apparatus, the primitive road infrastructure of the Soviet Union, and the different gauge used by the Russian railroad, all made for growing

---

[12] Figures in *GSWW*, vol. 4, 72–93, 199–224, esp. 218–23. On ideological determinants, see ibid., 30–38, 481–521.

chaos and eventually totally paralyzed the German Blitzkrieg. The fact that about half of the German divisions deployed in Soviet Russia relied solely on horse-drawn wagons for their provisions meant that even when supplies arrived at the railheads, it was difficult to bring them to the front. Considering these factors, as well as the shortage of spare parts for the modern elements of the army, and the lack of replacement horses for the more backward formations, one can only wonder how the Blitzkrieg got as far as it did.[13]

Once Blitzkrieg failed, production, industrial capacity, material and manpower resources, organization and technical skill, all became more important than tactics, training, and courage. Of course, Blitzkrieg itself depended on technology; indeed, it made a fetish of modern fighting machines. But now technological innovation had to be paralleled by quantities produced, while the initial psychological impact of mass (but spatially and temporally limited) use of modern weaponry lost much of its force. In this area Germany had no chance of competing successfully with its enemies. One interesting consequence of this change was a transformation of the image of the war, to be discussed below. But this change took time, and although in retrospect one could find its origins in the prewar period, it became increasingly obvious only during the latter part of the war.

The growing gap between Germany and the Allies can be gauged from some revealing figures. Between 1940 and 1941 Germany's tank production rose from more than 2,000 to well over 5,000. Consequently the Wehrmacht doubled the number of its armored divisions, but reduced the number of tanks per division by a third. Nevertheless, this expansion of the armored forces was insufficient in view both of the growing amounts of matériel on the Soviet side, and the immense losses of equipment suffered by the Germans. It is indicative, for instance, that while in 1940 less than 400 modern tanks were built in the Soviet Union, in the first half of 1941 alone their number rose to 1,500. Even more impressively, in the second half of that year, and despite the loss of Russia's primary industrial regions, almost 5,000 advanced models were turned out.[14] At this point Germany was apparently still not committed to fighting a total war, since between 1940 and 1941 its

---

[13] Ibid., 525–832, for German operations; 833–940, for the Soviet side; 936–1029, 1081–188 for the collapse of the economic *"Blitzkrieg* strategy"; logistics in M. van Creveld, *Supplying War*, 3d ed. (New York, 1980), 142–80.

[14] *GSWW*, vol. 4, 78–93 (Soviet), 217–20 (German).

expenditure on war production hardly rose (although this may be partly explained by its previously high investment in armaments). During the same period the expenditure on armaments in Great Britain, the Soviet Union, and the United States put together almost doubled; even more significantly, this total was already three times larger than that of the Reich, although the United States was certainly not close to the peak of its war effort.[15]

In the wake of the terrible fighting of winter 1941–1942, Germany greatly expanded its armaments production, and over the next few years also made significant improvements in the technology of its weapons. But by this point the nature of the fighting had already changed irreversibly. In the West it had been possible (though not without risks) to maintain military effectiveness with a few well-equipped divisions followed by the great bulk of infantry formations, but in the East, because of the vast spaces that had to be occupied, the infantry proved unable to keep up with the armor over such long distances. This meant that the armor had either to wait for the infantry or to operate independently from its support (and logistical apparatus). Both options meant the end of Blitzkrieg, since the first dictated loss of momentum, while the second weakened the power of the punch by dispersing the forces and exposing them to constant threat of encirclement and annihilation. Blitzkrieg operations could have been resumed only if the Wehrmacht had been motorized on a scale that was far beyond the capacities of the Reich. Hence, as a more or less stable front emerged in the East, it became clear that it had to be held by the Wehrmacht's ill-equipped infantry formations, joined now by a growing number of armored divisions which had lost most of their tanks over the winter and could no longer be replenished.

Some elite army and Waffen-SS units were, of course, constantly supplied with modern fighting machines, but attempts to bring about fundamental changes in the overall situation repeatedly failed. Thus, while the summer offensive of 1942 already limited itself to the southern sector of the Eastern Front (where it met with disastrous defeat), the summer offensive of 1943 (the last time the Eastern Army took the initiative) was limited only to the area of Kursk and was stopped within a few days without any hope of success. Similarly, the winter offensive of 1944 in the West relied chiefly on surprise and cloud cover,

---

[15] Ibid., 217.

and once more had to be given up shortly after it was launched. Consequently, during most of the years of fighting on the Eastern Front (where the bulk of the German army was engaged), conditions became increasingly similar to those on the Western Front of World War I. However, while the Wehrmacht had to contend with a growing demodernization of its front-line forces, the Red Army was rapidly modernizing as it prepared for its own Blitzkrieg to the West.[16]

A few figures will suffice to demonstrate that in spite of Germany's tremendous efforts to increase armaments production, it had little chance of catching up with its foes. If by 1944 the Third Reich had raised the annual production of tanks to 27,000, already in 1943 the Soviet Union had reached an annual production rate of 30,000 tanks, while the British produced 36,000 tanks in 1942–1943, and the total American tank production by the end of the war reached 90,000. Similarly, while Germany produced 40,000 aircraft in 1944, the Soviet Union was already producing aircraft at an annual rate of 30,000 in the last years of the war, and the United States put out a total of 100,000 fighters and 90,000 bombers, many of which were strategic four-engine aircraft of a type Germany was unable to produce. Add to this the four million vehicles of all kinds put out by the American motor industry, and we can see that Germany stood little chance of winning the war after it had been transformed into total world confrontation.[17]

Controversies and Historiography

Two main controversies have developed around the concept of Blitzkrieg, its causes, consequences, and implications. One has to do with the relationship between domestic pressures and foreign policy, especially the decision to go to war.[18] The second concerns the relationship between war and the implementation of criminal policies by the Nazi

[16] On the *Wehrmacht*'s failure to replenish its manpower and matériel, see *GSWW*, vol. 5, bk. 1, pts. 2–3. On the soldier's front experience, see S. Fritz, *Frontsoldaten: The German Soldier in World War II* (Lexington, KY, 1995); T. Schulte, *The German Army and Nazi Policies in Occupied Russia* (Oxford, 1989); O. Bartov, *Hitler's Army: Soldiers, Nazis, and War in the Third Reich* (New York, 1991); Bartov, *The Eastern Front, 1941–1945*, 2d ed. (New York, 2001).

[17] Ploetz, *Geschichte des Zweiten Weltkrieges*, 2d ed. (Würzburg, 1960), 448–53, 471, 499, 593–94, 613; *GSWW*, vol. 4, 856.

[18] See notes 1 and 3, above. See also E. M. Robertson, ed., *The Origins of the Second World War*, 5th ed. (London, 1979); A. J. P. Taylor, *The Origins of the Second World War* (New York, 1961).

regime, especially the decision on the "Final Solution."[19] Both controversies are crucial not merely for our understanding of the wider implications of Blitzkrieg but, more importantly, for the analysis of the nature of the Third Reich, and, even more generally, the relationship between modern war and the state.

For the first two decades following the end of World War II, it was generally believed that Blitzkrieg had been simply utilized as the most fitting strategy for the Third Reich to accomplish its policy of military expansion. There was no appreciation of the fact that this might have been a way to resolve or prevent domestic tensions, or to wage war without further exacerbating popular discontent. Because Germany had reaped such amazing successes in its first military campaigns in Poland, Scandinavia, the West, South-East Europe, and the initial phases of "Barbarossa," it was deemed natural that it had prepared a military machine most suitable for such battles, and that it was only due to unforeseen natural and political factors, as well as blunders by the political leadership of the Reich, that this series of triumphs finally turned into defeat.

In the mid-1960s, however, this convention was challenged by a number of historians who claimed, on the basis of either new evidence, or new interpretations of old evidence, that in fact both the timing of the German decision to go to war, and the nature of the war conducted by the Wehrmacht, were anything but a matter of choice. Rather, they argued, the Nazi leadership was compelled to follow this course by a combination of economic constraints, popular pressures, and political anxieties, along with the better-known aspirations of conquest and expansion. Surveys of the condition of the German economy during the initial phases of the war seemed to indicate that the Reich had not at all been as totally mobilized as had been assumed up to then. While it did build up an impressive military machine, and produced modern armaments for a portion of the armed forces, Germany failed to create the economic basis necessary to sustain a long-term military commitment, but rather used only certain sectors of industry, and even those could be shifted to peacetime production relatively rapidly.

The question thus arose, what were the reasons for this obvious lack

[19] C. R. Browning, *The Path to Genocide: Essays on Launching the Final Solution* (New York, 1992), chap. 5; C. Gerlach, "The Wannsee Conference," in *The Holocaust: Origins, Implementation, Aftermath*, ed. O. Bartov (London, 2000), 106–61.

of preparation in a country apparently set upon waging a large-scale war, indeed, a war that it had itself initiated? Further examination of economic conditions in Germany on the eve of the war appeared to show that a major transformation had taken place from a state of wide-spread unemployment in the early 1930s to severe shortages of labor and resources by 1938. It was also noted that the Nazi leadership, and Hitler in particular, were profoundly anxious about the possibility of popular anger and unrest in case the regime attempted to make the same demands on the population associated with the Great War, namely both blood sacrifices and domestic economic hardship and pri-vation. The German public, not unlike the population of France and England, was anything but enthusiastic about the prospect of another war, knowing full well the horrific toll it would take on each and every member of the nation (even if some suffered more than others).[20]

Combining all these findings together, a new interpretation of the re-lationship between domestic and foreign policy in Nazi Germany was proposed.[21] According to this thesis, by 1938 Hitler realized that he was faced with the choice of either slowing down the rapid rearma-ment of Germany, for which he had neither sufficient manpower nor resources, or unleashing a war which would bring in more (slave) la-bor and (requisitioned) resources from newly conquered territories. The first option entailed abandoning, or at least greatly postponing, his plans for expanding Germany's territories, an idea with which he was obsessed and therefore could in no way agree to give up, quite apart from the political repercussions such a decision might have had on his own stature and the Nazi regime in general.[22] The second option, how-ever, meant that Germany would have to go to war before it had com-pleted its rearmament program and hence at a point in which it was still unready for a full-scale, potentially two-front confrontation.[23]

[20] Works by Mason and Milward in note 1, above; *GSWW*, vol. 1, pt. 1.

[21] For a similar contemporary interpretation of Imperial Germany's policies, see F. Fischer, *Germany's War Aims in the First World War* (1961; London, 1967); Fischer, *War of Illusions* (1969; London, 1973).

[22] On the regime's structural tendency for "cumulative radicalization" and Hitler's fears about his approaching decline, see H. Mommsen, "The Realization of the Un-thinkable: The 'Final Solution of the Jewish Question' in the Third Reich," in H. Mommsen, *From Weimar to Auschwitz* (Princeton, 1991), 224–53; J. Fest, *Hitler* (Har-mondsworth, 1982), 607–21; I. Kershaw, *Hitler* (New York, 1999–2000), 2:1–60, 181–230.

[23] For the "Hoßbach memorandum" outlining Hitler's plans for war, see J. Noakes and G. Pridham, *Nazism 1919–1945* (Exeter, 1988), 1:680–88.

Moreover, while discontent, especially among the working class, was already troubling the Nazi regime, it was feared that total war would greatly increase such manifestations of opposition, to the point of threatening the stability of the regime.[24] The choice was therefore made, not untypically for Hitler, to unleash a limited, but ferocious war, against selected targets and along specific fronts, while doing everything possible to keep other nations out of the conflict until it was too late to intervene. This was to be carried out at a minimum cost to the population, without mobilizing the whole industrial infrastructure of Germany for war, but rather by producing, in certain sectors of industry, only those types of military hardware deemed necessary for the campaign. Hence, the idea was to fight a victorious war without paying the price Europeans had come to expect since 1914–18.[25]

This plan worked until the collapse of the German invasion of Russia in winter 1941–1942. At that point it became clear that if Germany wished to stay in the war, it had to strive in all earnestness for a total mobilization of its resources. Paradoxically, just as Hitler's natural inclination to avoid such measures, motivated by his fear of unpopularity, was overcome, and total war was both declared and eventually also practiced, the fate of Germany was sealed.[26] This was not, however, due to unrest among the German population, as Hitler had feared, nor to any attempted "stab in the back," but rather to the fact that the Reich could only hope to win in a series of Blitzkriege, a type of warfare which, ironically, had initially been chosen for reasons of domestic constraints, not strategic calculation. Not uncharacteristically for the murderous absurdity which increasingly dominated the Reich, it was now such cool, rational technocrats as Albert Speer who insisted on making ever greater efforts for total mobilization of the nation's resources, and thereby simply prolonged the war and the suffering and destruction it entailed without being able to prevent Germany's ultimate defeat, an outcome already anticipated by far less brilliant minds no later than winter 1941/42.[27]

[24] T. Mason, "The Workers' Opposition in Nazi Germany," *HJ* 11 (1981): 120–37.

[25] See retrospective essays on this theory by T. Mason, P. Hayes, and H. James, in *Reevaluating the Third Reich*, ed. T. Childers and J. Caplan (New York, 1993), 161–89, 190–210, 114–38, respectively.

[26] Total war was finally declared publicly in a speech by Joseph Goebbels only on February 18, 1943, following the catastrophe in Stalingrad.

[27] Speer, *Inside the Third Reich* (New York, 1971), pts. 2–3.

This complex analysis of the wider implications and underlying motives of Blitzkrieg has been accepted by a large number of scholars, and has served as an important interpretive tool in explaining both the domestic and foreign/military policy of the Reich. Only in recent years have the data on which it was established come under increasing scrutiny and criticism.

The argument has been made that there was no such widespread opposition to the regime among the working classes as had been previously assumed, that the labor and resources shortage was not as severe as it had been depicted, and that Germany had actually done its very best, under the circumstances, to mobilize as totally as it could. Hence Blitzkrieg was not practiced *instead* of total war, but was rather a new manner of deploying and employing forces without giving up the notion of total mobilization. In other words, Blitzkrieg was merely a tactical innovation, not a new strategy. The timing of the war, it has been said, had to do much more with the opportunities Hitler felt he had been presented with, than with the alleged domestic crisis, which in fact never existed, or at least was not perceived as such by the Nazi leadership.[28]

The criticism of the "domestic crisis" thesis is of some importance not only because it questions several of the basic contentions about the nature of Blitzkrieg, but also since it constitutes part of a larger trend in recent scholarship on the Third Reich. The previous Marxist-oriented interpretation of Blitzkrieg had rejected the Nazi notion of *Volksgemeinschaft* as a mere propagandistic myth, and strove to document the workers' adherence to their interests and consequent opposition to the regime. While this view of society under the Nazi regime appears now to have resulted, at least in part, more from wishful thinking than from a balanced analysis, recent interpretations have similarly questioned the *Volksgemeinschaft* as a social reality, preferring for their part to concentrate more on passive resistance to the regime by widespread (often middle-class) sectors of society, or on non-conformist fringe

---

[28] Criticism of economic interpretation in Overy, James, and Hayes, notes 3 and 25 above. Critiques of working class opposition in O. Bartov, "The Missing Years: German Workers, German Soldiers," and A. Lüdtke, "The 'Honor of Labor': Industrial Workers and the Power of Symbols under National Socialism," in *Nazism and German Society, 1933–1945*, ed. D. F. Crew (New York, 1994); A. Lüdtke, "The Appeal of Exterminating 'Others': German Workers and the Limits of Resistance," in *The Third Reich*, ed. C. Leitz (Oxford, 1999), 153–77.

groups made mainly of youths of both middle- and working-class origins.[29] From another perspective of inquiry, the insistence on the primacy of domestic factors, typical of Marxist interpretations, was also shown to be at least not as foolproof as it had seemed in the past.[30] Finally, Blitzkrieg has always remained for many political and military historians, soldiers, and intelligent laymen, a military tactic rather than the outcome of complex forces and pressures and the expression of a totalitarian regime in crisis.[31] To be sure, this criticism, persuasive as it is in many ways, has not been able to demolish altogether the previous interpretation, and has left untouched many of the more intricate and subtle connections drawn between war, society, totalitarian regimes and economic preconditions. What is most important in this critique for our own argument, however, is that it blurs the distinction between Blitzkrieg and total war, and presents the former only as a version or elaboration of the latter, without denying that it was a crucial aspect of the Nazi state.

In the meantime, the importance of the ties between war and domestic policy has been highlighted from a different, even more disturbing, but nevertheless related perspective. In the course of debating the origins of the so-called "Final Solution of the Jewish Question," it was suggested by some scholars that the decision to initiate mass murder had been taken only after the invasion of the Soviet Union. Consequently it was argued that the realization of genocide might well be related to the progress of the Russian campaign. The various versions of this interpretation belonged, generally speaking, to what has been called the "functionalist," or "structuralist" school, a term coined, interestingly enough, by the same scholar who had insisted on the relationship between the decision to go to war and domestic policy.[32] Conversely, the so-called "intentionalist" school viewed operation "Bar-

---

[29] M. Broszat and E. Fröhlich, *Alltag und Widerstand* (Munich, 1987); A. Klönne, *Jugendkriminalität und Jugendopposition im NS Staat* (Münster, 1981); D. J. K. Peukert, *Inside Nazi Germany* (New Haven, 1987). But the most recent scholarship again emphasizes consent and conformism. See R. Gellately, *Backing Hitler: Consent and Coercion in Nazi Germany* (Oxford, 2001); E. A. Johnson, *Nazi Terror: The Gestapo, Jews, and Ordinary Germans* (New York, 1999); and chapter 1, note 60, above.

[30] See, however, T. Mason, "The Primacy of Politics. Politics and Economics in National Socialist Germany," in Mason, *Nazism*, 53–76.

[31] Note L. Deighton, *Blitzkrieg* (London, 1979).

[32] T. Mason, "Intention and Explanation: A Current Controversy about the Interpretation of National Socialism," in Mason, *Nazism*, 212–30. And see note 19, above.

barossa" at best as the occasion, but certainly not the cause of or impetus for, the plan of genocide. Rather, the "intentionalists" argued that the plan had been conceived years earlier, perhaps even long before Hitler came to power.[33]

The "functionalists," however, precisely because they rejected such teleological interpretations, needed to find the point at which a decision *was* reached by the top echelons of the regime. Alternatively, since the more extreme representatives of this school maintained that genocide was first begun as a series of local initiatives from the middle ranks in the field and only then adopted and expanded as a general policy by the regime, it became necessary to provide the chronological and geographical context within which this process took place (the assumption being that there had in fact never been a specific decision on the "Final Solution").[34] Since there was no doubt that the killing of Jews by mass shootings began only following the invasion of Russia, and since the construction of death camps began only in the fall of 1941, with the first installations being put into operation in winter 1941-1942 and spring 1942, it seemed likely that there was some connection between the military operations and the "Final Solution."[35] But while it is clear that the occupation of a huge territory, and the vicious nature of the fighting in the East, provided the context in which genocide could be carried out, partly concealed and, more importantly, made acceptable to perpetrators and bystanders already brutalized by war, some scholars maintain that the course of the Blitzkrieg campaign in the Soviet Union had a much more direct and specific effect on the decision to implement the "Final Solution."

Two contradictory interpretations of the relationship between Blitzkrieg and genocide have been suggested. The first argues that the Nazi regime chose to carry out mass murder following its realization that the Blitzkrieg in the East, and therefore in the long run the war itself, had been lost. The recognition of the failure to defeat Bolshevism was of crucial importance, since the Nazi regime had unleashed its cam-

[33] G. Fleming, *Hitler and the Final Solution* (Berkeley, 1984), including the introduction by S. Friedländer; E. Jäckel, *Hitler's World View: A Blueprint for Power* (Cambridge, Mass., 1981).

[34] Mommsen, "Realization"; M. Broszat, "Hitler and the Genesis of the 'Final Solution': An Assessment of David Irving's Theses," in *Aspects of the Third Reich*, ed. H. W. Koch (London, 1985), 390–429.

[35] See note 19, above; Browning, *Genocide*, chap. 5; M. R. Marrus, *The Holocaust in History* (New York, 1987), chap. 3.

paign in the East as a crusade against what it perceived to be the enemies of humanity and culture (at least its Aryan representatives). Hence
there was an immense sense of frustration felt by the Nazis. It was this
frustration at having been unable to complete the task they had set
themselves, rather than any premeditated plan to annihilate the Jewish people, that made Germany turn against the Jews, the one "enemy"
they were capable of destroying. Thus the failure of the Blitzkrieg in
Russia is presented as being at the root of the "Final Solution." Had the
campaign against the Soviet Union succeeded, genocide might not
have taken place at all, and the Jews could have been expected to be
simply pushed further East, expelled from the German occupied parts
of Russia.[36]

This interpretation, despite its Marxist origins, has the curious characteristic of partly overlapping with a conservative revisionist thesis
on the German war against Russia and the origins of the "Final Solution." The latter argues that the Nazis waged war against Bolshevism
out of fear, since they were certain that otherwise Stalin and his "Asiatic Hordes" would overrun and destroy Germany. Having been informed of the atrocities committed by Stalin against his own people,
the Nazi and military leadership simply adopted (or "copied") his
methods as measures of self-defense. This revisionist thesis is anything
but original, since it is so closely related to the Nazis' own representation of reality. Moreover, it both implies, and in some places clearly asserts, not merely a seemingly logical connection between the war
against Bolshevism and the genocide of the Jews, but also an apparently reasonable course of action on the part of the Germans, since it
claims that the "Final Solution" was not "original," but only an imita-
tion of the real or perceived acts of the Bolsheviks, who were, after all,
seen by the Nazis as identical with the Jews. Hence we are presented
with a process whereby the Nazis both took an example from the enemy, and, having associated their victims with the same enemy from
whom they had allegedly learned these methods, felt they had a license to destroy them.[37]

---

[36] This is the central argument of A. Mayer, *Why Did the Heavens Not Darken?* (New
York, 1989).

[37] E. Nolte, "Between Historical Legend and Revisionism?" and "The Past That
Will Not Pass," in *Forever in the Shadow of Hitler?* (Atlantic Highlands, 1993), 1–15, 18–
23. On the German historians' controversy that set the context for these arguments, see
chapter 1, note 13, above.

Both the left-wing and the right-wing revisionist interpretations which view the "Final Solution" as a "by-product" of either the failure of Blitzkrieg or the nature of Stalinism are exceedingly problematic, since to a large extent they do not correspond to the evidence.[38] Thus the contrary thesis points out that the killing of the Jews began well *before* the Wehrmacht had suffered major military reverses; therefore, it has been argued that rather than deciding on the "Final Solution" out of a sense of frustration, the decision on the genocide of the Jews was taken precisely at the point when the Hitler felt that the war against the Soviet Union had been won and that therefore Germany's energies could be diverted to the next important mission, purging the world of the Jews. And, once that policy had been decided on and the first steps leading to its implementation were taken, there was no going back, due to the nature of the regime and to its previous fixation on the "Jewish Question."[39]

It should be pointed out, of course, that some interpretations reject such clear-cut connections between *Blitzkrieg* and the "Final Solution." Thus, for instance, while the "frustration" thesis tends to push the decision on genocide to as late as winter 1941–1942, and the "euphoria" thesis places it in the summer months of 1941, yet another thesis, though not necessarily "intentionalist," tends to predate the decision on genocide to before the attack on Russia.[40] Nevertheless, even this interpretation has to concede that the actual *killing* began only after the launching of "Barbarossa." Hence, while there is no consensus on the nature of the tie between the *decision* on mass murder and the course of the Blitzkrieg in Russia, there is almost complete unanimity on the connection (but not on the *nature* of that connection) between Blitzkrieg and the *implementation* of genocide.

This brings us, however, to yet another aspect of the relationship between war and genocide. Blitzkrieg, as we have seen, has been presented by some scholars as a determined attempt to avoid total war. However, there can be little doubt as to the ties between total war and the Nazi version of genocide, namely, industrial killing. It was, after

---

[38] On differences between "Stalinism" and "Hitlerism" see I. Kershaw, "'Working Towards the Führer': Reflections on the Nature of the Hitler Dictatorship," in *Stalinism and Nazism: Dictatorships in Comparison*, ed. I. Kershaw and M. Lewin (Cambridge, 1997), 88–106.

[39] Browning, *Genocide*, chap. 5.

[40] R. Breitman, *The Architect of Genocide* (Hanover, N.H., 1991).

all, the so called "Great War," the first modern, industrial, total war,
which introduced the notion and practice of industrial killing of millions of soldiers over a relatively short span of time. The death camps
of World War II would seem inconceivable without the mechanical
slaughterhouse of the Western Front between 1914–1918. Hence, I
would argue that while it is important to recognize the ties between
the strategic, political, and ideological aspects of Blitzkrieg, on the one
hand, and the nature of totalitarian regimes, domestic policy, and
genocide, on the other, we must also emphasize that this type of warfare cannot be divorced from total war as a phenomenon of modern industrialized society. Rather, Blitzkrieg should be viewed as an aspect,
or offshoot, of total war, an attempt to revise it or make it more effective without doing away with those features of the original deemed
crucial to the conduct of modern war. In this sense it can be argued that
while Nazi Germany attempted to avoid total war in the military and
economic sense, it certainly did all it could to accomplish a total psychological mobilization of the population, just as much as it strove for
a total elimination of its real and perceived enemies. The limits on war
were to be set only as far as the suffering of the population at home
and the German soldiers at the front were concerned. The foe could
expect either complete subjugation or total annihilation.[41]

The Nazi Blitzkrieg was therefore not an alternative to total war, but
rather an attempt to adapt modern war to existing domestic and foreign conditions, as well as to Germany's expansionist aims and ideological ends. The Nazi conception of war was predicated on total
domination and ruthless extermination. Hence the still-present admiration for the Nazi war machine, even when allegedly focused only on
its purely military aspects, is especially disturbing, since it carries
within it an implicit fascination with mass killing and total destruction.
It is this issue which I would like to address in the following section.

Images and Representation
The image of the quick, lethal, almost clinical German *Blitzkrieg*, that
combination of roaring tanks and screaming dive bombers, brilliant
staff officers and healthy, smiling troops singing as they march to vic-

---

[41] M. Geyer, "The Militarization of Europe, 1914–1945," in *The Militarization of the
Western World*, ed. J. R. Gillis (New Brunswick, N.J., 1989); K. Theweleit, *Male Fantasies*,
2 vols. (Minneapolis, 1987–1989).

tory, was first propagated among both the German public and the Reich's neighbors, friends and foes alike, during the initial phases of the war. It was a powerful and persuasive image, for it closely corresponded to events as they were experienced by the various parties involved in the conflict, even if their radically different implications depended on one's loyalties. Indeed, the perceived congruity between the propagandistic image of war as disseminated in films, newsreels, photographs, leaflets, radio programs, and its reality was perhaps the most shocking aspect of Blitzkrieg for a public grown skeptical about the correspondence between image and reality. For in reality, just as on the silver screen, the tanks roared, the Stukas screamed, and the Wehrmacht, though perhaps not made of smiling soldiers, marched on into victory.[42]

While Nazi propaganda produced such images of Blitzkrieg with the clear intention of both intimidating its enemies, prospective allies, and neutrals, and uplifting the spirits of a German public initially quite anxious about a possible repetition of the 1914–1918 ordeal, other nations found this image just as useful in explaining their own experience of the war. Thus the French, for instance, tried to justify or rationalize their humiliating 1940 débâcle by grossly exaggerating the overwhelming numerical and technological superiority of the Wehrmacht, drawing what seemed to a public just recovering from the actual manifestations of Blitzkrieg highly convincing sketches of endless streams of tanks and aircraft, followed by invincible, not to say superhuman Aryan troops (feared, even hated, but occasionally also envied and admired),[43] all descending in an unstoppable flood upon France's fair fields and towns, shrugging aside the courageous, amiable, but outnumbered and technologically outdated French *poilus* (who by implication had been betrayed by the corrupt republic). This utilization of Nazi propagandistic images was an easy way out for in-

---

[42] See notes 4 and 6, above. On French reactions to the German Blitzkrieg, see H. Amouroux, *Le peuple du désastre 1939–1940* (Paris, 1976); J.-P. Azéma, *1940 l'année terrible* (Paris, 1990); P.-A. Lesort, *Quelques jours de mai-juin 40: Mémoire, témoinage, histoire* (Paris, 1992); A. Horne, *To Lose a Battle: France 1940*, 2d ed. (London, 1969).

[43] Postwar ambiguity in portraying fascists and Nazis can be found in M. Tournier, *The Ogre* (New York, 1972); J.-P. Sartre, "The Childhood of a Leader," in J.-P. Sartre, *Intimacy* (New York, 1948), and in such films as L. Cavani's *The Night Porter*, L. Visconti's *The Damned*, R. W. Fassbinder's *Lili Marleen*, H. J. Syberberg's *Hitler*, L. Wertmuller's *Seven Beauties*, etc. Conversely, see Hitler's bizarre expressions of admiration for Stalin, in *Hitler's Table Talk 1941–44*, 2d ed. (London, 1973), 8, 587.

competent generals and weak or opportunistic politicians whose lack of insight, indecisiveness, and outright blunders had much more to do with the defeat than any material, numerical, or innate superiority of the enemy. Nevertheless, since this image proved to be so useful in explaining what would have otherwise been difficult to accept, it was generally taken at face value at the time and lingered long after the end of the war.[44]

As the war went on, and Blitzkrieg receded in the face of a more total, and much less swift and glorious war, its German image became increasingly ambiguous, until finally it was transformed, indeed reversed, with the wielders of technology now playing the role of inhuman automatons, while those lacking matériel but rich in courage took up the posture of the superman. Thus whereas in 1940 it was the Wehrmacht which won cheap victories with modern fighting machines, by 1944 it was the enemy who was flying and driving ever more sophisticated machines against the increasingly (at least in relative terms) ill-equipped troops of the Wehrmacht. Consequently Nazi propaganda now changed its tune, presenting the war as a struggle between the German spirit and the cold, inhuman technology of the enemy (symbolized by the strategic bomber, that one item of technology not produced by the German armaments industry). Thus whereas in 1940 spirit and machine were welded together into the German Blitzkrieg, in 1944 the German spirit confronted the alien machine, and *Geist* was naturally bound to win in this newly christened *Materialschlacht* (battle of material).[45]

This, of course, never happened. Nor did the previous image ever totally vanish, since the great heroes of the latter years of the war still remained to a large extent both the *masters* of machines, such as the Luftwaffe pilots, the submarine crews, and the tank troops or *Panzertruppen,* and the machines themselves, the superheavy "Tiger" and "Panther" tanks, the first jet planes such as the Messerschmitt 262, and, most of all, the V-1 and V-2 rockets, those wholly depersonalized weap-

[44] On images of the *poilus* between 1914–1940, see C. Rearick, *The French in Love and War: Popular Culture in the Era of the World Wars* (New Haven, 1997). Further on lingering images from the 1930s and Vichy, see O. Bartov, "The Proof of Ignominy: Vichy France's Past and Present," *CoEH* 7, no.1 (1998): 107–31.

[45] On demodernization see Bartov, *Hitler's Army,* 12–28. On propaganda, see J. W. Baird, *The Mythical World of Nazi War Propaganda, 1939–45* (Minneapolis, 1974); Z. A. B. Zeman, *Nazi Propaganda* (London, 1964); D. Welch, ed., *Nazi Propaganda: The Power and the Limitations* (London, 1983).

ons, the epitome of technological war, the wonder-weapons or *Wunderwaffen* which failed to bring about that change of fortune and total transformation of modern war that was finally accomplished in a different part of the world by the atom bomb.[46]

Hence, when the war ended, the Germans (but many other participants in the conflict as well) were left with two competing images of their war. The first, closely related to the end-phase of the fighting, portrayed hordes of well equipped enemies attacking the Reich from every conceivable direction, East and West, air and sea, held back by desperately tired but courageous troops, ill fed, sorely lacking in modern armaments, tough and cynical and proud.[47] The second evoked better times, and compared the orderly, efficient, neat victories of German arms with the messy, destructive, chaotic defeat. Naturally, this image was derived from the German perspective, whereby the destruction of Warsaw or Rotterdam was part of a swift triumph, while that of Hamburg and Berlin served as proof of the enemy's steamroller techniques and over-destructiveness. But this was a powerful and enticing image that cast the winner in an inferior moral role, allowing him only superiority of numbers and production capacity, not of human virtues and technological quality. Moreover, both images could to a large degree be disseminated rather easily in the West, since they played on liberal guilt feelings regarding the terror bombing of Germany and the conquest and political subjugation of Eastern Europe and Eastern Germany by the Red Army as an ally of the West. Both images also relied on the assumption, widely held in Germany and generally accepted in the West, that there was no correlation between the German soldier, who conducted a professional, "fair" war, and the criminal policies of the regime carried out by the SS and its various agencies.[48]

---

[46] On the quest for the heroic warrior even in modern war, see O. Bartov, *Murder in Our Midst: The Holocaust, Industrial Killing, and Representation* (New York, 1996), 15–32. See also J. W. Baird, *To Die for Germany: Heroes in the Nazi Pantheon*, 2d ed. (Bloomington, 1992). For a contemporary representation of heroism, see E. Jünger, *The Storm of Steel* (1920; New York, 1993).

[47] See H. Spaeter and W. Ritter von Schramm, *Die Geschichte des Panzerkorps Grossdeutschland* (Bielefeld, 1958), vol. 3; and such postwar films as G. von Radvanyi's *Der Arzt von Stalingrad* (1958) and F. Wisbar's *Hunde, wollt ihr ewig leben?* (1959).

[48] On postwar representations of the *Landser* (grunt) as victim of both the Nazi regime and its enemies, see R. G. Moeller, *War Stories: The Search for a Usable Past in the Federal Republic of Germany* (Berkeley, 2001).

Hence the image of Blitzkrieg continued to play an important role in the post-war period as well. Yet this role was not confined to Germany. Indeed, precisely because Blitzkrieg was always both a military tactic and an image, both a reality and a manner of representing that reality, it became, in a sense, the ideal (of) modern war. Thus anyone who imagined war, who propagated it, who represented it in film or art or fiction or conscription brochures, could draw upon this available image of Blitzkrieg. Although, as I have argued, in reality *Blitzkrieg* was merely a version of total war, it came to serve as a highly potent counter-image to that other memory of industrial, modern total war, that of the mechanical slaughter of the Western Front in 1914–1918. While the latter was to be avoided at all costs, the former remained horribly (whether perversely or naturally) attractive, especially to those young men of numerous nationalities and several generations who, given the opportunity, were always likely to try and reenact it. This is, after all, the popular image of war as portrayed in countless war films and novels. It is a heroic, fast, dangerous, exhilarating, glorious, and sensuous representation of a paradoxically fifty-year old futuristic war.[49]

This transformation of Blitzkrieg into the good war, that is, the kind of war everyone prefers to fight, at least if fighting can not be avoided, is not only the domain of over-enthusiastic teenagers, but also of sober (though ambitious) generals. The Israeli tank General Yisrael Tal (Talik), for instance, is said to have likened the 1967 Israeli desert war against Egypt to a Blitzkrieg and to have compared himself with Hitler's favorite Panzer general, Heinz Guderian.[50] Similarly, one cannot help feeling that the American General Norman H. Schwarzkopf was portrayed (not unwillingly, one would assume) as the leader of a 1991–style Blitzkrieg, which contained all the necessary elements of few losses, immense quantities of sophisticated matériel, quick results, and massive destruction to the enemy. But while the good war has thus come down to us from within a German historical context that bliss-

[49] See the creation of a new American hero after Vietnam, in S. Jeffords, *Hard Bodies: Hollywood Masculinity in the Reagan Era* (New Brunswick, N.J., 1994). On one of the earliest antiwar war films, see J. W. Chambers II, "All Quiet on the Western Front (1930): The Antiwar Film and Image of the First World War," *FRT* 14/4 (1994): 377–411.

[50] On Israeli "Blitzkrieg" see M. Handel, "Israel's Political-Military Doctrine," in *OPIA* 30, Center for International Affairs (Cambridge, Mass., 1973); and on its nemesis in 1973, see H. Bartov, *Dado: 48 Years and 20 Days* (Tel-Aviv, 1981).

fully ignores essential components of this type of warfare, such as terrorizing the population by concentrated bombing of open cities, we are now experiencing yet another disturbing transformation of Blitzkrieg, that of its becoming a media spectacle.

Since Blitzkrieg is essentially part image and part reality, its two fundamental components are military action and media representation. Propaganda was always crucial for the success of Blitzkrieg campaigns, just as harmless but frightening sirens formed an inherent element of dive-bombers whose demoralizing effect was much greater than their destructive power. Blitzkrieg itself was to some extent a frenzied, yet well planned, murderous spectacle in which the actors were supplied with live ammunition. But nowadays, since the introduction of live media coverage, we are experiencing another kind of theater. Now we can watch battles at close range, in real time, without knowing what their outcome will be, hence sharing the confusion of the battle scene with the participants. This is a play without a script, and while the reporting is live, the dead really die, and the blood really flows. Yet we view all this at an immense distance from the event, and though we know that it is happening just as we observe it, there is absolutely nothing we can do about it. We cannot give a drink of water to the wounded, or bandage a bleeding child. If Blitzkrieg was the first war which blended modern images and technology, which sold itself as a media event, war in the post(modern)war age has become even more immediate and direct, happening right in front of our eyes, yet simultaneously reinforcing our sense of complete detachment from the events unfolding on the screen, since they are, precisely due to their being broadcast in real time, so far from us that they can never touch our actual existence. Hence live reporting breeds indifference, not compassion, detachment, not empathy. We take it as a given that the war out there and our own reality are connected *only* through the television screen, and that the connection can be severed at any moment we choose by pressing a button.[51]

By way of conclusion, I would thus like to emphasize the links between the various aspects of Blitzkrieg discussed above. We have noted that while Blitzkrieg could have been motivated by a desire to

---

[51] See further in M. Hudson and J. Stanier, *War and the Media* (New York, 1998); S. Jeffords and L. Rabinovitz, ed., *Seeing Through the Media: The Persian Gulf War* (New Brunswick, N.J., 1994).

minimize the price of war as far as one's own population was concerned, it was simultaneously closely related to the unleashing of a policy of genocide toward other populations. That is, while trying to be a limited war domestically, it was a total war vis-à-vis its real and perceived enemies. We have also seen that Blitzkrieg's reliance on images was not only a necessary precondition for its success, but has also played a role in perpetuating its fascination for postwar generations. Thus we may say that there is a link between the anesthetized image of Blitzkrieg disseminated in the popular media, and the current "real-time" reporting on war and violence whose effect seems to be detached curiosity and indifference, rather than compassion and political mobilization. In recognizing these links, we would be justified to feel profound unease about the potentialities of own civilization.

To take just one hypothetical example, how would we react today to a live CNN report from Auschwitz, showing us the gas chambers in operation, the smoking crematoria, the arrival of new transports, all in real time? How would that reality affect our own? We think of the real-time reports from Rwanda, Bosnia, Kosovo, Somalia, China, as well as the inner cities of the United States, and we know the answer. In this sense we can perhaps argue that Blitzkrieg was much more than a new strategy, for it was part of a process in the development of modern humanity which perfected our capacity to participate and yet remain detached, to observe with fascination and yet remain indifferent, to focus on an extraordinary explosion of energy and passion, and then calmly switch it off and go about our business. Perhaps *this* is the essence of Blitzkrieg, since it was, after all, an attempt to wage destructive war while pretending that nothing of importance (at least for the domestic population) was actually going on. In this sense we may even argue that Blitzkrieg was the perfect manifestation of modernity, since it presupposed normality as a simultaneous and essential component of atrocity, or, in our own terms, it anticipated the phenomenon of the "real-time" report, the symbol of contemporary humanity's indifferent acceptance of, and detached fascination with, death and destruction.

THE APPROPRIATION OF HISTORY
Particularly since the end of World War II, military history has acquired the reputation of being a somewhat dubious undertaking, and those who practice it have not infrequently been dismissed as second-rate scholars concerned more with tales of heroic battles than with se-

rious historical research. This bias can be traced back both to general postwar trends in public taste and sensibilities, and to more specific developments in the historical profession. It is, however, also closely related to the self-imposed limits and focuses of inquiry evident in the research and writing by military historians themselves, quite apart from the inherent characteristics and available topics of investigation in a sub-discipline devoted to the study of war. To be sure, popular military histories, battle accounts, biographies of great warlords, picture books on tanks and airplanes, and so forth, retain an immense public appeal, and often reach best-seller dimensions (a phenomenon which in turn makes scholars of history all the more suspicious of this genre). But by and large, within the scholarly community, military history has a bad name. This is true in most Western countries; and yet, distinctions should and can be made.

While in Britain and the United States (and to a lesser extent also in France), war and the military are (or are at least perceived as being) far from the most crucial element in these nations' own history, in Germany the relationship between war and society, as well as between soldiers and politics, has been accepted as a main factor in German history throughout the modern era. Conversely, while British and especially American scholars have begun to transform traditional military history into a wholly new and fascinating area of research, not least thanks to the increasing interest in war and violence shown by non-military historians, in Germany military history has—with a few recent exceptions—by and large remained in the hands of the traditionalists. To be sure, German military historians have raised some contentious political issues, and have courageously brought the military institution under a searing critique. But both in terms of their methodology, and in terms of their openness to new developments in historical scholarship, they have made little progress. Moreover, even in confronting sensitive political, ideological, and conceptual issues, they have shied away from drawing more radical conclusions from their own findings, and have failed seriously to address some of the most difficult and potentially explosive questions, such as the mental make-up of the soldiers and the involvement of the army in the Holocaust. Indeed, the few German scholars who, in the last few years, have cc ifronted these issues have all too often found themselves professionally and politically penalized.[52]

---

[52] For examples of new, often politically contentious, cultural and social military

The following pages will therefore concentrate on several aspects of military history writing in the Federal Republic of Germany since 1945, while keeping in mind some of its common characteristics with, and differences from, the historiography of war in other nations. In writing on this issue, I will attempt to take up the position of the insider as outsider, as one who belongs to the group (whether that of military historians, German historians, or historians in general), and yet who is also out of it (being neither a "pure" military historian, nor a German, nor exclusively a German historian). This potentially fruitful vantage point entails, of course, the possibility of shirking one's own responsibility for the group or for one's activities within it. At the same time, however, it is far from an untypical position for historians, especially military historians, to take, not least due to the low esteem in which this branch of the profession is currently held. Hence while I will subject German military history writing to a general critique (noting both merits and limitations), I will admit right at the outset that I see myself too as subjected to this critique and criticism, and not "outside" or "beyond" it. Nevertheless, I do view this specific group of historians and their writings largely as an outsider, as, indeed, I believe I am also seen by its members. Hence I can exercise empathy without being tied down by group loyalty.

Writing War

Before turning to the German scene, let me begin with a few words on the general context. As noted above, since 1945 military history in most Western countries has been on the defensive. While heroic war films and popular histories have always found a ready audience, professional historians tended to shy away from this field. This was both because of the general abhorrence of war following the terrible carnage of World War II, and to a growing extent due to the fact that a younger generation of historians, who had not served in the military and had

---

history in Germany, see R.-D. Müller and H.-E Volkmann, eds., *Die Wehrmacht: Mythos und Realität*, pt. 5 (Munich, 1999); H. Heer, *Tote Zonen: Die deutsche Wehrmacht an der Ostfront* (Hamburg, 1999). But as reactions to the exhibition "Crimes of the Wehrmacht" show, there are still strong ideological and methodological taboos. See O. Bartov, "The Wehrmacht Exhibition Controversy: The Politics of Evidence," in O. Bartov et al., *Crimes of War: Guilt and Denial in the Twentieth Century* (New York, 2002), 41–60; *Besucher einer Ausstellung: Die Ausstellung* "Vernichtungskrieg. Verbrechen der Wehrmacht 1941 bis 1944" in *Interview und Gespräch*, ed. Hamburger Institut für Sozialforschung (Hamburg, 1998); and R. Beckermann's documentary film, *Jenseits des Krieges* (1998).

not experienced war at close quarters, felt estranged from anything related to soldiering and the military establishment. Moreover, military history came to be associated with the official, commissioned histories of World War I, in which particular national and political biases were emphasized at the cost of a more detached, scholarly view of events, thereby exposing the more lamentable aspects of the state's ability to mobilize the intellectual community to its service.

This does not mean, of course, that no one wrote military history, but rather, that the field was left open either to historians more interested in the purely military, operational, tactical, and technological aspects of war, or to scholars who focused on strategy, politics, economics, and international relations. Consequently, military history tended to become isolated, divorced from new approaches to historical investigation and writing in the rest of the profession. Thus, while social, intellectual, and cultural historians avoided themes related to war, military historians stuck to the most conventional methodologies and closed themselves off from their colleagues' innovative ideas and concepts.

This is lamentable, since it impoverished the field of military history, and deprived history writing in general of a deeper understanding of the impact of war and the military on modern society. After all, in the past, historians had recognized that war was as an immensely important element in human civilization, and its study had indeed exercised some of the very best scholarly, intellectual, and philosophical minds.[53] Neglect of this aspect of human history did not, of course, diminish the role of war itself in our own time, but simply left us with only limited tools to analyze it. And while serious scholars pursued other avenues in the past, those who resisted this trend either felt obliged to apologize for not joining the multitude, or reacted by willfully ignoring their colleagues' contributions to historical research. Institutionally this meant that while the best minds often chose not to study war and the military, those who did could only find positions in military colleges and research institutes. This in turn diminished the reputation of military history even further, and often did indeed also narrow the horizons of such historians or put them under institutional

---

[53] A. Gat, *A History of Military Thought: From the Enlightenment to the Cold War* (Oxford, 2001); P. Paret, ed., *Makers of Modern Strategy: From Machiavelli to the Nuclear Age* (Princeton, 1986).

pressures which prevented them from expanding their historical perceptions and trying out more innovative approaches. For these reasons, whatever their personal political and professional biases might have been, military historians became increasingly conservative in their approach to the writing of history and, by extension, often also in their views of human society and politics.

This should not be seen as an obvious, self-evident development. Before World War II military historians had at times been highly original in their analyses of the past and radical in their politics. To mention just one case from German historiography, the revolutionary theses of the young historian Eckart Kehr in the 1930s, which were rediscovered and expanded during the 1960s and 70s, were based on a close and highly sophisticated analysis of the construction of the Imperial Navy and its political, economic, and social context.[54] Yet it took close to two decades after the end of World War II before new (or renewed) approaches to the study of war and the military began changing this convention, and even then their impact has remained limited. Ironically, the same country which had produced the first modern military historian, Hans Delbrück, in the first two decades of the last century, has been especially tardy in rejuvenating this sub-discipline.[55]

In Britain, and even more so in America, the last two to three decades have seen great changes in the study of war. Examples of new approaches to this field have interestingly not come necessarily from military historians, indeed, have sometimes not come from historians at all. Thus the highly influential *The Great War and Modern Memory* (1975) was written by a professor of English, Paul Fussell, and *A War Imagined* (1991) by another professor of English, Samuel Hynes. Nor were Modris Eksteins's *Rites of Spring* (1990) or Robert Wohl's *The Generation of 1914* (1979) written by military historians, while William McNeill's *The Pursuit of Power* (1983) was anything but a traditional military history, encompassing as it does several continents and a thousand years of human civilization.[56] As John Chambers and, in a more qualified manner, also Peter Paret have argued, there is room to speak today of

---

[54] E. Kehr, *Battleship Building and Party Politics in Germany* (1930; Chicago, 1973), E. Kehr, *Economic Interest, Militarism and Foreign Policy* (Berkeley, 1977).

[55] H. Delbrück, *History of the Art of War (1900–1919)*, 4 vols., 2d ed. (Lincoln, Neb., 1990).

[56] See also the fascinating study, N. F. Dixon, *On the Psychology of Military Incompetence* (London, 1976).

a "new" military history, though I would agree that it is still both young and limited, and suffers from severe intellectual, institutional, and theoretical constraints that will take many years to overcome.[57] In fact, it seems that only a new *cultural* military history, even more ambitious than that previously undertaken, will stand a chance of establishing itself as an intellectually vigorous, analytically and methodologically innovative, and academically respectable sub-discipline.

In Germany, however, even these early beginnings seem to be still a matter for the future. Excepting such fascinating works as Klaus Theweleit's *Male Fantasies* (which is neither by a military historian nor directly on the military, and yet can serve as a uniquely instructive model for military historians concerned with the mentality and psychology of their protagonists),[58] much of current German military history seems to plod along conventional, traditional methodological and analytical lines, unimpressed either by influences from abroad or by its own much more illustrious past. This condition needs to be further examined, not least because the *study* of military history, as well as the *actual* military institution, let alone the phenomenon of war itself, have had such a tremendous impact on German history.

Writing Germany's War

For the first two decades or so after the collapse of the Third Reich German military history consisted in large part of either very technical, tactically or strategically oriented works, or of a large host of memoirs, chronicles, and battle accounts by former members of the Wehrmacht.[59] This literature was often useful as far as the documentary and personal material it provided was concerned, though on the analytical level it often suffered from severe handicaps traceable back to strong

[57] J. W. Chambers II, "The New Military History: Myth and Reality," *MH* 55 (July 1991): 395–406; P. Paret, "The History of War and the New Military History," in P. Paret, *Understanding War: Essays on Clausewitz and the History of Military Power* (Princeton, 1992), 209–26. See also J. Lynn, "Clio in Arms: The Role of the Military Variable in Shaping History," *MH* 55 (January 1991): 83–95.

[58] Theweleit, *Fantasies*.

[59] For memoir literature and formation chronicles, see Bartov, *Eastern Front*, 164, notes 1–2. For technical studies, see R. Absolon, *Wehrgesetz und Wehrdienst, 1935–45* (Boppard / Rhein, 1960); G. Tessin, *Formationsgeschichte der Wehrmacht 1933–1939: Stäbe und Truppenteile des Heeres und der Luftwaffe* (Boppard / Rhein, 1959); H. Meier-Welcker, *Untersuchungen zur Geschichte des Offizierkorps: Anciennität und Beförderung nach Leistung* (Stuttgart, 1962).

apologetic tendencies and endemic, occasionally quite explicit prejudices carried over from the war itself. As for the historical method applied, the scholarly components of this large body of literature were
crafted in a highly traditional, conservative mould, accepting the implicit assumption that the past as it had "really" happened could be reconstructed simply by reference to official documents, while the array
of memoirs seemed to imply that their writers' participation in the
events they recounted was sufficient proof for the veracity of their accounts.

What most of these works had in common was that they by and large
accepted, confirmed, and recapitulated the official Wehrmacht view of
the war, notwithstanding the fact that both the Wehrmacht and the
regime it had served no longer existed. As such, this was quite a remarkable phenomenon, and one which must have had at least something to do with the great reluctance of either participants in the war
or those writing about it (often the same people) to subject both their
own experiences and the national experience as a whole to a fundamental critique (quite apart from reflecting the extent to which many
of these men had internalized the National Socialist perception of the
war without even being aware of having done so). Hence the legend
of the army's aloofness from the regime, the soldiers' professionalism,
"correctness," and devotion (to the Fatherland, not the Führer), the
generals' abhorrence of and opposition to the crimes of the SS, their
rigidly upright conduct and their strict adherence to moral codes and
soldierly standards, was perpetuated and largely accepted also by
many sectors of the non-German public and not a few military historians, especially in Britain and the United States,[60] all this notwithstanding the fact that as early as the Nuremberg trials the army (or at
least its top echelons) was shown to have been both deeply implicated
in the crimes committed by the Nazi regime, and strongly committed
to the "cause" it had espoused.[61]

This situation changed significantly during the 1960s and 1970s.
With the publication of several important studies on the Wehrmacht,
its relationship with the Nazi regime, its educational policies, and its
involvement in National Socialist crimes, the traditionally apologetic

---

[60] A good example is B. H. Liddell Hart, *The German Generals Talk* (New York, 1948).

[61] See, most recently, M. R. Marrus, ed., *The Nuremberg War Crimes Trial, 1945–46: A Documentary History* (Boston, 1997).

view was substantially revised, and the focus shifted from tactics and strategy to politics and complicity.[62] To be sure, much as these studies have contributed to our knowledge of the army's collaboration with the regime, they were neither forerunners in this field nor had they ever totally relinquished both previous traits, namely, fascination with military operations and ambivalence regarding the army's criminal actions. Indeed, these works, innovative as far as German scholarship was concerned, had been preceded by earlier British and American scholarly studies, which even if often less well documented, had already presented the main arguments on the role of the German military in politics and the implementation of National Socialist criminal policies.[63] In fact, these German studies were notable for their general reluctance to acknowledge the contribution of non-German scholars to the debate. What is more, they manifested a strong predilection to avoid issues still deemed sensitive by the German scholarly establishment, the media, the political community, and the public at large. This tendency, on which I will have more to say below, can still be seen in Germany today.

A second important area, separate from and yet closely related to the first, in which German scholarship on the Wehrmacht has shown only slight progress, and has hardly even begun the process of integration into the larger field of historical studies, is that of the range of scholarly and intellectual preoccupations of military historians and the resulting narrow and constricting methodology they apply to their sources. Over the last couple of decades we have seen social and cultural history move to the forefront of historical writing. As a result, official documents traditionally viewed as the primary sources of history have been subjected to much closer textual analysis and scrutiny and have been supplemented, if not replaced, by other, more varied and far less conclusive types of evidence.[64] "Objective" historical facts are now viewed as suspect by many historians; instead, they seek to uncover the conscious or

[62] For a review of the literature, see O. Bartov, "German Soldiers and the Holocaust: Historiography, Research, and Implications," in *The Holocaust: Origins, Implementation, Aftermath* (London, 2000), 162–84.

[63] J. Wheeler-Bennett, *The Nemesis of Power: The German Army in Politics 1918–1945* (London, 1945); G. A. Craig, *The Politics of the Prussian Army 1640–1945* (Oxford, 1955); A. Dallin, *German Rule in Russia 1941–1945: A Study of Occupation Policies* (London, 1957); F. L. Carsten, *The Reichswehr and Politics 1918–1933* (Oxford, 1966).

[64] G. G. Iggers, *New Directions in European Historiography*, rev. ed. (Hanover, N.H., 1984); L. Hunt, ed., *The New Cultural History* (Berkeley, 1989); P. Burke, ed., *New Perspectives on Historical Writing* (University Park, PA, 1992).

unconscious motivations of those who had manufactured the evidence at our disposal. They concern themselves as much with *perceptions* of reality among their protagonists as with what that reality "really" was.

In this context, German military historians appear at times like a throwback to another period, clinging to their documents with the tenacity of a retreating army aware of the catastrophe that awaits it at the end of the road. Instead of trying to learn from other German, and especially foreign scholars, about new concepts and approaches to historical studies, many of these military historians have increasingly insulated themselves from such influences. They have reacted by ever more detailed expositions of facts and numbers, documents and maps, to the point that even the powerful analytical potential of this kind of approach has gradually become submerged in a morass of printed sources with few interpretative remarks. In a way, their texts have become so similar to the documents on which they are based, that they have lost much of their effectiveness, and can serve only as sources and not as interpretations.

Whose History Is It, Anyway?

In order to demonstrate the problems noted above more specifically, let me turn to the single most important and comprehensive work of German military history since the collapse of Hitler's regime, the multi-volume series *Germany and the Second World War* (*GSWW*), of which up to now seven volumes have appeared covering the entire period between 1939–1945 (with some omissions to be treated in the forthcoming three volumes). The first six volumes have already come out in an English translation.[65]

In one sense, this vast collection, encompassing at present well over 7,000 tightly printed pages—it is projected to reach almost double that

---

[65] The series, published by the Militärgeschichtliches Forschungsamt since 1979, will have ten volumes (some made of two tomes). The translated volumes are: *Germany and the Second World War: The Build-up of German Aggression*, vol. 1 (Oxford, 1990); *Germany's Initial Conquests in Europe*, vol. 2 (Oxford, 1991); *The Mediterranean, South-East Europe, and North Africa, 1939–1941*, vol. 3 (Oxford, 1995); *The Attack on the Soviet Union*, vol. 4 (Oxford, 2000); *Organization and Mobilization of the German Sphere of Power*, vol. 5, bk. 1 (Oxford, 2000); *The Global War*, vol. 6 (Oxford, 2001). Published German volumes not yet translated are: *Das Deutsche Reich und der Zweite Weltkrieg: Organisation und Mobilisierung des deutschen Machtbereichs*, vol. 5, bk. 2 (Stuttgart, 1999) and *Das Deutsche Reich in der Defensive: Strategischer Luftkrieg in Europa, Krieg im Westen und in Ostasien 1943–1944/45*, vol. 7 (Stuttgart, 2001).

number by the time it is completed—makes the claim of being an authoritative study of Nazi Germany (a term judiciously avoided in the German and English title) in World War II by its sheer weight—physical, scholarly, and thematic. In another sense, these volumes imply that history, at least the writing of *this* history, "belongs" to the group of scholars who have been composing these volumes since the 1970s in the Militärgeschichtliches Forschungsamt (MGFA, or Military History Research Institute) in Freiburg (moved to Potsdam following German reunification). Moreover, since the MGFA was located, until recently, right next to the Bundesarchiv-Militärarchiv (BA-MA), where the largest collection of German military documents is kept, this series of volumes also asserts the authority of being the official interpretation of the Truth, at least so long as we accept that this elusive entity can in fact be found in, or reconstructed from, the documents of the Wehrmacht. This physical proximity to the primary sources thus creates what I would consider the illusion that the members of the MGFA are merely giving "objective" history a voice, and are indeed uniquely situated to do what any other historian, who is neither part of the group nor maintains the same intimate relationship with the documents (and the bureaucrats who control them—and provide the MGFA with free access to them), is by definition barred from achieving.

The *GSWW* is a remarkable accomplishment. It has been recognized as such not merely by the narrower circles of scholars interested in military history, but also beyond, both in Germany and abroad, as indicated by the decision of Oxford University Press to translate the entire mammoth series into English. The series is extraordinary not only due to the immense amount of material covered by the members of the MGFA, but also because it indeed provides a highly informed, and yet critical view of wartime Germany, and manages to demolish many of the conventions hitherto staunchly held by German (as well as some non-German) historians. Especially the chapters on the military, economic, and propagandistic preparation of Germany for war in the first volume, as well as on the ideological roots, military and economic planning for, and initial phases of Germany's war of destruction against the Soviet Union in the fourth volume, have had a major impact on all subsequent work concerned with these events.

Furthermore, the *GSWW* is a landmark publication in that despite the fact that it was produced by members of an official institute with close ties to the German military and Ministry of the Interior, its authors have maintained a high degree of academic independence and have insisted on their right to be critical of formerly accepted, and far more convenient "truths." Hence this quasi-official publication has managed to retain a high scholarly standard, a rather rare, if not unique phenomenon where national histories of war produced by official institutions are concerned. This was not achieved without much wrangling, conflict, and some compromises, the signs of which can be detected in many of these volumes, both in the somewhat uneven quality of the contributions, and in the stark contradictions between the arguments (and, ironically, "truth" claims) made by the different historians writing for the very same volume. But by and large, and within the parameters of what it had set out to do, up to now this has been a most successful historiographical venture.

What the future holds for this series is far less clear. Now that the MGFA has moved to Potsdam, against the wishes of many of its original members, there are indications that those in charge of the Institute are trying to bring about a major shift in the focus of its publications and the general control over the research and writing undertaken by its members. This will obviously take time, but as members of the old group have been drifting out to other academic posts or to retirement, one may expect that their replacements will not be given the same academic freedom enjoyed by the original team (and may be selected according to criteria that will ensure greater conformism). This may mean that the prospective volumes of the series will assume a somewhat different, and much less critical, if more uniform character, depriving them thereby of much of their previous merit, rooted precisely in that precarious balance between official sanction and support, on the one hand, and commitment to criticism and scholarship, on the other. Moreover, one should not overlook the obvious fact that relocating to Potsdam perforce evokes certain associations with Prussian traditions which were not known to criticize the military establishment. However, rather than speculating about the future, let us instead concentrate on what the MGFA has already produced, or rather, on those issues with which the series has failed to come to grips.

For, much as there is a great deal to admire in the *GSWW*, there is also much to criticize; and although we may lament its anticipated transformation in the future, we must also emphasize the limits of its achievement, not least because it seems that there is little chance that these limits will be surpassed in the near future.

Precisely because, as I have already noted, the *GSWW* implicitly claims the status of a definitive work, it is necessary to point out its shortcomings in three major areas. This is especially pertinent, since it is here that the series reflects, rather than resolves, a general problem in military history writing (and in some respects also in other sub-disciplines of history) in Germany. These areas include:

1. A conservative methodology, based on the assumption that a rigorous and faithful analysis of official archival documentation would suffice to reconstruct past events; that the veracity of this reconstruction would be "self-evident"; and that therefore there is no need for any further explanation, verification, or theoretical justification of this reconstruction of the past. This methodology, I would argue, fails to confront some of the most intriguing, as well as crucial questions of history in general, and of the period and events discussed in the *GSWW*, in particular.

2. An almost complete disregard of social and cultural history and all that they might bring to such an undertaking, presumably derived from the assumption that they belong to a wholly different, and therefore irrelevant, group of sub-disciplines, which cannot effectively be applied to military history. This intentionally rigid definition of the MGFA's disciplinary location within the historical profession greatly impoverishes the scope of the undertaking and bars its scholars from raising a host of both fascinating and central questions related to their work.

3. An almost complete absence of any discussion of the Holocaust, supposedly on the assumption that it is not directly related to the theme of Germany in World War II. Quite apart from being a false assumption, which most recent (German and foreign) studies of the Holocaust and German occupation policies have by now firmly dismissed,[66] this glaring absence sheds a disturbing light on the whole enterprise: it raises queries regarding the pressures which might have led to this exclusion; and, perhaps more troubling, it raises is-

[66] Browning, *Fateful Months: Essays on the Emergence of the Final Solution* (New York, 1985), 39–56; D. Cesarani, ed., *The Final Solution: Origins and Implementation* (London, 1994), pt. 2; H. Heer and K. Naumann, eds., *War of Extermination: The German Military in World War II, 1941–1944* (1995; New York, 2000); W. Manoschek, *"Serbien ist judenfrei." Militärische Besatzungspolitik und Judenvernichtung in Serbien 1941/42* (Munich, 1995); B. Chiari, *Alltag hinter der Front: Besatzung, Kollaboration und Widerstand in Weißrußland 1941–1944* (Düsseldorf, 1998); C. Gerlach, *Kalkulierte Morde* (Hamburg, 1999); U. Herbert, ed., *National Socialist Extermination Policies: Contemporary German Perspectives and Controversies* (New York, 2000), chaps. 5, 6, 8, 9; Heer, *Tote Zonen.*

sues regarding the views held by this group of historians on the connection between the Holocaust, the war, and the "German" Reich. In other words, an inevitable question would be, to whom *does* the history of the Holocaust belong? In this context it should be added that, judging by the plan of the rest of the series issued by the MGFA, we should not expect that the "Final Solution" will be addressed in *any* of the future volumes, at least not as a major concern that merits a separate volume or a substantial contribution.[67] To be sure, scholarly and public criticism, along with the appearance in the last decade of major studies by German historians of the links between the military and genocide, may compel the MGFA to revise its publication plans. But the conservative trend of the Institute in recent years seems to be moving strongly in the other direction. Be that as it may, as things stand now we can conclude that the MGFA views the Holocaust as only marginally relevant to the German military history of the war.

If we restate now the question implied by the title of this section, we can say that according to the *GSWW*, the military history of Germany in World War II belongs to military historians (the MGFA); these military historians have little or nothing to do with any other kinds of historians and history writing, and therefore neither does the military history of Germany; and this same history has little to do with the genocidal policies of the Nazi regime, at least as far as the "Final Solution of the Jewish Question" is concerned. That history, it appears, belongs to someone else (historians of the Holocaust? Jewish historians? Non-German historians?).[68]

Mentality and Genocide

At this point, I will briefly point out in what way a greater openness to outside influences, both of other sub-disciplines of history and of other social sciences, both from within Germany and especially from abroad, may contribute to enhancing the importance and deepening the insights of German military history, if only by enabling it to come to grips

[67] The working titles of future volumes are: vol. 8: *Das Deutsche Reich in der Defensive: Der Krieg im Osten und Südosten 1943–1944/45;* vol. 9: *Staat und Gesellschaft im Kriege:* pt 1: *Innenpolitik und "Volksgemeinschaft" 1939–1944/45,* pt. 2: *Das militärische Instrument;* vol. 10: *Das Ende des Dritten Reiches.*

[68] On this question, see M. Broszat and S. Friedländer, "A Controversy about the Historicization of National Socialism," in *Reworking the Past,* ed. P. Baldwin (Boston, 1990), 102–34; Kershaw, *Dictatorship,* 80–107, 180–217.

with some of the most troubling and most profound questions of war in the modern era.

First, a less rigidly Rankean approach to history is needed, one that takes greater distance from and a more critical attitude toward archival sources, along with a higher degree of skepticism regarding the objective truth value of both official documents *and* one's own reconstruction of events based on such documents, for this would open up a whole series of questions generally ignored by such works as the GSWW. The 7,000 pages of this study have, after all, merely given us a *version* of Germany's history in World War II, a version culled largely from the documents found in the Federal Military Archive. This is neither the Truth, nor the whole Truth, nor anything but the Truth. Not only has this history given us only a partial view of the events, it has also given us much which is merely conjecture, interpretation, and reconstruction on the basis of partial, indeed biased information, something that is the case of *any* history. Nor is this a question of space merely, because neither five, nor ten, nor twenty thousand pages on any given historical period or geographic location would ever suffice. Total history is, at best, an ideal; it is not an achievable goal, and definitive histories, to the extent that they are possible, are time and place bound. Precisely because of this limitation, it might be better to deal in less detail with some aspects of the war, and devote more attention to others.

What, then, are these other aspects that have been neglected? Let us ask, for instance, about the mentality of the soldiers who took part in this war. The volumes of the GSWW tell us a great deal about their conscription, equipment, losses, the orders they carried out, the defeats they sustained. But as far as their mentality is concerned, we do not proceed much further than some vague generalities. If any individual is discussed in greater details, it is invariably a general, or a politician. The rank and file get about as much mention as they do in any traditional military history written since Caesar and Tacitus. Nor is this an impossible task; indeed, some such studies have been written, initially by non-German scholars, but now also by young German historians, yet they receive scant or no mention in the mammoth academic apparatus of the GSWW.[69] This is not for lack of material, or even lack of in-

---

[69] Bartov, *Hitler's Army;* Schulte; and K. Latzel, *Deutsche Soldaten—nationalsozialistischer Krieg? Kriegserlebnis—Kriegserfahrung 1939–1945* (Paderborn, 1998).

terest. It simply does not fit into the historical-conceptual framework
of these volumes. This makes for a gaping hole in this vast venture,
since the result is very much a history from above, written, as it were,
from the green-tables of the staff officers and generals, not from the
view of the men who did the fighting.

Second, this Rankean mixture of history from above and rigid adherence to what are, after all, highly suspect documents, is closely associated with the scant regard given to social and cultural history. It is,
one must say, a great pity that such a fine group of historians, working
for a considerable period of time on the war, has made such a meager
contribution to the social and cultural history of the Wehrmacht, a subject recognized as one of major importance already quite a few years
ago. We still know precious little about the social composition of the
Wehrmacht and the relationship between the background of the soldiers and their conduct during the war; nor do we know much about
the effect which the troops' experience in the war had on their postwar
social status, political affiliations, or self-perception. Similarly, we still
know very little about the existence and nature of a "front culture," relations between the soldiers within their units and between subordi-
nates and superiors, political convictions and resistance, as well as
contacts between the front and the rear, soldiers' patterns of marriage
and divorce, rape and prostitution, fraternization and brutality vis-à-
vis occupied populations. All of these issues have not been addressed
to a sufficient degree, and if they were, then not by the members of the
MGFA. One also wonders whether at some later stage the series will
address the issue of women in the war. A social, as well as a cultural
history of the German army in World War II, a history that cannot be
based merely on the files of the BA-MA, or on Rankean methodology,
is still waiting to be written.[70]

[70] For recent progress, see Müller and Volkmann, pts. 4 and 5. See also F. Seidler,
*Prostitution, Homosexualität, Selbstverstümmelung: Probleme der deutsche Sanitätsführung
1939–45* (Neckargemünd, 1977); J. Stephenson, "'Emancipation' and its Problems: War
and Society in Württemberg 1939–45," *EHQ* 17 (1987): 345–65; *"Die Jahre weiß man
nicht, wo man die heute hinsetzen soll": Faschismuserfahrungen im Ruhrgebiet,* ed. L. Niethammer (Bonn, 1983), essays by M. Schmidt and A.-K. Einfeldt; C. Essner and E. Conte,
"'Fernehe,' 'Leichentrauung' und 'Totenscheidung': Metamorphosen des Eherechts
im Dritten Reich," *VfZ* 2 (1996): 201–27; T. Kühne, "Zwischen Männerbund und Volksgemeinschaft: Hitlers Soldaten und der Mythos der Kameradschaft," *ASG* 38 (1998):
165–89; Moeller, *War Stories;* F. Biess, "Survivors of Totalitarianism: Returning POWs
and the Reconstruction of Masculine Citizenship in West Germany, 1945–1955," in *The
Miracle Years Revisited: A Cultural History of West Germany,* ed. H. Schissler (Princeton,
2001), 57–82.

Third is that most obvious and striking absence in the *GSWW* regarding the Holocaust. This lacuna is, moreover, related on at least two levels to the problems mentioned previously. For on the one hand, the relationship between the Wehrmacht and the Holocaust can in fact be quite well documented by means of the archival holdings in the BA-MA; that is, it can be confronted with the traditional methodology employed by the members of the MGFA. On the other hand, the reluctance of the *GSWW* to deal with the mentality of the soldiers (which cannot be easily penetrated merely with archival sources and traditional methodology) may well be rooted in a more or less conscious awareness of the potential political repercussions of such an investigation.

Indeed, the conclusions which might be drawn from a frank and rigorous inquiry into the mental make-up of German troops during the Nazi regime could well prove to be as unsettling and politically uncomfortable as those one might expect from an additional volume devoted solely to the question of the Wehrmacht's role in the "Final Solution" (no such volume is planned). This is the realization that the young men of the Wehrmacht, who later became the founding generation of the new German Federal Republic, were deeply involved in the ideological assumptions and political actions of the Nazi regime. That is, not only that the lower ranks of the Wehrmacht were a crucial component of the realization of the "Final Solution," but that this mass complicity, precisely because it involved many hundreds of thousands, nay, millions of soldiers, was perforce reflected in attitudes (whether openly expressed or, more often, powerfully suppressed) among the young generation of the FRG, that very generation which soon emerged as the political, economic, and intellectual elite of West German democracy.

Conclusion: Toward a New Military History
All this is not intended simply to criticize the *GSWW* which, as already noted, remains an admirable accomplishment. It is to say that had this series sacrificed some of its detailed analyses in favor of a deeper examination of the soldiers' mentality, and had it devoted more attention to the connection between the war and the Holocaust, it would have greatly enhanced its historical value, quite apart from rendering a crucial educational and political service. For in Germany, memory still exercises a great deal of influence on people's attitudes, and history is still a major player on the political scene. And since war, ideology, and

genocide have had such a prominent role in Germany's recent past, one would do much better to confront them head on than to sweep their nastier aspects under the carpet by retreating into the old defensive line of professional compartmentalization or invoking dusty arguments on the alleged function of the historian as a detached, objective "*Wissenschaftler.*"

Hence I would like to end with a plea to young German scholars concerned with their nation's military history to go back to the example of some of their great predecessors of the interwar period and before: to approach their field with an open mind to developments in the historical profession at large, as well as in other social sciences, in Germany and especially abroad; to resist the debilitating, servile attachment to documents as the sole source of historical research, and to enhance their critical, literary, and political sensibilities; to realize that more (documents, footnotes, pages) is not always better, and that adherence to well-tried methods, though perhaps politically safe (both vis-à-vis the historical guild and on the national scene), does not necessarily bring one closer to the truth—nor does it make for a clearer understanding of the past; and finally, that while these days there is growing pressure in Germany to look back at past events with pride, there is still a great deal of room for explaining why such major portions of that past are so utterly shameful.

If German military historians wish to carve out for themselves a significant and influential niche in the scholarly debate on the past, they can no longer afford to ignore the excellent work being done by their German and foreign colleagues. Whether this is in the area of oral or social history, whether it concerns eclectic works of great originality or major contributions to the cultural history of war, general works on the experience of whole societies in total war, or analyses of memory, commemoration, gender, and faith, and much, much more, there is now a vast array of scholarship which must inform any serious work on modern war.[71]

---

[71] A few examples: J.-J. Becker et al., eds., *Guerre et cultures, 1914–1918* (Paris, 1994); M. R. Higonnet et al., eds., *Behind the Lines: Gender and the Two World Wars* (New Haven, 1987); J. Winter and E. Sivan, eds., *War and Remembrance in the Twentieth Century* (Cambridge, 1999); J. Bourke, *An Intimate History of Killing: Face-to-Face Killing in Twentieth-Century Warfare* (New York, 1999); P. Lagrou, *The Legacy of Nazi Occupation: Patriotic Memory and National Recovery in Western Europe, 1945–1965* (Cambridge, 2000); A. Weiner, *Making Sense of War: The Second World War and the Fate of the Bolshevik Revolution* (Princeton, 2001).

To be sure, this is not simply a German problem. In many other nations military history has been marginalized, or has managed to marginalize itself. But I believe that in Germany, both due to the importance of the subject, and because of certain institutional constraints and political sensibilities, the problem is even more urgent, and the present limitations and deficiencies are more visible. It is therefore high time for a new military history to emerge from Germany.

PART TWO
Extermination Policies

[3]

Killing Space
THE FINAL SOLUTION
AS POPULATION POLICY

PARADIGMS OF HOLOCAUST SCHOLARSHIP

Recent developments in Holocaust scholarship have done away with many conventional interpretations. It appears that the paralyzing effect of the horror on any attempt to explain its origins has gradually diminished. More and more historians are willing now to examine the roots of the Holocaust with a good measure of detachment. Careful archival research, the meticulous reconstruction of past circumstances, and sober evaluations of their protagonists' perceptions and motivations have largely—though by no means entirely—replaced earlier assertions of incomprehension and ineffability, of moral indignation and accusatory wrath.

Generally speaking, one can only welcome this calmer trend in the historiography of Nazism and the Holocaust. Since more scholars than ever before, in the United States, Europe, and Israel, are engaged in research on this period, and since previously inaccessible archives in Eastern Europe and the former Soviet Union are at last open to them, our knowledge and our understanding of modern genocide has been tremendously enhanced.[1] Indeed, we have shown ourselves to be far better at explaining past atrocities than at preventing present atrocities, which should cast some doubt on the notion of humanity's ability to learn from history's lessons.

[1] For a gist of recent research, see U. Herbert ed., *National Socialist Extermination Policies: Contemporary German Perspectives and Controversies* (New York, 2000). See also *Darstellungen und Quellen zur Geschichte von Auschwitz*, 4 vols., ed. Institut für Zeitgeschichte (Munich, 2000); K. Orth, *Das System der nationalsozialistischen Konzentrationslager: Eine politische Organisationsgeschichte* (Hamburg, 1999); U. Herbert, K. Orth, and C. Dieckmann, eds. *Die Nationalsozialistischen Kozentrationslager*, 2 vols. (Göttingen, 1998).

Still, the new expansion of knowledge and interpretation has neither augmented the scholarly consensus nor significantly diminished the professional, national, and ideological biases so characteristic of modern historiography. Indeed, some of the biases and deficiencies of contemporary Holocaust scholarship may be traced back to the conflicts and the traditions of the very period under scrutiny. The two most influential schools of interpretation of Nazism and the Holocaust have been labeled "intentionalism" and "functionalism."[2] The former stresses the centrality of Hitler and views the destruction of the Jews as a long-term project planned well in advance; the latter dwells on the structural characteristics of the Third Reich and presents the Holocaust as the outcome of intra-governmental rivalries and self-imposed logistical constraints. Intentionalists insist on ideological imperatives and the realization of a genocidal program; functionalists dismiss Hitler's role and emphasize the logic of modern bureaucratic norms and procedures, while relegating abstract ideological tenets to the level of empty rhetoric.

This division is not, of course, so tidy. In recent years, both sides in the debate have moved closer to their antagonists and have given up some of their more extreme positions; some of the vehemence that characterized the controversy in the 1970s and 1980s has abated.[3] And yet we can still tell the intentionalists from the functionalists. Despite some notable exceptions, moreover, we can also identify the origins of these positions, and their implications for individual and national identity, and therefore what they tend to miss, overlook, or purposely leave out.

Intentionalism has been promoted largely by non-German scholars. Intellectually, it may derive from a belief in the unique nature of Prussian authoritarianism, German antisemitism, or Nazi racism. If it is propounded by not a few Jewish scholars, this is mainly owing to the fact that many of those writing on the Holocaust are Jews, and that

[2] Coined by T. Mason, "Intention and Explanation: A Current Controversy about the Interpretation of National Socialism," in T. Mason, *Nazism, Fascism and the Working Class*, ed. J. Caplan (Cambridge, 1995). Further in C. R. Browning, *Fateful Months: Essays on the Emergence of the Final Solution* (New York, 1985), chap. 1; and also see C. R. Browning, *The Path to Genocide: Essays on Launching the Final Solution* (New York, 1992), chap. 5.

[3] O. Bartov, "Introduction," and S. Friedländer, "The Extermination of the European Jews in Historiography: Fifty Years Later," in *The Holocaust: Origins, Implementation, Aftermath*, ed. O. Bartov (London, 2000), 1–18 and 79–91, respectively.

most Jews writing on the Holocaust do not live in Germany. One prominent exception to this rule is the German historian Eberhard Jäckel, who is often attacked by his colleagues for insisting on the centrality of Hitler's ideology and political role; but even Jäckel has not gone beyond an analysis of Hitler's writings and speeches either to examine German public opinion (that is, Hitler's reception) or to reconstruct the creation of the "concentrationary universe" (that is, Hitler's function as leader).[4] Some intentionalists, such as Lucy Dawidowicz, have paid a great deal of attention to the Jewish victims, to their perceptions and misperceptions of German policies, to their struggle to survive, and to the conditions of their destruction.[5] Others, such as Daniel Jonah Goldhagen, have insisted on the manner in which the perpetrators' antisemitism motivated them not merely to kill, but also to derive pleasure from the killing.[6] Neither perspective is common among German scholars.

Functionalism is the product and remains at the basis of German scholarship on the Holocaust. The most important and the most influential historians of the Third Reich and the Holocaust in West Germany in the 1970s were Martin Broszat and Hans Mommsen. They are commonly considered to be the founders of functionalism, or "structuralism," as the fundamental interpretive paradigm of Nazism in Germany. In this reading, ideology is recognized and then dismissed as irrelevant; the suffering of the victims is readily acknowledged and then omitted as having nothing to tell us about the mechanics of genocide; and individual perpetrators, from Adolf Hitler, Heinrich Himmler, and Reinhard Heydrich to the lowliest SS-man, are shoved out of the historical picture as contemptible but ultimately unimportant pawns in the larger scheme of a "plutocratic state" whose predilection for "cumulative radicalization" was a function of its structure rather than the product of intentional planning or self-proclaimed will.[7]

Again, there are important exceptions to this rule. The influential

---

[4] E. Jäckel, *Hitler's World View: A Blueprint for Power* (Cambridge, Mass., 1981).

[5] L. S. Dawidowicz, *The War Against the Jews 1933–1945* (New York, 1975).

[6] D. J. Goldhagen, *Hitler's Willing Executioners: Ordinary Germans and the Holocaust* (New York, 1996).

[7] See H. Mommsen, "The Realization of the Unthinkable: The 'Final Solution of the Jewish Question' in the Third Reich," in H. Mommsen, *From Weimar to Auschwitz* (Princeton, 1991), and M. Broszat, "Hitler and the Genesis of the 'Final Solution': An Assessment of David Irving's Theses," in *Aspects of the Third Reich*, ed. H. W. Koch (London, 1985), 390–429.

German historian Andreas Hillgruber emphasized Hitler's role in planning and directing Germany's war. Yet, except for a few short essays, Hillgruber never did research on the Holocaust, and toward the end of his life he insisted on the need of Germans to identify with their own history and not with the history of their victims.[8] Raul Hilberg's magnum opus, *The Destruction of the European Jews*, which first appeared in 1961 and in a revised and expanded version in 1985, can be seen in some ways as the originator of functionalism, although Hilberg came to the United States before the war as an Austrian Jewish refugee. In fact, however, Hilberg's book is very much concerned with the deeper roots of Nazism, which he identifies in the first chapter with a long anti-Jewish Christian tradition, and is deeply preoccupied with the reactions of the Jews to Nazi policies.[9] (Indeed, his statements on the alleged absence of Jewish resistance and the complicity of community leaders in the genocide have subjected him to incessant attacks by many other Jewish scholars.)[10] Furthermore, the American scholar Christopher Browning calls himself a moderate functionalist, but his best-known work, *Ordinary Men*, which appeared in 1992, ventures into an area that no German functionalist had hitherto approached, namely, the actions and the motivations of face-to-face killers.[11] Browning coolly zeroed in on the horror of the killing rather than remaining with the so-called *Schreibtischtäter* (desk-murderers) so beloved of German functionalists.

GENOCIDE AND ETHNIC CLEANSING

Götz Aly belongs to a younger generation of German scholars who have been busily revising much of what their elders wrote, but without wholly rejecting some of their assumptions. Born after the war, between the late 1940s and early 1960s, such hard-working historians are extremely adapt at archival work, and they are less wary about exploding national myths and apologetic conventions than the previous generation (whose own mentors were more often than not complicit

---

[8] A. Hillgruber, *Hitlers Strategie: Politik und Kriegführung, 1940–1941* (Frankfurt/M., 1965); A. Hillgruber, *Zweierlei Untergang: Die Zerschlagung des Deutschen Reiches und das Ende des europäischen Judentums* (Berlin, 1986).

[9] R. Hilberg, *The Destruction of the European Jews*, 3 vols., rev. ed. (New York, 1985).

[10] O. Bartov, *Mirrors of Destruction: War, Genocide, and Modern Identity* (New York, 2000), 129–32.

[11] C. R. Browning, *Ordinary Men: Reserve Police Battalion 101 and the Final Solution in Poland* (New York, 1992).

with the Nazi regime). And yet these younger scholars do not entirely depart from the tradition in which they were raised; consequently, their prose is often inaccessible to laymen, their methodology is conservative, and their *Fragestellung* is in most cases limited in scope and ambition.

However, Aly is one of the most original, prolific, and controversial figures in this cohort of historians. This may partly explain his "outsider" status in the German historical guild, his public reputation notwithstanding. Aly's *"Final Solution,"* his finest achievement so far, came out in German in 1995.[12] Since then he has become involved a major controversy in Germany over the complicity of German historians in planning the Third Reich's policies of ethnic cleansing and resettlement in the East (to which there are some brief references in this book), and the cover-up of this episode both by those scholars and by their students in the postwar years.[13]

Aly relishes such disputes; the spirit of '68 wafts through his polemic. Yet his arguments cannot be dismissed easily, since he is an indefatigable researcher and a powerful writer. To be sure, his prose has a way of shifting from not entirely supportable generalizations to excessively meticulous presentations of documents and bureaucratic procedures, but his conclusions are always challenging and provocative. Nevertheless, for all his standing as the *enfant terrible* of his field, Aly remains part of the German scholarly discourse on the Holocaust. He disagrees with, and fiercely criticizes, many of his colleagues, but his own perspective is very much in line with the reigning consensus over the main paradigms of Nazi historiography in Germany.

Aly makes several crucial assertions in *"Final Solution."* For a start, he claims that by focusing primarily on "the inner workings of the perpetrators,"[14] his study differs radically from most other works on the Holocaust, which "have made the victims' perspective their own." While "the view from the perpetrators' perspective is bound to be upsetting," he observes, "the subject matter—the decision-making

---

[12] G. Aly, *"Endlösung": Völkerverschiebung und der Mord an den europäischen Juden* (Frankfurt/M., 1995); Aly, *"Final Solution": Nazi Population Policy and the Murder of the European Jews* (New York, 1999). His most controversial previous study is G. Aly and S. Heim, *Vordenker der Vernichtung: Auschwitz und die deutschen Pläne für eine neue europäische Ordnung* (Hamburg, 1991).

[13] G. Aly, *Macht-Geist-Wahn: Kontinuitäten deutschen Denkens* (Berlin, 1997).

[14] Aly, *"Final Solution,"* 1.

process leading to the Holocaust—forces us to look inside the minds of the administrators and planners."[15] He is right, of course, about the need to understand the motivation of the perpetrators; but he is quite wrong in claiming to be the first to have formulated or pursued this objective. Most German scholarship on the Holocaust, and much of the rest of the historiography of this period, is concerned with the perpetrators, which can be demonstrated bibliographically and anecdotally.[16] So in this sense Aly flatters himself.

But this first argument is closely linked to a second, and two-sided, argument. On the one hand, Aly claims, "what to the victims must have seemed the horrible efficiency of the bureaucracy of death appeared . . . in the eyes of the perpetrators . . . as an unbroken series of defeats, an inability to approach their goals, once established"; or to put it more bluntly, "the activities of Himmler, Heydrich, and Eichmann can thus be described as a chronology of failure."[17] On the other hand, while the alleged persistence of the victims' "one-sided view" of the Holocaust is "understandable," Aly believes that it "leads historical analysis astray and causes it to almost ignore the 'positive' aspects of Nazi population policies," that is, the extent to which the Nazis believed that they were constructing a better world even as they were murdering millions of human beings.[18]

This is, to say the least, a problematic assertion. A proper understanding of the Holocaust, to be sure, requires that its implementation be viewed also from the perspective of the organizers; and there is little doubt that—as Himmler asserted in his infamous speech in Posen in 1943—they believed themselves to be engaged in a glorious undertaking of conquest, demographic restructuring, and resettlement of a

[15] Ibid., 59.

[16] Seminars on the Holocaust at the universities of Freiburg and Göttingen in the late 1990s discussed exclusively studies on the perpetrators. American courses often stress the victims' experience. See R. L. Millen et al., eds., *New Perspectives on the Holocaust: A Guide for Teachers and Scholars* (New York, 1996). From G. Reitlinger, *The Final Solution: The Attempt to Exterminate the Jews of Europe, 1939–1945* (New York, 1953), to P. Longerich, *Politik der Vernichtung: Eine Gesamtdarstellung der nationalsozialistischen Judenverfolgung* (Munich, 1998), most major studies of the Holocaust focused on the perpetrators. An attempt to integrate both narratives is S. Friedländer, *Nazi Germany and the Jews*, vol. 1 (New York, 1997).

[17] Aly, "Final Solution," 59.

[18] Ibid., 246.

new *Lebensraum* by members of the "Aryan" race.[19] But surely the genocide that this entailed was not merely the "negative" side of this otherwise "positive" program. It was also what made the SS "strong," the true elite and vanguard of the *Volk*. Hence the Germans' "living space" became everyone else's killing space. Aly's focus on the Nazi sense of failure in their population policies as the source of the Holocaust leads him to neglect the remarkable feeling of triumph that the murder of the Jews engendered in the Nazis.

And this leads us to the core of the book, and Aly's third and central argument. Using a mass of documents from Himmler's offices in his capacity as Reich Commissioner for the Consolidation of German Nationhood (*Reichkommissar für die Festigung deutschen Volkstums,* or RKF), along with other sources on resettlement and deportation, as well as on the systematic murder of the mentally handicapped, Aly demonstrates in chilling detail the elaborate links between these policies and the emergence of the "Final Solution." (German scholars tend to put such terms as "Final Solution" or "Führer" in inverted commas, lest readers take them literally, and also to indicate their own distance from the Nazi vocabulary.)

Between 1939 and 1941, as Aly persuasively argues, several key Nazi agencies, including the SS and the Führer's Chancellery, were engaged in an attempt to change radically the demographic structure of the occupied parts of Poland. For this program, three elements became crucial: bringing ethnic Germans from the East (under agreement with the Soviet Union and other countries) to be resettled in the Greater German Reich; making room for those new "Aryan" arrivals by pushing out the Polish population; and ridding Germany and its newly annexed or occupied territories of the Jews. At the same time, the regime murdered some 70,000 inmates of insane asylums in Germany and tens of thousands more in occupied Poland (and later in occupied Soviet territory). These actions were presented as a cleansing of the "Aryan" genetic pool, as a means to save taxpayers money, and as the inevitable consequence of the need to free hospital beds for soldiers and to provide temporary housing for newly arrived ethnic Germans who could not yet be resettled on farms requisitioned from deported Poles.

---

[19] Himmler's speeches to SS leaders in Posen on October 4, 1943, and to army generals in Sonthofen on May 5, 1944, in J. Noakes and G. Pridham, eds., *Nazism, 1919–1945: A Documentary Reader,* 4 vols. (Exeter, 1988), 3:1199–1200.

The "positive" sides of this policy were a total failure. Indeed, these actions often contradicted each other. Ethnic Germans spent long periods waiting for their promised farms in what increasingly came to resemble concentration camps. Plans to deport Jews from Germany, Austria, Bohemia, and the annexed provinces of Poland had to be postponed, because priority was given to deporting Poles from their farms to make room for ethnic Germans, and because there were neither enough trains available nor sufficient space in which to "dump" them. Hans Frank, the man in charge of the Generalgouvernement (the part of German-occupied Poland not annexed to the Reich), had bigger plans for his fiefdom and refused to turn it into a "dumping ground" of the regime's undesirables, especially since the army was now claiming vast territories there for training and then for staging areas in preparation for the attack against the Soviet Union.[20]

By the summer 1940, it seemed that Himmler's grandiose demographic plans had come to a total standstill. Not knowing what to do with "their" Jews, but certain that they would eventually have to go "somewhere," the Nazi authorities in Poland concentrated them in a few major ghettoes, such as Warsaw and Lodz, and awaited a decision from the top. First they hoped to deport them to the so-called Lublin reservation in the Generalgouvernement, but Frank would not relent. Then, after the defeat of France, the idea of deporting the Jews to Madagascar was floated, soon to sink again when Britain, which still ruled the waves, refused to lay down its arms. By then, however, plans were already being hatched for the attack on the Soviet Union. The demographic experts of the SS now saw an opportunity vastly to expand the scope of their project, renamed the General Plan East (*Generalplan Ost*, or GPO), whereby tens of millions of Poles, Russians, and Jews would be deported and murdered, and many other millions of Slavs subjugated, so as to facilitate the creation of a huge new "living space" in Western Russia.

That the Jews would die in vast numbers was already clear to these "ethnocrats" long before the invasion of Russia was launched on June 22, 1941. During the early months of the campaign, however, only Soviet Jews were being killed en masse by the *Einsatzgruppen* (the murder squads of the SS and SD), first men only and soon thereafter whole

[20] See also Y. Lozowick, *Hitler's Bureaucrats: The Nazi Security Police and the Banality of Evil* (Jerusalem, 2001), 55–83 (In Hebrew.)

communities, whereas other Jews were supposed to be worked to death as slave labor or to be deported farther East into the depths of the Soviet Union. It was not until the tide turned in the Russian campaign—here Aly rejects Christopher Browning's "euphoria of victory" theory about the decision on the "Final Solution"[21]—when it transpired in the fall of 1941 that the Wehrmacht would not defeat the Red Army in a rapid Blitzkrieg, that the SS developed and began to build more sophisticated killing facilities for Jews.

All that remained, then, of the ambitious demographic plans of the regime and its innumerable experts (many of whom held academic degrees and continued their careers long after 1945) was the "final solution of the Jewish question."[22] For Aly, and this is his fourth and final argument, there was no decision on what we now know as the Holocaust. The genocide of the Jews developed almost imperceptibly as the outcome of everything that occurred before it: the failed resettlement project, the inability to defeat the Red Army, and the skill acquired in killing the handicapped and shipping masses of people from one part of the Nazi empire to another. In Aly's account, the Holocaust was the result of a new organizational expertise, an indifference to human life, and a habituation to brutality, all combined with frustration and a growing desire to succeed after so many mishaps and disappointments.

Here Aly is in general agreement with the older functionalists. Still, he proposes some significant modifications. He insists that one cannot analyze the emergence of the Holocaust in isolation from other ethnic and eugenic policies of the regime between 1939 and 1941. He also rejects the early functionalist argument that the Holocaust originated in a series of initiatives by low and middle level officials on the ground who carried out local murder operations, and that it was only later systematized into state-organized genocide. Aly shows, rather, that a genocidal urge was evident in all echelons of the Nazi administration even before the war in Russia, and he suggests that precisely the most radical proposals emanating from officials of various ranks were

[21] For his most recent statement on this issue, see C. R. Browning, *Nazi Policy, Jewish Workers, German Killers* (Cambridge, 2000), 170–75.

[22] On two SS "wonder boys" and their postwar careers, see L. Hachmeister, *Der Gegnerforscher: Die Karriere des SS-Führers Franz Alfred Six* (Munich, 1998); U. Herbert, *Best: Biographische Studien über Radikalismus, Weltanschauung und Vernunft 1903–1989* (Bonn, 1996).

widely circulated, discussed, and eventually adopted, in a kind of collective quest for a final solution to an irksome problem. Aly also, and quite rightly, dismisses the distinction made by such functionalists as Martin Broszat between the "positive" and "negative" aspects of the regime. For the seemingly progressive policies of the Third Reich—such as better housing and social services—were predicated on the exclusion, the deportation, or the elimination of those undesirable racial and political "elements" which allegedly had prevented the racial utopia of the *Volksgemeinschaft,* or national community, in the first place.

But finally, and very much in keeping with the functionalist consensus of the German historiography of the Holocaust, Aly believes that Hitler never gave an order to unleash the "Final Solution." He adds that the Führer, beyond his promises to back up those who came up with the most effective and extreme "solution" to the "problem" posed by the Jews, was not especially interested in the details of their extermination.

GENOCIDE AND IDEOLOGY

"Final Solution" is an important addition to the literature on the origins of the Holocaust, and it should be read by anyone who wishes to understand the context within which the genocide of the Jews occurred. Since "population policies" and "ethnic cleansing" have become almost a regular feature of world politics in the twentieth century, it is crucial to comprehend their relationship to mass murder.[23]

Of course, it is precisely the importance of Aly's book that makes it necessary to point out its limitations, the main problem lying not so much with what he says, but rather with what he does not say, lacunae that are themselves very much part of the German functionalist tradition. Some of these shortcomings are not lost on Aly himself; however, the paragraph in which he demonstrates his awareness of his omissions is curiously absent from the German original, and appears only in the English translation.

---

[23] N. M. Naimark, *Fires of Hatred: Ethnic Cleansing in Twentieth-Century Europe* (Cambridge, Mass., 2001). The English translation of Aly's book is occasionally imprecise and generally awkward. See Aly, *"Final Solution,"* 152, where Army Group Center and Army Group South appear as "Central Army Division" and "South Army Division." Within the Nazi context, *Volkspolitik* should probably be translated as "racial policies," not as "ethnic policies."

Aly argues that the German leadership, in putting an official halt to the "euthanasia" campaign in August 1941 (but without actually stopping the secret mass murder of the mentally handicapped throughout the war in other places and in other forms), "reacted subtly and flexibly to the public 'mood.'" And he proceeds to the following assertion:

> Conversely, this meant that Hitler, Himmler, and Heydrich felt sure of the support, or at least the passivity, of the overwhelming majority when they began the comprehensive murder of European Jewry a few weeks later. We can do no more than pose the question here, as the apparatus of authority is the focus of this book. A study on what the Germans thought of the "solution of the Jewish question" in 1941 has yet to be written. It would be methodologically difficult, but should without question be attempted.[24]

Now, it is false that such studies of German public opinion do not exist. Several studies published both before and after Aly's book examined precisely the question of German public knowledge of, and opinion about, the mass murder of the Jews.[25] Moreover, the fact that Aly's book is concerned with "the apparatus of authority" should in no way eliminate the question of public opinion. After all, if this apparatus was influenced by public opinion in the case of the murder of the handicapped—indeed, if the regime was greatly interested in the public "mood" and devoted much energy to gauging it, as we know it did—how can this issue be dismissed in the case of the Holocaust?[26]

And how is it that Aly, who is especially interested in middle-ranking officials, has nothing to say about their own attitudes toward those they were killing? He writes that these "technocrats" were anything but "spineless functionaries," that "at the intermediate and lower levels, there were committed people involved who were convinced of the ne-

---

[24] Aly, "*Final Solution*," 205. But in Aly, "*Endlösung*," 316, this passage is missing.
[25] J. Wollenberg, ed., *The German Public and the Persecution of the Jews, 1933–1945: "No One Participated, No One Knew"* (1989; Atlantic Highlands, N.J., 1996); D. Bankier, *The Germans and the Final Solution: Public Opinion under Nazism* (Oxford, 1992); Bankier, ed., *Probing the Depths of German Antisemitism: German Society and the Persecution of the Jews, 1933–1941* (New York, 2000); E. A. Johnson, *Nazi Terror: The Gestapo, Jews, and Ordinary Germans* (New York, 1999); R. Gellately, *Backing Hitler: Consent and Coercion in Nazi Germany* (Oxford, 2001).
[26] H. Boberach, ed., *Meldungen aus dem Reich: Die geheime Lageberichte des Sicherheitsdienstes der SS 1938–1945*, 17 vols. (Herrsching, 1984). E. Fröhlich et al., eds., *Die Tagebücher von Joseph Goebbels*, 24 vols. (Munich, 1993–).

cessity and rightness of their actions. They did not view themselves as tools, but as active, recognized protagonists."[27] So much for the banality of evil. And yet, Aly never inquires into their antisemitic motivation as has the German scholar Dieter Pohl, who has exhaustively studied the Holocaust in Eastern Galicia, and has discovered that many of those Nazi functionaries were indeed committed antisemites.[28]

Aly's assertion that this issue ought to be the focus of another study is akin to investigating slavery in the United States while leaving the question of racism to some other time. He does concede that "ideology did . . . remain important in so far as it sufficiently undermined the moral and legal barriers in the minds of the perpetrators, serving as a justification for their murderous acts." Yet he insists that "a purely ideological explanation . . . did not play any significant role in the actual decisions made."[29] A purely ideological explanation would indeed be sorely deficient; but this is just as true about an interpretation of the events that leaves ideology entirely out. In any case, human motivation is surely too complicated to be "purely" explained by anything.

Moreover, Aly's description of Hitler as largely uninvolved in the decision-making process about the extermination of the Jews is hardly consistent with what we know about his fanatic antisemitism and his insistence on the need to destroy the Jews, especially if a world war were to break out (an eventuality for which he began preparing as soon as he "seized power" in Germany).[30] Aly himself cites some of Hitler's pronouncements in this vein. We also know that Hitler played a key role in the "euthanasia" campaign, and that he signed a written authorization to murder the mentally handicapped.[31] To assume that Hitler was happy to step aside and let the "Final Solution" somehow occur, while throughout his "career," from the early 1920s to his political testament written on the eve of his suicide in April 1945, he saw the Jews as the most formidable evil threatening Germany, simply makes no sense at all.[32]

[27] Aly, *"Final Solution,"* 29.

[28] D. Pohl, *Nationalsozialistische Judenverfolgung in Ostgalizien 1941–1944: Organisation und Durchführung eines staatlichen Massenverbrechens* (Munich, 1996), 83–93.

[29] Aly, *"Final Solution,"* 29.

[30] C. Gerlach, "The Wannsee Conference," in *The Holocaust: Origins, Implementation, Aftermath,* ed. O. Bartov (London, 2000).

[31] H. Friedlander, *The Origins of Nazi Genocide: From Euthanasia to the Final Solution* (Chapel Hill, 1995), 67–68.

[32] On both Hitler's antisemitic obsession and his frequent attempts to remain aloof

Aly makes a convincing case for the evolution of anti-Jewish policies in Poland from the project of "ethnic cleansing" and resettlement during the first two years of the war; but surely this fails to explain, as Saul Friedländer has noted, why the deportation of Jews from Central and Western Europe, even from the farthest Greek islands, to the crowded ghettoes, camps, and killing installations in the East would have had anything to do with the demographic restructuring of Eastern Europe.[33] Nor is it at all clear why the failure of *Volkspolitik* in 1941 "naturally" led to the genocide of the Jews, if we accept Aly's assertion that ideology played no role in the decision-making process. Only a prior ideological commitment to a Europe cleansed of Jews (*judenrein*) would have made the move from "ethnic policies" to genocide appear as obvious as it indeed did to the perpetrators.

There can be no doubt that in the Nazi mind the Jews differed essentially from all other real or imagined enemies. Aly himself cites a number of documents that indicate the regime's interest in "re-Germanizing" Slavs, such as Poles, Czechs, and Slovenes, who appeared to Himmler's "race-experts" as having "Aryan" features. Hitler was not opposed to assimilating some Poles and believed that the majority of the Czech people could be "Germanized."[34] Indeed, according to Aly, "the Germans treated Poles and Jews quite differently in their deportation to the Generalgouvernement, especially with regard to material expropriation; it affected the Jewish population, right from the beginning of the occupation, incomparably more severely than the Polish." For one thing, mass theft of Jewish property constituted a crucial component in financing the entire resettlement program. Worse still, writes Aly,

> the expropriation of Jewish property, in contrast to that of the majority of the Poles, was not dependent on concrete resettlement; it was anticipatory. That is, the Jews—and only the Jews—were robbed of almost their entire means of subsistence and thus turned into a "superfluous," "unproductive" population; but, because of a lack of deportation opportunities, they at first remained in the country. Thus was the

---

from the decision-making process on genocide, see I. Kershaw, *Hitler*, vol. 2 (New York, 1999–2000).

[33] Friedländer, "The Extermination of the European Jews," 88.

[34] Aly, *"Final Solution,"* 100, note 3; 118. See also J. Connelly, "Nazis and Slavs: From Racial Theory to Racist Practice," *CEH* 32, no.1 (1999): 1–33.

material basis for the image of the filthy, loafing Jewish black marke-
teer created.[35]

Yet having acknowledged the "special" status of the Jews in the German racial hierarchy, Aly explains neither its origins (after all, antisemitic stereotypes existed long before the Jews were robbed of all
their possessions) nor its relative role in his tale of "ethnic policies."
The Jews were never subjected to such racial screening as were other
peoples occupied by the Germans; they were not *Untermenschen* (subhumans) like the Russians and the Poles, but rather the anti-race
(associated for many people with the Anti-Christ and with church
teachings on the Jews as a condemned people), and as such they had
to be completely eradicated. The decision to murder the Jews, rather
than to somehow make them disappear into a far-off land, the timing
of that decision, and the manner in which the genocide was ultimately
carried out, were obviously influenced by the context of events, among
which Himmler's plan of racial restructuring was a major component.
But to argue that one can explain the origins of the Holocaust without
any attempt to analyze the impact of traditional antisemitism, the
regime's anti-Jewish propaganda and indoctrination, and the attitudes
of the men who were actually organizing the genocide, is to misun-
derstand much of what the Holocaust was about.

Curiously, several documents cited by Aly point in precisely this direction, though they are interpreted differently by him. Peter-Heinz
Seraphim, one of Himmler's "ethnocrats," wrote in October 1940 that
the Generalgouvernement, the very area supposed to serve as a "dumping ground" for the Jews, was "already essentially oversaturated with
Jews." Consequently, he claimed that "the Jewish question has become
a first degree problem of mass population policy," and concluded that
"this gives rise to one long-term goal: the demographic cleansing of
this area, which can only be hinted at here."[36] Aly also provides documentation to show that in the killing of inmates of mental institutions,
the treatment of Jewish patients "clearly differed from the murder of
'Aryan' patients. While the Germans were killed selectively, according
to criteria that included length of hospital stay, ability to work, and
medical diagnosis and prognosis, the Jews became victims of 'euthanasia' collectively, solely on the basis of their racial classification."[37]

[35] Aly, *"Final Solution,"* 77–79.
[36] Ibid., 114–15.
[37] Ibid., 120.

All this notwithstanding, Aly's book remains under the spell of earlier German works on National Socialism and the Holocaust. His book is predicated on the notion that antisemitism was marginal to the entire undertaking, and that public attitudes, and the ideological disposition of the officials involved in the organization and implementation of genocide, were a negligible factor in the determination of policies. This insistence is all the more curious since Aly's book reconstructs a quasi-realized plan that required the deportation of Poles to make room for ethnic Germans, and the "emigration" of Jews so as "to make more room for Poles," as Himmler put it in December 1940.[38]

Since the Jews had to disappear, but had nowhere to go, they were first ghettoized and then murdered. And when all other plans fell through, even when the fronts were collapsing and Germany was about to be invaded, the Jews remained what they had been from the very beginning: Germany's first and primary target. The economic calculations that were supposedly at the root of this vast demographic upheaval were initially used to legitimize the murder of the Jews, but they were discarded as soon as they appeared to indicate the need to preserve the Jews as extra labor. As the German scholar Ulrich Herbert and others have written, the Nazi idea of *Vernichtung durch Arbeit*, or destruction through labor, may have applied to the Jews for part of the time, but the systematic killing of millions of productive human beings capable of contributing to Germany's war effort was ideologically determined.[39] The "ethnocrats" of the SS may have come up with ingenious arguments to justify killing as an economically sound means to prevent overpopulation and to bring about a modernization of the economy and a Germanization of the Reich's *Lebensraum* in the East, but there can be no doubt that, from the standpoint of the German war effort, this was a disastrous decision. And yet this decision was taken and implemented.

CONSENSUAL GENOCIDE

On July 16, 1941, Rolf-Heinz Höppner, charged with "resettlement affairs" in Posen and already involved in the murder of thousands of mentally ill patients in the Warthegau, the renamed annexed western province of Poland, wrote a memorandum to his boss, Adolf Eichmann:

[38] Ibid., 167.
[39] U. Herbert, "Labour and Extermination: Economic Interest and the Primacy of *Weltanschauung* in National Socialism," *P&P* 138 (1993): 144–95.

There is a danger that, in the coming winter, it will become impossible to feed all the Jews. It must seriously be considered whether the most humane solution is to finish off the Jews unfit for labor through some fast-acting means. This would definitely be more pleasant than letting them starve to death."[40]

This was one kind of rationalization of genocide: mass murder as a humane solution to an economic impasse. But another rationalization was offered for the mass murder of those Jews who were fit for labor. Since the invasion of the Soviet Union a few weeks earlier, all Jewish men of military age (and hence fit for work) were being massacred by the *Einsatzgruppen* as a security risk and as potential Bolsheviks. Following this "first sweep," the SS was charged with killing the remaining women, children, and old men, as "unproductives" or "useless mouths to feed."[41]

For Aly, the "Final Solution" was the last phase of a long process in which the Jews increasingly came to be seen as a population that had to be done away with so as to make possible the implementation of the demographic restructuring that had bogged down due to military and logistical failure. In the summer and the fall of 1941, "the term 'evacuation' became a synonym for murder," and all that was needed were a few "last remaining—minuscule—steps in the building of a complete extermination machine." In early October, Hitler "requested" that the Jews be moved "farther East" to areas not clearly defined. At this point Himmler and Heydrich ordered the construction of extermination camps that would serve as those destinations in the "East" to which the Jews would be "evacuated." And so Aly believes that "the final step between making the political decision and actually carrying out the plans was an extremely small one . . . under the conditions of this dictatorship . . . [and since] the technological prerequisites for mass extermination had long since been tested on the mentally ill."[42]

It follows, in Aly's view, that the Wannsee conference, which was convened on January 20, 1942, after several postponements, was merely Heydrich's successful attempt to gain the political consensus by "all . . . central institutions directly involved with these issues in respect to bringing their goals into line" (as the Conference records put

[40] Aly, *"Final Solution,"* 214.
[41] See more in Browning, *Nazi Policy.*
[42] Aly, *"Final Solution,"* 230–31.

it), the issue being "the evacuation of the Jews to the East." The meeting ensured cooperation between various government agencies, and no less important it "incorporate[d] the 'final solution' into the daily bureaucratic and political routines of the German state and organize[d] a division of labor." This "made it possible for each person to avoid any individual responsibility, instead entering into partly active, but generally passive, complicity with the government."

As Aly forcefully puts it, "nothing more was demanded of the individual. Nothing more was necessary in Germany."[43] Viewed from the perspective of public opinion, Aly argues that both the "euthanasia" campaign and the later "Final Solution" were a "secret Reich matter" that "was actually public." This ambiguity of definition, to his mind, must "be understood as an offer to Germans in general, and to the indirect participants in particular, to avoid responsibility and enter into an unconfessed, passive complicity that did not weigh on the conscience." Since the "euthanasia" campaign aroused no opposition among the thousands of officials involved, it gave the state leadership "the certainty that systematically planned mass murder, organized according to a division of labor, was essentially possible to achieve with the German government apparatus and the German public."

To be sure, Aly concedes that "the decision on the 'final solution of the Jewish question' was indisputably interwoven with the antisemitic doctrine of the German state at the time." But he insists that "any analysis will miss the mark if it is based only on the explanations offered time and again by Hitler and his Propaganda Minister and if it takes them at face value." Specifically, Aly is adamant that "Nazi ideology gained its effectiveness not from isolated, government-controlled hatred of Jews or the mentally ill, Gypsies or Slavs, but from the totalitarian unity of so-called negative and positive population policies." What Himmler liked to call "the socialism of good blood" really amounted to the racist superstition that the Jews "counted as a world enemy, the so-called anti-race per se"; but still Aly insists that "it was not the ideology itself that was historically unique, but the fact that it succeeded within a short time in becoming the central principle of a modern state."[44]

[43] Ibid., 233. See also K. Pätzold and E. Schwarz, *Tagesordnung: Judenmord. Die Wannsee-Konferenz am 20. Januar 1942. Eine Dokumentation zur Organisation der "Endlösung"*, 3d ed. (Berlin, 1992).

[44] Aly, "Final Solution," 244–46.

Much of this is accurate. But what it excludes is just as important, historically and morally, as what it includes. For it is a fact that there was opposition in Germany to the killing of "Aryan" inmates of insane asylums, just as there was opposition to the regime's attempt to take out the crosses from classrooms in Bavaria. The government was highly sensitive to public opinion: it stopped the "euthanasia" campaign (even though it continued it secretly elsewhere); it relented from confronting the Catholic population of Bavaria; it worried about rationing luxury items, let alone food, and therefore robbed the occupied countries and doomed them to famine and mass death; it employed millions of slave workers so as to lighten the load for the Germans. Even bureaucrats, as Aly himself shows, were anything but passive puppets of their seniors. They actively participated in formulating policy. Their opinion mattered.

But there was one issue, and only one issue, on which there seemed to be a general consensus and absolutely no debate: the persecution, the exclusion, the isolation, the expropriation, and finally the murder of the Jews. Some voices were raised about the utility of their labor potential, but those voices were weak and unimportant. Bishop Clemens August Graf von Galen of Münster, who protested so eloquently about the murder of the mentally ill, uttered not a single public word about the murder of the Jews.[45]

How this consensus was created, and what its effects on the formulation and the implementation of policy were, is not a marginal issue in trying to understand the mechanism whereby a state carries out genocide. It is possible that, as Aly writes, "Hitler's role . . . cannot be described as that of an inexorable giver of orders, but as that of a politician who gave his people free rein, encouraged them to develop the imagination to make the apparently impossible possible, and backed them unconditionally." Yet the controlling fantasy of Hitler's existence was the eradication of the Jews, and it was this fantasy, and the imagination of a total extermination, that he provoked in the public and encouraged his functionaries to realize.

There are many letters from German soldiers on the Eastern front that approvingly cite Hitler's speech in which he promised to exterminate European Jewry if "they" unleashed another world war; and these letters are just one measure of the extent to which the Führer's

---

[45] B. A. Griech-Polelle, *Bishop von Galen: German Catholicism and National Socialism* (New Haven, 2002).

genocidal fantasies came to be shared by millions of Germans.[46] Indeed, Aly himself asks whether "the machinery of extermination would not have been stopped, or at least slowed, had serious opposition and difficulties in legitimation arisen in the initial weeks and months. This," he rightly notes, "leads to questions about the behavior of the Germans, in particular." But he himself relents from pursuing this troublesome avenue of inquiry any further. "These questions are not the subject of this book," he lamely explains, "but must be posed in the same measure that we take leave of the exculpatory idea of a 'Führer order.'"[47]

A young German scholar, Christian Gerlach, has recently put forward a new interpretation of the Wannsee Conference. According to Gerlach, the original purpose of the meeting was to debate the status of German Jewish *Mischlinge*, or "half-breeds," individuals with both "Aryan" and Jewish ancestry. But following the Soviet counter-offensive before Moscow on December 5, 1941, and the Japanese attack in Pearl Harbor two days later, Hitler apparently decided to extend the mass killing of the Jews which was already taking place in the occupied parts of the Soviet Union into a continent-wide, and perhaps universal "final solution of the Jewish question." This, argues Gerlach, was related to Hitler's above-mentioned speech of January 30, 1939, in which he warned that in the case of a world war he would murder all the Jews of Europe. Hitler repeatedly referred to this speech in later years (though he tended to post-date it to the outbreak of war in September 1939). According to Gerlach, it was only in December 1941 that Hitler came to think of the war as a world war, and consequently ordered the genocide of the Jews.[48]

Thus Gerlach makes a clear distinction between the mass shootings of Soviet Jews in the summer of 1941, where the victims were murdered wherever they were found, and the "Final Solution," in which Jews were brought over thousands of miles to previously built death camps and killed there with ever greater speed and efficiency. He, too,

[46] O. Bartov, *Hitler's Army: Soldiers, Nazis, and War in the Third Reich* (New York, 1991), 106–78.

[47] Aly, *"Final Solution,"* 259. For comparisons with Italian and French attitudes toward the Holocaust, see J. Steinberg, *All or Nothing: The Axis and the Holocaust 1941–43* (London, 1990); Lozowick, 149–92.

[48] Gerlach, "Wannsee." See also, most recently, M. Roseman, *The Wannsee Conference and the Final Solution* (New York, 2002).

has found no "Hitler order," and yet he makes a powerful argument in favor of Hitler's centrality in the making of the decision to exterminate totally; and thereby he undermines not only older functionalist interpretations but also Aly's notion of a more or less smooth transition from "ethnic policies" to genocide, and Hitler's relative marginality to this process.

On February 24, 1942, Hitler proclaimed in a speech to the members of the Nazi Party: "Today . . . my prophecy shall hold true that it is not the Aryan race that will be destroyed in this war, but rather it is the Jew who will be exterminated. Whatever comes with the struggle, however long it will last, this shall be its final outcome. And only then, after the elimination of these parasites, will a long period of international understanding and thus true peace spread over the suffering world."[49] Such statements were greeted in Germany not with equanimity, but with enthusiasm. There were those who disliked them; but they remained silent about them, and thus complicit with them.

In order to understand the origins of the Holocaust, we must understand the origins of this public attitude in Germany. For it was a combination of technocratic activism and public complicity that made the great crime possible, and the former would not have accomplished much without the latter. And if we are to understand the nature of the killing, we must also go beyond the neat desks of the *Schreibtischtäter* and observe the physical encounter between the perpetrators and their victims. This must be seen from the perspective of the victims, and this perspective, contrary to Aly's assertion, has received very little scholarly attention, especially in Germany.

By including the voices of those who were subjected to persecution, humiliation, torture, and murder, we may realize the extent to which hatred and ideological conviction were at the root of the events and were constantly fueled by the very encounter that they originated. From where the victims stood, there was no doubt in their minds that they were not being killed merely as bureaucratic abstractions, but as the worst enemy of the Germans and as the lowliest creatures on earth: as Jews.

[49] Aly, *"Final Solution,"* 265.

[4]

Ordering Horror
CONCEPTUALIZATIONS OF THE
CONCENTRATIONARY UNIVERSE

THE CONCENTRATION CAMP AS SOCIOLOGICAL CONSTRUCT

The historiography of the Holocaust has been written almost exclusively in two distinct narratives. The first, to which German historians have made an especially important contribution in recent years, is concerned with the planning, the organization, and the perpetration of genocide. The second, written in large part by Jewish scholars, some of whom specialize in literature rather than history, focuses largely on the victims. And this predilection for telling two different stories about the same event imposes serious limits on our understanding of the "Final Solution."[1]

To be sure, the problem is not unique to this subject. Many nations have tended to tell only their side of the past, ignoring or marginalizing the role and the fate of other groups that influenced or were touched by their history. The traditional historiography of imperialism deprived the peoples whose freedom was taken away by European colonization also of their identity and their history. Similarly, the complicated, sometimes disastrous, but in many cases also fruitful relationship between European Jewry and the Christian population in whose midst it lived for many centuries earned only a few cursory remarks in the national histories that have been an important influence in defining European identities since the nineteenth century.[2]

---

[1] Compare P. Longerich, *Politik der Vernichtung: Eine Gesamtdarstellung der national-sozialistischen Judenverfolgung* (Munich, 1998) and R. Ogorreck, *Die Einsatzgruppen und die "Genesis der Endlösung"* (Berlin, 1996), to L. Yahil, *The Holocaust: The Fate of European Jewry* (New York, 1990), and L. L. Langer, *Preempting the Holocaust* (New Haven, 1998).

[2] Colonial destruction of identity in F. Fanon, *The Wretched of the Earth* (New York, 1963), and S. Lindqvist, *"Exterminate All the Brutes"* (New York, 1996); creation of national identity in G. Eley and R. G. Suny, *Becoming National: A Reader* (New York, 1996).

Historians are always caught between their professional duty to reconstruct the past as accurately as they can, and their personal, national, and ideological motivations. While scholarly integrity depends on presenting all the protagonists of a given historical event, the identity of the individual historian sets limits to his or her interests and sensibilities. Still, most historians would agree by now that telling the tale from the perspective of only one side must distort the picture and hamper the understanding. We may accept that, to some extent, this is inevitable, but we must think it a regrettable consequence of our limitations. In the case of the Holocaust, however, there is little evidence of such regret. Many of the scholars writing on the perpetrators or on the victims tend to justify the persistence of this double narrative. One might even argue that if most scholars of the Holocaust agree on anything, it is on the merits of separating the murderers and the murdered, as well as on the historical and moral perils of combining the two perspectives into a single narrative.

Writing a comprehensive history of the Holocaust that takes into account both the organization of genocide and the manner in which it was experienced by the victims is, of course, an almost impossibly vast undertaking.[3] Merely mastering the tremendous documentation, the ever-growing secondary literature, and the variety of languages in which all this material was written, may well be beyond the capacities of a single scholar. These technical limitations are themselves a measure of the scale of the genocidal ambitions of the Nazis, and the extent to which they were in fact realized.

Consider the case of the fine German historian Dieter Pohl. His recent book on the genocide of the Jews in Eastern Galicia is one of the most important regional studies of the Holocaust in the last few years. Pohl has made extensive use of newly available documents in Poland, Ukraine, and Russia, as well as of East European scholarly literature that was rarely invoked in previous works by Western historians. And yet, although he is concerned with a relatively small region, Pohl admits to having written his study only from the perspective of the perpetrators, expressing the hope that the story of the victims will be

---

[3] S. Friedländer, *Nazi Germany and the Jews*, vol. 1 (New York, 1997), 67–68, has attempted this for the 1930s. M. Gilbert, *The Holocaust: A History of the Jews of Europe during the Second World War* (New York, 1985), focuses on the victims; R. Hilberg, *The Destruction of the European Jews*, 3 vols., rev. ed. (New York, 1985), is on the perpetrators.

written by another historian equipped with the required scholarly and linguistic abilities.[4]

The persistence of this double narrative can be traced also to a jumble of historical assumptions. It has been argued that there is no need to represent the victims in order to explain the planning and the implementation of their murder. Similarly, analyses of the victims' experience have often seen no need to dwell on the organization of genocide or the motivations of the perpetrators. And these vexations are not merely methodological. They reflect also an anxiety regarding the moral impact of acknowledging the humanity of both groups by putting them, so to speak, face-to-face with one another—though the reality of genocide made contact between them unavoidable.

German scholars have insisted that since the perpetrators totally dehumanized their victims, no amount of knowledge about the objective reality of the latter will tell us anything of value about the motivations of the former. Moreover, claiming that the perpetrators might have recognized the humanity of those they killed is seen as morally dubious, since it may lead to a humanization of the killers. A similar fear is implicit in the resistance of those concerned with the perspective of the victims. They are reluctant to combine their narrative with that of the murderers, since this might create empathy with individuals whose actions took them beyond the fold of civilization. And there is also the worry that a comprehensive account might lead to highly disturbing assertions about the complicity, in some cases the collaboration, of the victims in the murder itself.[5]

Still, by insisting on this rigid separation of narratives, scholars are paradoxically in danger of accepting the dehumanization that was at the very heart of the genocide. This is not to say that the perpetrators often saw their victims as fellow human beings, though some such

[4] D. Pohl, *Nationalsozialistische Judenverfolgung in Ostgalizien 1941–1944: Organisation und Durchführung eines staatlichen Massenverbrechens* (Munich, 1996), 15, 410.

[5] Some Jewish historians have confronted collaboration: Y. Gutman, ed., *Patterns of Jewish Leadership in Nazi Europe 1933–1945* (Jerusalem, 1979); in Hebrew. I. Trunk, *Judenrat: The Jewish Councils in Eastern Europe under Nazi Occupation*, 2d ed. (Lincoln, Neb., 1996). But German historian Martin Broszat, "A Plea for the Historicization of National Socialism," in *Reworking the Past*, ed. P. Baldwin (Boston, 1990), 78, argues that the narrative of Nazism undermines "the pleasure of narration," and the historiographical introduction to *National Socialist Extermination Policies: Contemporary German Perspectives and Controversies*, ed. U. Herbert (New York, 2000), 1–52, never even raises the question of a double narrative.

cases have been documented, nor that the victims were in a position to view their murderers as anything but the embodiment of evil. But it is precisely the process of dehumanization that we need to understand, and this cannot be achieved without analyzing the relationship between the two groups, however profoundly disturbing this may be for our perception of our own humanity.

No Community of Suffering

Wolfgang Sofsky's pathbreaking study, *The Order of Terror,* is one of the first systematic attempts to break out of these paradigms, and provide a comprehensive interpretation of the "concentrationary universe."[6] It is a remarkable book, filled with important ideas, based on a mass of published documents, memoirs, and secondary works. It is quite unrelenting in its determination to penetrate the reality and the logic of the concentration camp system by focusing on the relationship between and among the perpetrators and the victims. What Sofsky tells us about human behavior in extreme situations is profoundly disturbing, and his book should be read by anyone who wishes to gain a deeper understanding not only of Nazi terror, but also of the dark potential of modern society.[7] And yet Sofsky has written a highly problematic book whose unified narrative is structured around an evasion, even a dismissal, of National Socialism's most fundamental characteristics: its ideological underpinnings and its genocidal dynamics.

Sofsky shows little interest in the controversy between the "intentionalist" and the "functionalist" interpretations of Nazism.[8] Nevertheless, as a sociologist, he focuses on the structures and the functions of the Nazi concentration camp system, which he sees as increasingly

---

[6] W. Sofsky, *The Order of Terror: The Concentration Camp* (Princeton, 1997), orig. pub. as *Die Ordnung des Terrors. Das Konzentrationslager* (Frankfurt/M., 1993). Earlier attempts include E. Kogon, *The Theory and Practice of Hell* (New York, 1950); H. G. Adler, "Gedanken zu einer Soziologie des Konzentrationslagers," in Adler, *Die Erfahrung der Ohnmacht* (Frankfurt/M., 1964), 210–26; F. Pingel, *Häftlinge unter SS-Herrschaft. Widerstand, Selbstbehauptung und Vernichtung im Konzentrationslager* (Hamburg, 1978). See now K. Orth, *Das System der nationalsozialistischen Konzentrationslager: Eine politische Organisationsgeschichte* (Hamburg, 1999) and U. Herbert, K. Orth, and C. Dieckmann, eds., *Die nationalsozialistischen Konzentrationslager: Entwicklung und Struktur,* 2 vols. (Göttingen, 1998).

[7] See also G. M. Kren and L. Rappoport, *The Holocaust and the Crisis of Human Behavior,* rev. ed. (New York, 1994).

[8] See above, chap. 3, note 2, and I. Kershaw, *The Nazi Dictatorship,* 3d ed. (London, 1993), chap. 5.

isolated from the rest of society, and only marginally influenced by the ideology of the regime. In this sense, there are definite "functionalist" echoes in his argument.

The concentration camp, Sofsky argues, was a place in which absolute power was given to a group of people whose growing separation from their environment, and whose gradual independence from the center, meant that their actions were primarily governed by an awareness of the unlimited power that they held, by their ability to exercise terror against their victims without any outside control. At the same time, the closed society of the camp made for the appearance of a unique relationship between the perpetrators and the victims, whereby the perpetrators depended on the complicity of some victims to maintain their control, while the victims could hope to survive only through some collaboration with their potential murderers.

Sofsky's description of the camp leaves very little room for comradeship and solidarity among the inmates. Indeed, while he never loses sight of the difference between the guards and the prisoners, Sofsky shows how the interaction between the different "classes" of inmates facilitated the effective operation of the system as a whole, despite the small numbers of SS men on the ground.

> This was not a *Leidensgemeinschaft*—there was no community of suffering here. The laws of the jungle prevailed in the daily struggle for survival . . . Frequently, the only way to survive was at the expense of others. One prisoner's death was another's bread . . . Solidarity is based on the principle of mutual aid and sharing. But where there is nothing to share, except at the cost of common destruction and doom, solidarity lacks a material basis . . . Absolute power is based on a cleverly devised system of classification and collaboration, gradation of power, and privilege . . . [It] thrusts individuals into a condition where what is ultimately decisive is the right of the stronger.[9]

At the top of the hierarchy of prisoners were the "greens" and the "reds," that is, the criminals, who were mostly German, and the "politicals," who were mostly communist.[10] These two groups vied for control of the rest of the camp population, in which Jews, Gypsies,

---

[9] Sofsky, *Terror*, 162–63.

[10] For a demystification of the heroic communist narrative of anti-fascism, see L. Niethammer, ed., *Der "gesäuberte" Antifaschismus. Die SED und die roten Kapos von Buchenwald. Dokumente* (Berlin, 1994).

Poles, and Russians were at the bottom. Even in the case of these "lower" categories, once the "aristocracy" of communists or criminals was weak or absent, it was the Poles and the Russians who came to control the lowest of the low, of which the Jews were the vast majority. Homosexuals also ranked quite low in the hierarchy, though they could improve their conditions by having sex with the upper echelons of the male population or with women. Inmates imprisoned for their religious convictions, including Jehovah's Witnesses, were initially treated very badly; but later on, due to their obedience in all matters not touching directly on their faith, as well as to their "Aryan" status, their situation greatly improved.

Where solidarity existed, as in the case of the communists, it was employed to save other comrades from punishment and death by manipulating the lists. This had the inevitable result that other inmates were killed instead.[11] In order to "maintain themselves over the longer term," Sofsky writes, "the prisoner-functionaries had to give preferential treatment to the group that supported them, while excluding the others from support."[12] To be sure, the final arbiter was always the SS, and all inmates were in danger of being murdered by the guards at any given moment. The Kapos and block leaders also killed inmates in order to demonstrate their power and status. Indeed, the SS was dependent on the prisoner hierarchy for control of the camp, just as those prisoners fortunate enough to gain a position of power knew that their status spelled the difference between life and death: extra food, better clothes and quarters, less work and more rest. Sofsky's book powerfully demonstrates that absolute power produces atrocity, that absolute power is an essential condition for the mental and physical destruction of human beings, by creating perpetrators for whom atrocity is normality, and murder merely part of a day's routine, punctuated by lunch breaks and social activities.

Sofsky does not deny that this condition of omnipresent murder attracts and breeds sadists, and he furnishes some hair-raising examples. In Sachsenhausen, Jews were drowned in the latrine, and others were killed by attaching water hoses to their mouths; in Dachau, prisoners were locked in "dog cells" too small to either stand or sit in; in Buchen-

---

[11] Two exemplary memoirs on solidarity and exclusion among communist inmates are J. Semprun, *Literature or Life* (New York, 1997) and M. Buber-Neumann, *Milena* (New York, 1988).

[12] Sofsky, *Terror*, 142.

wald, prisoners' legs were torn asunder by hanging them from doors, and their genitals were burned, frozen, and crushed. Thousands of inmates were "bathed to death" in ice-cold water. Prisoners were suspended from poles by their arms after they had been tied behind their backs, mauled by dogs, thrown into quarries, pushed into swamps, buried and burned alive.[13]

But what is even more terrifying in Sofsky's account is the normality of both the murder and the complicity by those who could thereby postpone their own death by a few weeks, days, or hours. Hence his insistence that "moral depravity and sadistic brutalization" apart, "the violence of the aristocracy had a clear social meaning . . . It documented the prerogative they enjoyed to beat, torment, and kill . . . By means of brutality, many prisoner-functionaries demonstrated that they were still alive, while so many others were not."[14]

Sofsky also dispels the notion that the concentration camp was a site of order and rules, clearly defined goals and an efficient bureaucracy. He argues instead that the very essence of absolute terror is its combination of endlessly elaborate rules and regulations with perpetual chaos and improvisation. In the concentrationary universe, no one knew what would happen next. What had saved an inmate from death on one occasion could prove to be his or her undoing the next day.

Sofsky's focus on the camp as an institution enables him to pay close attention to all major components of that infernal world. He notes how the inmates' perception of time and space was transformed into an eternal here and now, in which any memory of the past or thought of the future could spell disintegration and extinction. He analyzes work in the camps, which he rightly distinguishes from slavery by stressing that its ultimate aim was always the murder of the prisoners, even if they were at times expected to benefit the economy of the Reich or to satisfy the greed of their guards on their way to annihilation. And he examines the ubiquitous violence and death that was the single most characteristic feature of the camps.

The Concentration Camp versus the Holocaust
And yet this book is seriously flawed. Indeed, it raises fundamental questions about the use and abuse of grand explanations and abstract

---

[13] Ibid., 223–40.
[14] Ibid., 148–49.

categories, and about the role of ideology, theory, and identity in per-
petrating and interpreting evil. Sofsky's analysis of the concentration
camp as an institution enables him to categorize it as a typical product
of modern civilization, structurally and organizationally related to
other modern institutions such as military barracks, prisons, insane
asylums, and so forth, but radically different from them in that its sole
function was the destruction of humanity. By insisting on this model,
however, Sofsky obscures some of the most distinct features of the
Nazi system, and fails to clarify what made it different from other totalitarian regimes in our century.

Sofsky's way of regarding absolute terror leaves unexplained the
genocidal enterprise of the Nazis against the Jews. He shows convincingly that the combination of chaos and power created the terror that
was the main characteristic of the camps. But when he finally arrives
at the "Final Solution" in the very last chapter of his book, significantly
entitled "The Death Factory," it becomes clear that his analysis is insufficient to explain the radically different, wholly murderous logic of
what the Nazis called the "extermination of the Jews."

Sofsky is not alone in finding a great deal of improvisation in the
Nazi attempt to murder an entire people.[15] And yet the Nazi policy
was ruled by one simple principle, understood and accepted by all
those involved in this enterprise: each and every Jew, man, woman,
and child, was to be killed. This principle did not apply to any other
category of people tortured and often murdered by the Nazis.[16] The
regime encountered a great deal of opposition to the euthanasia of the
physically and mentally handicapped; and though it was secretly continued, the Nazis also resorted to other measures such as steriliza-
tion.[17] German communists, being "Aryan," could in many cases be
"re-educated" and returned to the fold. Homosexuals were not con-

[15] H. Mommsen, "The Realization of the Unthinkable: The 'Final Solution of the
Jewish Question' in the Third Reich," in H. Mommsen, *From Weimar to Auschwitz*
(Princeton, 1991) and M. Broszat, "Hitler and the Genesis of the 'Final Solution': An
Assessment of David Irving's Theses," in *Aspects of the Third Reich*, ed. H. W. Koch
(London, 1985), 390–429.

[16] E. Jäckel, "The Impoverished Practice of Insinuation: The Singular Aspect of National Socialist Crimes Cannot Be Denied," in *Forever in the Shadow of Hitler?* (Atlantic
Highlands, 1993), 74–78.

[17] H. Friedlander, *The Origins of Nazi Genocide: From Euthanasia to the Final Solution*
(Chapel Hill, 1995); B. A. Griech-Polelle, *Bishop von Galen: German Catholicism and National Socialism* (New Haven, 2002).

sistently persecuted, and could improve their treatment by demonstrating heterosexual behavior. Even the majority of Poles and Russians, although they were categorized as *Untermenschen*, were to be enslaved rather than killed. And, as Michael Zimmermann and Guenter Lewy have recently shown in their studies on the Gypsies, debates about the "racial composition" of the Sinti and Roma (who were considered to have once been "pure Aryans") limited the extent to which they were pursued and murdered by the Nazis, and made for a rather haphazard policy of persecution.[18]

It was *only* in the case of the Jews that there was a determination to seek out every baby hidden in a haystack, every family living in a bunker in the forest, every woman trying to pass herself off as a Gentile. It was only in the case of the Jews that vast factories were constructed and managed with the sole purpose of killing trainload after trainload of people. It was only in the case of the Jews that huge, open-air, public massacres of tens of thousands of people were conducted on a daily basis throughout Eastern Europe.[19]

Paradoxically, Sofsky's last chapter, itself an acute analysis of the death camps, causes his own thesis to collapse. Treblinka and Sobibor, Chelmno and Belzec have little in common, as he points out, with the typical concentration camp, to whose analysis the main bulk of his book is devoted. Only Birkenau bears some resemblance to those other camps, since it served both as a death camp and as a concentration camp. But in this case, too, the camp did not exist as such for the vast majority of the Jews transported there in the latter stages of the extermination, since they were immediately selected for the gas chambers and turned into ashes within hours of their arrival.[20]

For Sofsky's argument to hold—namely that the concentration camp was the most typical and unique feature of the Nazi regime—he

[18] Orth, *Das System*, 23–66; R. Gellately and N. Stoltzfus, eds., *Social Outsiders in Nazi Germany* (Princeton, 2001); U. Herbert, *Hitler's Foreign Workers: Enforced Foreign Labor in Germany under the Third Reich* (Cambridge, 1997); M. Zimmermann, *Rassenutopie und Genozid: Die nationalsozialistische "Lösung der Zigeunerfrage"* (Hamburg, 1996); G. Lewy, *The Nazi Persecution of the Gypsies* (New York, 2000).

[19] See Pohl, *Ostgalizien*, 144–47; T. Sandkühler, *"Endlösung" in Galizien: Der Judenmord in Ostpolen und die Rettungsinitiativen von Berthold Beitz 1941–1944* (Bonn, 1996), 150–52.

[20] Y. Arad, *Belzec, Sobibor, Treblinka: The Operation Reinhard Death Camps* (Bloomington, 1987); Y. Gutman and M. Berenbaum, eds., *Anatomy of the Auschwitz Death Camp* (Bloomington, 1994); Richard Glazar's testimony in G. Sereny, *Into That Darkness: An Examination of Conscience* (New York, 1983), 213–14.

needs to show at a minimum that the death camp was a natural out-growth of the concentration camp system, that the incarceration of real or imaginary political opponents, "asocials," criminals, and "deviants," all of whom were individual adults and none of whom were imprisoned along with their families, had something in common with the genocide of the Jews. He needs to show, indeed, that the one thing led to the other. And this is precisely what he cannot show.

Such an argument was made in the early years of scholarship on the Nazi regime,[21] but it has meanwhile become increasingly contested, since we now know that the death camps were constructed merely as a more efficient way of killing Jews following the technical and psychological problems encountered in mass open-air killings during the first phase of the Holocaust, and in view of the fact that those who organized the death camps came from the administration of the T-4 operation, that is, the "euthanasia" campaign, rather than from the concentration camps.[22] In any case, Sofsky does not even attempt to substantiate his implied assumption that the "Final Solution" was an outgrowth of the concentration camp. And so his harrowing last chapter seems tacked on to the rest of a book, almost as an afterthought, unwittingly betraying his recognition that something was lacking in his analysis all along.

These problems and inconsistencies in Sofsky's half-hearted distinctions between categories of camps and victims (until his last chapter the Jews are usually placed on the same level as Poles and Russians) are especially egregious in a study whose most important contribution is its penchant for categorization. But this brings us to another problem, which is Sofsky's persistent use of abstract categories, especially his term "absolute power." Reading his book, one begins to feel that "absolute power" has a life of its own, independent of any person's will, ideology, passions, and prejudices; that it is itself an external force that rules over everyone's fate, perpetrator and victim alike, and that there is no escaping it. The effect is completely ahistorical.

Focusing on the closed environment of the concentration camp, Sofsky dismisses the impact on the perpetrators of ideological training

---

[21] Kogon; Orth, 9–21; Herbert, Orth, and Dieckmann, 1:17–40; Y. Gutman et al., eds., *The Nazi Concentration Camps: Structure and Aims. The Image of the Prisoner. The Jews in the Camps* (Jerusalem, 1984), 3–36, in Hebrew; Sofsky, *Terror*, 28–43.

[22] E. Klee, W. Dressen, and V. Riess, eds., *"The Good Old Days": The Holocaust as Seen by Its Perpetrators and Bystanders* (New York, 1991), 4–5.; Friedlander, 284–302.

and traditional prejudices, of loyalty to a regime and hatred of real or imagined enemies. He argues that "to link what was actually happening inside the system—the motivational structure propelling the perpetrators and the dynamics of excessive power—to *ideology* is unconvincing." For absolute power, ideology "is not just superfluous, but obstructive." Indeed, "to take recourse in ideology is a false interpretation *post festum*, nourished by the mistaken belief that there always has to be an intellectual reason, that everything has some historical meaning." Consequently, Sofsky asserts that "to attempt to derive the brutality of the associates of the SS from the images of the enemy propagated by regime propaganda would be naive: it would mean being taken in by the ideology of the system," whereas in fact "absolute power has no enemies that could endanger it."[23]

Sofsky has no interest in history and biography, in individual recollection and collective memory. His protagonists are weirdly faceless, lacking a past and a future, an identity and a name. They function as they do because of the system into which they have been thrown, because of the status that has been allotted them, because nothing they might do could conceivably change the reality of their present condition. In that sense, everyone is caught in an eternal present that Sofsky calls "camp time," where the past is irrelevant and the future cannot be anticipated. Most disturbing, perhaps, is the fact that the prisoners appear in his study as abstract entities, as "reds," "greens," "Jews": they are precisely the identities that were imposed upon them by the perpetrators, and are denied any unique human features.

To some extent this reflects the nature of Sofsky's book, a sociological study whose insistence on making distinctions forces it into a framework that leaves no room for personal choice and personal identity. But finally this gives his study a strangely apologetic tone. While a similar order of terror was constructed by other regimes in this century, Sofsky insists on the unique features of the Nazi case—but he desists from discussing the political, ideological, and historical origins of Nazism, presents the camp as a site for the destruction of an undifferentiated mass of human beings (however complex their social organization), and fails to discuss systematically the concrete case of the Jewish genocide. In this way, Sofsky ends up by dissociating the order of terror from anything particularly German. Despite his last-minute

[23] Sofsky, *Terror*, 20–21, 235.

effort to correct this impression, he tends to associate the fate of the Jews with that of all other victims of the regime.

The Penultimate Horror

From this perspective, *The Order of Terror* is not really about the Holocaust at all. The "ideal" concentration camp constructed by Sofsky is modeled on such camps as Buchenwald, Sachsenhausen, Mauthausen, and Dachau. Those were horrific institutions in which thousands of men and women were tortured and murdered. Some of them were Jews, but most belonged to the other categories of human beings persecuted by the Nazis, the majority of whom were considered political opponents. Only toward the end of the war did those camps change their identity, as the collapse of the front forced the Nazis to dismantle the camps associated with the "Final Solution" in the East and send their inmates on death marches to the West. The survivors of the death marches crowded the camps in Germany, transforming them into sites of mass dying; and even then, it should be noted, the "politicals" were kept apart from the Jews and lived in relatively better conditions.[24]

During most of the Third Reich, however, the older camps in Germany and Austria differed substantially from the concentration camps, the ghettos, and especially the death camps in the East. The main difference was that in the East the camp system served primarily one goal: the killing of Jews. That the Jews were perceived and treated by the Nazis as essentially different from all their other "enemies" is certainly implied in Sofsky's description of them as being the lowest of the low in the camp hierarchy, as constituting the vast majority of the *Muselmänner,* the walking dead of the camps, who could never gain any position of privilege or power. But even these adult and mostly male Jewish prisoners were not typical of the fate of Jews in Nazi-occupied Europe, the vast majority of whom, men, women and children, died in the ghettos, or were shot in mass executions, or were sent to the death camps. And this enormous genocidal structure constructed by the Nazis has only an incidental role in Sofsky's analysis, for the simple

---

[24] Orth, 270–336; essays by D. Blatman, A. Strzelecki, I. Sprenger, and E. Kolb in Herbert, Orth, and Dieckmann, 2:1063–1138; S. Krakowski, "The Death Marches at the Phase of the Camp Clearance," in Gutman, *Concentration Camps,* 373–84; R. H. Abzug, *Inside the Vicious Heart: Americans and the Liberation of Nazi Concentration Camps* (New York, 1985); J. Reilly, *Belsen: The Liberation of a Concentration Camp* (New York, 1998); J. Bridgman, *The End of the Holocaust: The Liberation of the Camps* (Portland, Ore, 1990).

reason that his book is about the system of terror against everyone but the Jews.

Sofsky seems to believe that he has given us a definitive interpretation of the entire Nazi system. He is mistaken. His "order of terror" explains a great deal about one of the most terrifying institutions of the Nazi regime, and it trenchantly reveals the extent to which it was the product of social structures and conceptions of humanity that are still with us today; but it tells us very little about the genocide of the Jews. Sofsky scants the link between ideology and action, and in the German case between National Socialism and the system of terror it constructed against (but also with the collaboration of) masses of Germans and non-Germans alike.[25] He also scants the link between the camps and the more comprehensive phenomenon of genocide, between the Nazi "concentrationary universe" and the singular event of mass murder of an entire people. The camps that Sofsky describes may be compared with the Soviet gulag, with the Chinese, Cambodian, and other camp systems, which flourished in the twentieth century.[26] The Nazi concentration camps were about as bad as some of their predecessors and their successors; but the horror of genocide stands apart from all of them. It is this horror, the very worst horror that humanity has yet devised, that Sofsky has neither explained nor dispelled.

THE CONCENTRATION CAMP AS HISTORICAL CONSTRUCT

Even as the genocide of the Jews was unfolding, Rabbi Yitzhak Nissenbaum, writing in the ever-diminishing Warsaw Ghetto, attempted to distinguish between past persecutions of Jews and the "Final Solution." His point, however, was not merely to categorize different types of exclusion, inhumanity, and butchery, but to set new parameters for the manner in which the persecuted ought to react to this new and unprecedented assault: "This is a time to sanctify life (*kiddush hakhayim*) and not to sanctify God (*kiddush hashem*) through death. In the past the enemies demanded the soul and the Jew sacrificed his soul to sanctify God; now the oppressor demands the body of the Jew, and it is the Jew's duty to defend it, to protect his life."[27] This crucial distinction,

---

[25] R. Gellately, *Backing Hitler: Consent and Coercion in Nazi Germany* (Oxford, 2001).

[26] D. Rousset, *L'univers concentrationnaire* (Paris, 1946); S. Courtois et al., *The Black Book of Communism: Crimes, Terror, Repression* (Cambridge, Mass., 1999); J. Kotek and P. Rigoulot, *Le siècle des camps: Détention, concentration, extermination* (Paris, 2000).

[27] E. Pfefferkorn, "Bruno Bettelheim and Lina Wertmuller's 'Seven Beauties,'" in

between those who fought to die with honor, and those who struggled to survive as human beings, had both immediate existential implications and profound long-term ramifications for Jewish identity. And yet, in a Europe occupied by a regime sworn to destroy each and every Jew, survival ultimately depended much more on coincidence and luck than on any consciously chosen mode of conduct. And as luck was in short supply, the majority of European Jewry perished.

The tension between *kiddush hashem* and *kiddush hakhayim* has haunted Jewish memory and identity ever since the Holocaust. But from a more universal perspective, it is the distinction between "human" and "inhuman" that has remained at the core of the event. The Nazis, of course, categorized humanity according to genetic and racial components and their alleged social and moral implications. Thus the handicapped became "life unworthy of life," homosexuals, "habitual criminals," and the "work-shy" became "asocials" and "degenerates." Russians were defined as "subhumans," and Gypsies represented an offensive mix of asocial behavior and racial impurity.[28] Yet the Jews were by far the worst enemy of all because of their supposed mission to pollute all other races and take over the world. Hence the Jews were an "anti-race," a living contradiction of and a mortal threat to "noble humanity" as embodied in the "Aryans." Their destruction was an ideological *sine qua non* and became a major goal of Germany's wartime policies.[29]

Conversely, both in Soviet Russia and among the Western Allies there were those who insisted during the war on the inherently evil or at least sick "nature" of the German people, while others (who eventually won out) stressed that the Germans themselves were victims of a criminal dictatorship from which they too had to be liberated. But

---

Gutman, *Concentration Camps*, 535, citation of N. Eck, *Wanderers on Death's Paths: Experience and Thought in Days of Annihilation* (Jerusalem, 1969); in Hebrew. See also in S. Esh, "The Dignity of the Destroyed," *Judaism* 11, no. 2 (1962): 106–7; Y. Valk, "The Religious Leadership during the Holocaust," in Gutman, *Jewish Leadership*, 330–331. Nissenbaum was leader of the Zionist religious Mizrachi party. See *Scroll of Agony: The Warsaw Diary of Chaim A. Kaplan* (Bloomington, 1999), 107.

[28] See note 18, above; H. Friedlander; M. Burleigh, *Death and Deliverance: "Euthanasia" in Germany, 1900–1945* (Cambridge, 1994); J. Connelly, "Nazis and Slavs," *CEH* 32, no. 1 (1999): 1–33.

[29] E. Jäckel, *Hitler's World View: A Blueprint for Power* (Cambridge, Mass., 1981); Friedländer, *Nazi Germany*, 73–112. See also J. Weiss, *The Ideology of Death: Why the Holocaust Happened in Germany* (Chicago, 1996), 325–41; and D. Bankier, ed., *Probing the Depths of German Antisemitism: German Society and the Persecution of the Jews, 1933–1941* (New York, 2000).

following the collapse of the Third Reich, and the exposure of the horrors of the concentration camps, it was difficult to avoid the question: who carried out these atrocities, in whose name, with what kind of conviction, for what ends? Moreover, one was faced with the dilemma of defining the humanity of the perpetrators: were they sadists, insane, ideological fanatics, or were they normal human beings just like the rest of us, indeed, just like their victims? And what were the implications of either conclusion for the understanding of modern tyranny and genocide?[30]

The response by the late Israeli poet and Holocaust survivor, Dan Pagis, to this question, should echo in our minds whenever we confront the "concentrationary universe." As he writes in the poem Testimony:

> No no: they definitely were
> human beings: uniforms, boots.
> How to explain? They were created
> in the image.
> I was a shade.
> A different creator made me.
>
> And he in his mercy left nothing of me that would die.
> And I fled to him, floated up weightless, blue,
> forgiving—I would say: apologizing—
> smoke to omnipotent smoke
> that has no face or image.[31]

For Pagis, then, the question is not the humanity of the perpetrator, which is, after all, perfectly visible in his overpowering lethal presence and decisive fateful actions. The question has to do with the humanity of the victim. For on the one hand, the perpetrator strives to deprive the victims of their human attributes so as to deny their existence even before he murders them. But on the other hand, the victims desperately hold on to these attributes to maintain a sense of humanity and a reason to survive; yet, at the same time, they long to escape the killer's gaze, to vanish from sight as individual human entities. Writes Pagis:

[30] The best historiographical surveys of the vast literature on this issue are Kershaw, *Dictatorship*, and M. R. Marrus, *The Holocaust in History* (New York, 1987).
[31] Translated from the Hebrew in L. L. Langer, *Art from the Ashes: A Holocaust Anthology* (New York, 1995), 590.

He stands, stamps a little in his boots,
rubs his hands. He's cold in the morning breeze:
a diligent angel, who worked hard for his promotions.
Suddenly he thinks he's made a mistake: all eyes,
he counts again in the open notebook
all the bodies waiting for him in the square,
camp within camp: only I
am not there, am not there, am a mistake,
turn off my eyes, quickly, erase my shadow.
I shall not want. The sum will be all right
without me: here forever.[32]

These questions, however, are hardly at the center of the massive
new collection, *The National Socialist Concentration Camps*, edited by Ulrich Herbert, Karin Orth, and Christoph Dieckmann, the generally
high scholarly level of its chapters notwithstanding.[33] This is somewhat curious, especially considering the fact that the preface, by Bar-
bara Distel, is a plea for the importance of the survivors' testimony in
the historical reconstruction of life in the concentration camps.[34] To be
sure, some of the contributors do draw on testimonies and other documents by camp inmates and survivors. But the main thrust of this
work lies elsewhere. What it is about, and what it both consciously and
unconsciously sets itself against, can be gleaned from a passing remark
in the main introduction by the editors. For while this collection indeed
presents the results of a great deal of new research conducted in Germany, Poland, Lithuania, France, Austria, Italy, Israel, and the United
States, and thus constitutes a crucial addition to our knowledge, it is
also predicated on looking at the Nazi camps from a specific perspective. As the editors note, the chapters in the two volumes are based on
papers delivered at a conference that was held in Weimar, Germany, in
1995. This was the first such international meeting on the Nazi camps
since the 1980 conference at Yad Vashem in Jerusalem, which was, according to the editors, "primarily preoccupied with the meaning of the
concentration and death camps for the Holocaust and the fate of the
Jewish inmates."[35]

[32]"The Roll Call." Ibid., 589.

[33] Herbert, Orth, and Dieckmann. See note 6, above.

[34] B. Distel, "Das Zeugnis der Zurückgekehrten. Zur konfliktreichen Beziehung
Zwischen KZ-Überlebenden und Nachgriegsöffentlichkeit," in Herbert, Orth, and
Dieckmann, 1:11–16.

[35] Ibid., 32.

This new German collection thus maintains a complex relationship with its predecessor, the 1984 Hebrew language publication of the Yad Vashem proceeding.[36] While the assertion that the Israeli volume is mainly concerned with the fate of the Jews is a somewhat unfair exaggeration, there is no doubt that the Holocaust, as a general term for the specific event of the genocide of the Jews, plays a larger role in it than in the more recent German publication.[37] Moreover, the Yad Vashem collection differs in that it goes beyond the chronological parameters of the historical events in order to evaluate their repercussions both on survivors and on later generations by way of sociological and psychological studies and by analyzing representations of the Holocaust especially in memoirs and fiction. Conversely, the new German study adheres strictly to the historical reality of the concentration camp system, and pays far more attention to the organization of the camps from the perspective of the perpetrators than to the manner in which they were experienced by the inmates. Indeed, this publication manifests a certain degree of ambivalence toward the relationship between the Holocaust (as the genocide of the Jews) and the concentration camps (as a system of political repression, labor exploitation, and murder). Put differently, these volumes have little to say either on the origins or on the legacy of the camps; they are only marginally concerned with the death camps (which claimed by far the largest share of the victims of the "concentrationary universe," and the vast majority of whose victims were Jews); and they are inconsistent about and uncomfortable with the specific fate of the Jews in the Nazi system.

This is related to another issue about which there is a more or less general consensus among the contributors, namely, the assertion that ideological factors played at best a minor role in the conceptualization and implementation of the "concentrationary universe." Hence, for instance, antisemitism is hardly ever mentioned, whereas such notions as logistical constraints, economic pressures, bureaucratic procedures, and competition between agencies are greatly highlighted. There is nothing very surprising in this interpretive predilection, based as it is on a "functionalist" tradition in German scholarship on the Third Reich, however much this paradigm has been revised and modified

[36] Gutman, *Concentration Camps.* See note 21, above.
[37] About a third of the twenty-eight contributions do not deal at all with the Jews; the rest are focused primarily but not exclusively on Jews or their representation.

over the last few years.[38] Yet considering recent debates over the role of antisemitism in the Holocaust, the centrality of the "Final Solution" for the Third Reich, and the motivation of and relationship between perpetrators and so-called "ordinary Germans" or "ordinary men," it is somewhat perplexing that little attention is paid to such questions in this new collection, a massive work certain to have a major impact on future research in Germany and elsewhere.[39]

Another characteristic feature of these volumes is their almost obsessive preoccupation with facts and general timidity in gauging their findings' more general implications. Again, this is part of a larger trend in German historical scholarship, which is especially understandable in the case of research on the camps. In the last decade or so, young German scholars have, for the first time, carried out extensive archival research and thereby undermined many of the theoretical assumptions of their elders, which often had little to do with the "facts on the ground" and the documents in the archives.[40] One also sympathizes with the psychological and methodological difficulties of working on this topic, and the tendency to prefer a detached, dry, scholarly approach so as to avoid the empty rhetoric and simplifications of the early postwar years.[41] But the result is still rather disappointing, since too many of the essays in these volumes read as lists of facts sorely in need of analysis and contextualization. Fortunately, the editors have included the closing comments made by more mature scholars at the end of each panel. In most cases, these more general essays do attempt not merely to criticize the papers but, even more important, to locate them within a larger historiographical context and interpretive framework. Even if one does not necessarily agree with the commentators' own interpretations, they are extremely useful in giving the raw material of documentation some sense, meaning, and direction.

Looked at from a different perspective, this new collection of essays was conceived as a response to Wolfgang Sofsky's *The Order of Terror*. In this sense, while most of the contributors distance themselves from

---

[38] See notes 8 and 15, above.

[39] See J. H. Schoeps, ed., *Ein Volk von Mördern? Die Dokumentation zur Goldhagen-Kontroverse um die Rolle der Deutschen im Holocaust* (Hamburg, 1996) and R. R. Shandley, ed., *Unwilling Germans? The Goldhagen Debate* (Minneapolis, 1998).

[40] An English-language gist is in *Extermination*, ed. U. Herbert.

[41] Broszat, "Historicization"; S. Friedländer, "Reflections on the Historicization of National Socialism," in S. Friedländer, *Memory, History, and the Extermination of the Jews of Europe* (Bloomington, 1993), 64–84.

what they see as an overly committed and engaged approach to the study of the Holocaust by Jewish scholars, they simultaneously set themselves apart from the perceived abstractions and insufficient sensitivity to historical dynamics of Sofsky's sociological method. And yet, while there is plenty of room to disagree with Sofsky's interpretation—not least because, as I have noted above, he too cannot fit the genocide of the Jews into his model of the "concentration camp"—his ability to isolate the main facets of camp society, and his powerful analysis of the function of power and control in the camp, succinctly summarized in his concluding chapter to *The National Socialist Concentration Camps,* far supersedes the imperfectly digested facts and figures the fill many of the preceding thousand pages.

This being said, there can be no doubt that these two volumes are an indispensable source for anyone wishing to write on the Nazi camps. The unifying conceptual historical paradigm of this collection is Falk Pingel's 1978 thesis on the development of the camps (featured prominently also in the 1984 Yad Vashem volume).[42] According to Pingel, the history of the camps can be divided into three more or less distinct phases:

1. 1933–36, when concentration camps were used mainly for the suppression and re-education of real and imaginary domestic political opponents.
2. 1936/7–1941/2, in which the camps were transformed into tools for the elimination of so-called asocial and criminal elements and increasingly also for racial persecution.
3. From 1942 to the end of the war, during which the camps became pools of forced labor under the conditions of total war and a growing lack of manpower, and, at the same time, facilitated the extermination of millions of undesirable human beings.

Much of the debate on the role of the concentration camps concerns the implications of this historical development. Thus while the camps had succeeded in suppressing political opposition by 1936, and from this point of view could be dismantled, they were in fact greatly expanded as a means to purge society of undesirables and to justify the

[42] F. Pingel, "Konzeption und Praxis der nationalsozialistischen Konzentrationslager 1933 bis 1938," in Herbert, Orth, and Dieckmann, 1:148–63; Pingel, "The Place of the Concentration Camps in the National Socialist Regime," in Gutman, *Concentration Camps,* 3–14; Pingel, *Häftlinge.*

central role of the SS within the state. Even more crucially, by the latter years of the war an inherent contradiction between forced labor and mass killing in the camps seemed to develop. What the SS called "destruction through labor" (*Vernichtung durch Arbeit*) could be seen as exemplifying the Nazi state's self-destructive dynamics; conversely, it may also reflect its inner, if murderous, logic. From our own perspective, it is difficult to understand why a regime in such dire need of labor would simultaneously sanction the direct or indirect murder of so many camp inmates. One answer is that, in the final analysis, ideological arguments—particularly in the case of the Jews—always took precedence over economic factors.[43] Most contributors to these volumes, however, argue that the "logic" of "destruction through labor" was derived from the seemingly inexhaustible supply of new inmates. They did not die because the regime wanted to kill them, but because it did not care if they lived and saw no reason to invest in their survival, since until late in the war they were easily replaceable. In this sense, the term "slave labor" is a misnomer; neither acquiring working inmates nor losing them through death had a price tag. This was an economy based on free labor and an extraordinarily high turnover of manpower whose life expectancy was a mere few months (with the partial exception of a few sorely needed skilled workers whose living conditions were consequently somewhat better).

This is a convincing argument as far as non-Jewish inmates are concerned, but as many other recent studies have shown (and some essays in these volumes too) in the case of the Jews ideological factors were paramount; Jews were either plucked out of the labor force and murdered, or were subjected to intentional "destruction through labor."[44] Indeed, as can be read in this collection, there was a certain degree of improvement in the general treatment of concentration camp inmates between 1942 and 1944, when labor was in high demand and food provisioning and accommodation could still be assured. Only in 1944–45, due to the disintegration of the Nazi state and the evacuations of labor and concentration camps away from the front-lines in horrendous "death marches," did the death-rate climb again to unprecedented lev-

---

[43] U. Herbert, "Labour and Extermination: Economic Interest and the Primacy of *Weltanschauung* in National Socialism," *P&P* 138 (February 1993): 144–95; C. R. Browning, *The Path to Genocide: Essays on Launching the Final Solution* (New York, 1992), chap. 3.
[44] Browning, *Nazi Policy, Jewish Workers, German Killers* (Cambridge, 2000), 170–75.

els.[45] And yet, it was precisely during the period of 1942–44 that the mass of Europe's Jewish population was murdered. Moreover, the genocide continued until the last possible moment: between May 15 and July 8, 1944, 147 trains deported 437,000 Hungarian Jews to Auschwitz; in the course of these fifty days, over 300,000 men, women, and children were murdered in the four gas chambers of Birkenau, a daily average of between 8,000 and 9,000 human beings.[46] To be sure, some other Hungarian Jews were taken to labor camps, such as the Mittelbau-Dora complex, in which they died in vast numbers digging underground facilities for Germany's V rockets. But there was obviously no relationship whatsoever between the numbers of able-bodied men and women murdered and the labor needs of the Reich's economy.[47]

The fundamental difficulty in the interpretive thrust of these two volumes is therefore that they fail to integrate the Holocaust into the general explanation of the concentration camp system. Had the Nazi regime not conducted the genocide of the Jews, but rather treated the Jews more or less in the same manner as all other political, ethnic, and national groups it was busily exploiting and murdering, then the approach proposed by these volumes would have appeared quite reasonable. Indeed, we would have had to conclude that the Nazi camp system was substantially similar to that of other totalitarian states, not least the Soviet Union.[48] It is possible to argue, of course, that in the Nazi case we have two separate, though related, developments: the concentration camp system, on the one hand, and the persecution and genocide of the Jews, on the other. But since neither the editors nor the contributors of this work propose such an approach, one is left unclear as to how these events and developments fit together and what is the relationship between them.

Here, to be sure, different scholarly and national traditions offer their own solutions. Polish scholars (both in the new German collection and in the earlier Israeli volume) are keen to point out the sacri-

---

[45] Herbert, Orth, and Dieckmann, vol. 2, sec. 4.

[46] R. L. Braham, *The Politics of Genocide: The Holocaust in Hungary* (Detroit, 2000), 152–53, 251–54; M. Gilbert, "The Debates and Reactions Regarding the Demands to Bomb Auschwitz," in Gutman, *Concentration Camps*, 352, note 52.

[47] J.-C. Wagner, "Das Außenlagersystem des KL Mittelbau-Dora," in Herbert, Orth, and Dieckmann, 2:707–29.

[48] N. Werth, "A State against Its People: Violence, Repression, and Terror in the Soviet Union," in Courtois, 203–15.

fice of the Polish nation and the help rendered by Poles to Jews in escaping or fighting the Germans.[49] These historians are reluctant to concede the antisemitism that pervaded 1930s and 1940s Poland, and tend
to underplay the differences between German anti-Polish and anti-
Jewish policies. Conversely, a fair number of Israeli and non-Israeli
Jewish scholars stress the uniqueness of Jewish fate in the war and the
role of antisemitism in determining the course and nature of the Holocaust.[50] Such views, however, are at best under-represented in this
massive collaborative work, especially as regards antisemitism. Indeed, most German contributors relegate ideological motivation and
traditional prejudice to a secondary role, and appear intent on re-
dressing a perceived imbalance in the scholarship on the camps that
over-stresses the case of the Jews.

One could conclude by saying that those who wish to survey the full
array of current research, trends, and debates in scholarship on the
Nazi camps and the Holocaust, would do well to read all 2,000 pages
in the German and Israeli collections, as well as some other new works
on the topic.[51] But there is one last important issue that is unfortunately only fleetingly referred to in the *National Socialist Concentration
Camps,* namely, the long-term impact of the camps on our current existence. Considering the public debates in Germany over the legacy of
Nazism, it is a pity that these volumes avoid any discussion of such
crucial topics as postwar justice in Germany, the politics of "overcoming" the past, the individual and collective psychological impact of
Nazism on the Germans, and the teaching and representation of that
period. It is, after all, well worth asking why, fifty years after the event,
a new generation of German scholars has undertaken to study Nazism
with such zeal and energy.[52]

[49] See H. Świebocki, "Spontane und organisierte Formen des Widerstandes in Kon-
zentrationslagern am Beispiel des KL Auschwitz," in Herbert, Orth, and Dieckmann,
2:959–77; K. Donin-Wonsowicz, "Forced Labor and Sabotage in the Nazi Concentraion
Camps," in Gutman, *Concentration Camps,* 105–13.

[50] W. W. Hagen, "Before the 'Final Solution': Toward a Comparative Analysis of Political Anti-Semitism in Interwar Germany and Poland," *JMH* 68/2 (1996): 351–81; Y.
Lozowick, *Hitler's Bureaucrats: The Nazi Security Police and the Banality of Evil* (Jerusalem, 2001), 55–70, in Hebrew. Y. Gutman and S. Krakowski, *Unequal Victims: Poles
and Jews during World War Two* (New York, 1986).

[51] See Orth; N. Frei et al., eds., *Darstellungen und Quellen zur Geschichte von Auschwitz,*
4 vols. (Munich, 2000).

[52] For some observations, see A. H. Rosenfeld, ed., *Thinking about the Holocaust: After Half a Century* (Bloomington, 1997), chaps. 9–10.

In his 1969 novel, *Man Son of Dog*, the Israeli writer Yoram Kaniuk described the impact of the Holocaust on Israeli society:

> Who is left? Burnt remnants, wretched nervous wrecks . . . Halved people, quartered people . . . All of us—moaning and yawning and striving to make money, build houses, hurry, quick quick, but all this happens during the daytime. At night we wake up in the spacious houses, the modern apartments, the elegant cars, at night we have nightmares and we scream, because the devil scratched blue numbers on our arms. Do you know . . . what kinds of screams fill this country in the middle of the night? Powerful screams . . . all those numbers, screaming and weeping, not knowing why and for what reason and how and when . . . there is no escape. Therefore they scream, they weep with burning humiliation. The knowledge . . . that they were raw material in the most sophisticated factory in Europe, under a heaven in which God sat as an exiled foreigner . . . That knowledge drives us insane—and we have become a country which is the greatest insane asylum on earth.[53]

This harrowing passage illustrates the need to integrate the aftermath of the camps into any historical work that wishes to analyze their meaning for our time. Indeed, nothing would widen the perspective of German scholars writing on Nazism more than a new focus on its long-term impact on the victims. For it is only in this manner that we can come to realize the extent to which the crimes of the Third Reich have stamped our entire civilization throughout the second half of the twentieth century and beyond.

[53] In Hebrew, Y. Kaniuk, *Man Son of Dog* (Tel Aviv, 1969), 46, cited in G. Shaked, "Between the Wailing Wall and Massada: The Holocaust and the Self-Consciousness of Israeli Society," in *Major Changes Within the Jewish People in the Wake of the Holocaust*, ed. Y. Gutman (Jerusalem, 1996). 521–22, in Hebrew. Kaniuk's novel appeared in English as *Adam Resurrected* (New York, 1971).

[5]

Ordinary Monsters
PERPETRATOR MOTIVATION AND
MONOCAUSAL EXPLANATIONS

THE BACKGROUND

Even before the Nazi murder machine ground to a halt under the pressure of the greatest military alliance ever assembled, scholars, intellectuals, and thinking people throughout the world began applying themselves to the crucial questions: How was "the nation of Goethe and Schiller" transformed into a barbarous, genocidal dictatorship, and what was at the root of the Third Reich's attempt to annihilate the Jews? Since 1945, the constant preoccupation with this central event of the twentieth century has produced a virtual flood of explanations, interpretations and theories, historical monographs and biographies, psychological analyses and personal memoirs, works of fiction and documentaries.[1] If this immense intellectual effort has until now failed to yield a wholly satisfactory answer, it has not been for lack of trying. The difficulty can be traced back to the horror, the complexity, and the magnitude of the event itself. The Holocaust is not ineffable and unexplainable. But no single explanation or representation seems to encompass the phenomenon as a whole.[2]

The attempts to explain Nazism and the Holocaust have followed very different paths. In 1945, the British historian A. J. P. Taylor pub-

[1] Recent surveys in W. Benz, *The Holocaust* (New York, 1999); O. Bartov, ed., *The Holocaust: Origins, Implementation, Aftermath* (London, 2000). See further in R. Rosenbaum, *Explaining Hitler: A Search for the Origins of his Evil* (New York, 1998); Y. Bauer and N. Rotenstreich, eds., *The Holocaust as Historical Experience* (New York, 1981); A. H. Rosenfeld, ed., *Thinking about the Holocaust: After Half a Century* (Bloomington, 1997); E. Sicher, ed., *Breaking Crystal: Writing and Memory after Auschwitz* (Urbana, Il., 1998); S. D. Ezrahi, *By Words Alone: The Holocaust in Literature* (Chicago, 1980).

[2] For thoughtful essays on this issue, see S. Friedländer, *Memory, History, and the Extermination of the Jews of Europe* (Bloomington, 1993).

lished a book entitled *The Course of German History* in which he traced the roots of Nazism all the way back to Luther. As far as Taylor was concerned (at least at the time: he changed his opinion later), the German penchant for authoritarianism, obedience, and brutality was already a long-established fact by the time Hitler came to power; it was this special path of German history that explained the horrors of the Third Reich.[3] This notion of a special path was elaborated upon and greatly expanded in numerous studies by German scholars in the 1960s and 1970s, and it has become known as the *Sonderweg* theory. Hans-Ulrich Wehler, one of the most prominent proponents of this theory, claimed that Germany had taken a different turn in the latter part of the nineteenth century, and thereby developed unique and pernicious traits which made it increasingly different from more "normal" western societies such as Britain and France. It was this abnormality of German history, reflected in its political, social, and economic structure, that was at the root of Nazism's "seizure of power."[4]

While many German historians spent the better part of two decades debating and finally rejecting the *Sonderweg* theory, other scholars, mainly Marxist ones, proposed that the Holocaust was merely an aspect of European fascism, which was itself seen as one of the death throes of capitalism. Still others, among whom Hannah Arendt stands out most prominently, asserted that genocide was inherent to what they called the totalitarian state, which was most perfectly represented by Hitler's Germany and Stalin's Soviet Union.[5] Conversely, many Jewish historians, such as Shmuel Ettinger and Shmuel Almog, argued that the Holocaust must be traced back to the Christian-European tradition of antisemitism. Acknowledging the transformation of traditional religious and socio-economic anti-Jewish sentiments into political and racial antisemitism in the late nineteenth century, such scholars of Jewish history nevertheless argued that no structural interpretation of Nazism and the Holocaust was plausible without admitting the central role of a pernicious anti-Jewish imagery, theology,

[3] A. J. P. Taylor, *The Course of German History: A Survey of the Development of Germany since 1815* (London, 1945). But A. J. P. Taylor, *The Origins of the Second World War* (New York, 1961) presents Hitler's foreign policy in the 1930s as perfectly reasonable.

[4] H.-U. Wehler, *The German Empire, 1871–1918* (1973; Providence, 1993).

[5] D. Blackbourn and G. Eley, *The Peculiarities of German History: Bourgeois Society and Politics in Nineteenth-Century Germany* (New York, 1984); I. Kershaw, *The Nazi Dictatorship*, 3d ed. (London, 1993), chap. 2; H. Arendt, *The Origins of Totalitarianism* (New York, 1951).

and demagoguery, dating back to the Middle Ages and greatly enhanced by the pseudo-scientific discourse of social-Darwinism and eugenics in the modern era.[6]

Over the years, many other theories and interpretations have been proposed. The two main paradigms of the debate were the "intentionalist" interpretation, which placed Hitler and his long-term maniacal antisemitism at the center of the event, and the "functionalist" school, which stressed the "polycratic" structure of the Nazi regime and its predilection for "cumulative radicalization" rather than any premeditated decision on genocide.[7]

In recent years there has been a tremendous surge of interest in the Holocaust, expressed in numerous films, novels, museums and, not least, works of scholarship. Much of the new scholarship on Nazism and the Holocaust has been of remarkable quality, making use of newly discovered documents and new methodologies. New interpretations, based on extensive archival research, of the origins and course of Nazi Germany's eugenic, racial, demographic, and genocidal policies, by such scholars as Michael Burleigh and Ian Kershaw in Britain, Christopher Browning and Gordon Horwitz in the United States, and Götz Aly and Hannes Heer in Germany, have made it necessary to revise our understanding of the Holocaust and its perpetrators.[8] Similarly, works on the memory and representation of the event, its impact on the survivors, and its use and abuse by states and various political interests, written by such scholars as Lawrence Langer, Berel Lang, James Young, and Saul Friedländer, have greatly deepened our knowledge of the victims, the bystanders, and the role of commemoration in the post-Auschwitz era.[9]

---

[6] S. Ettinger, *Modern Anti-Semitism* (Tel Aviv, 1978), in Hebrew; S. Almog, ed., *Antisemitism Through the Ages* (Oxford, 1988). See also J. Katz, *From Prejudice to Destruction: Anti-Semitism, 1700–1933* (Cambridge, Mass., 1980), and, most recently, J. Carroll, *Constantine's Sword: The Church and the Jews* (Boston, 2001). The opposite view is in A. S. Lindemann, *Esau's Tears: Modern Anti-Semitism and the Rise of the Jews* (Cambridge, 1997). On racism, see G. L. Mosse, *Toward the Final Solution: A History of European Racism* (Madison, Wisc., 1985).

[7] See in more detail above, chapter 3, first section, and references therein.

[8] M. Burleigh, *The Third Reich: A New History* (New York, 2000); I. Kershaw, *Hitler*, 2 vols. (New York, 1999–2000); C. R. Browning, *Ordinary Men: Reserve Police Battalion 101 and the Final Solution in Poland* (New York, 1992); G. J. Horwitz, *In the Shadow of Death: Living Outside the Gates of Mauthausen* (New York, 1990); Aly, *"Final Solution": Nazi Population Policy and the Murder of the European Jews* (1995; New York, 1999); H. Heer, *Tote Zonen: Die deutsche Wehrmacht an der Ostfront* (Hamburg, 1999).

[9] L. L. Langer, *Holocaust Testimonies: The Ruins of Memory* (New Haven, 1991); B.

THE BOOK

Published in 1996, Daniel Jonah Goldhagen's *Hitler's Willing Executioners* is a big and ambitious work.[10] It is big in every respect: its physical size, its historical reach, the magnitude of the audience that it seeks (and has managed) to attract, the volume of scholarship that it dismisses, the intensity and scale of its condemnation, and, not least, its sense of its own importance. Goldhagen makes big claims, disdaining qualifications and subtleties, often making sweeping generalizations so as not to allow any culprits to get away. The writing is passionate, often angry. The book is almost obsessively repetitive, hammering the same point over and over again.

It should be stressed that Goldhagen's book takes up some very important issues. In some of its parts, it makes a useful contribution and provides a necessary correction to the existing literature. But precisely because it is so replete with wrath, accusations, finger-pointing, insinuations, and self-righteousness, it does a disservice to the considerable work invested in researching and writing it and to the issues it seeks to introduce into the debate. This is history in black and white, and it pleases those impatient with careful argument and weighing of evidence. As for scholars who have spent a lifetime of research and writing on Nazism and the Holocaust, its dismissive attitude toward their work has made it exceedingly difficult for them to sympathize with its more important arguments.

Goldhagen makes a powerful case for a version of one of the oldest, most traditional, and in the previous couple of decades largely discredited interpretations of the Holocaust. He should be praised for his courage in doing so. Paradoxically, he also claims to present a completely new interpretation of the event, which supersedes anything that has been written so far. This bewildering claim for originality is based on his insistence that he is the very first scholar ever to have written on the perpetrators; that he can thereby, and for the very first time, conclusively demonstrate that the vast majority of the German population were murderers, actually or potentially; and that, in contradiction to an alleged scholarly consensus, he has finally proven that the main moving engine, the principal motivation, the factor that explains

---

Lang, *The Future of the Holocaust: Between History and Memory* (Ithaca, 1999); J. E. Young, *The Texture of Memory: Holocaust Memorials and Meaning* (New Haven, 1993); Friedländer, *Memory*.

[10] D. J. Goldhagen, *Hitler's Willing Executioners: Ordinary Germans and the Holocaust* (New York, 1996).

all facets of the Holocaust, was European antisemitism in general, and its specific German variety in particular.

There is nothing original in claiming that antisemitism was at the core of the Holocaust.[11] Moreover, quite apart from the voluminous scholarship that has advanced this assertion over the years, this has always been the "common sense" view in much of Europe, the United States, and Israel. Not surprisingly, it has always been the opinion of traditional Jews and remains the single most influential interpretation of what orthodox Jews (and a considerable number of secular Hebrew-speakers) call the *churban,* or the Destruction. Associating the Holocaust with the destruction of the Temple (*churban beit ha'mikdash*), and linking both to the eternal hatred of the Gentiles for the Jews (and to the Jews' sins against God), is crucial to the interpretation of the Nazi genocide by a community which would otherwise have to confront the question of God's tolerance of, if not direct complicity in, the near-total destruction of His people.[12]

This being said, however, it is not necessary to claim originality of interpretation in order to stress once more the importance of antisemitism, in its traditional and in its modern, racist forms, as an arguably crucial and (in recent mainstream scholarship) somewhat underemphasized condition of the Holocaust. Still, antisemitism as such is not a sufficient condition for explaining the specific nature of the Nazi-attempted genocide of the Jews. That many Germans were imbued with antisemitic ideas and images, especially after years of exposure to Nazi propaganda and indoctrination, may seem obvious, but it needs reiterating in view of several influential interpretations of Nazism and the Holocaust that have generally downplayed this factor.[13] In this sense, Goldhagen was quite right to bring back the old ar-

---

[11] See L. Poliakov, *Harvest of Hate: The Nazi Program for the Destruction of The Jews of Europe* (Philadelphia, 1954); P. Pulzer, *The Rise of Political Anti-Semitism in Germany and Austria* (New York, 1964); S. L. Gilman and S. Katz, eds., *Anti-Semitism in Times of Crisis* (New York, 1991); R. S. Wistrich, *Antisemitism: The Longest Hatred* (New York, 1991).

[12] Further in O. Bartov, *Murder in Our Midst: The Holocaust, Industrial Killing, and Representation* (New York, 1996), 54–60; E. L. Fackenheim, "The Rebirth of the Holy Remnant," and D. Michman, "The Impact of the Holocaust on Religious Jewry," in *Major Changes Within the Jewish People in the Wake of the Holocaust,* ed. Y. Gutman (Jerusalem, 1996), 603–12 and 613–56, respectively, in Hebrew; G. Greenberg, "Orthodox Jewish Thought in the Wake of the Holocaust: *Tamim Pa'alo of 1947*," in *In God's Name: Genocide and Religion in the Twentieth Century,* ed. O. Bartov and P. Mack (New York, 2001), 316–41.

[13] The most recent evaluation of this issue is Bankier, ed., *Probing the Depths of German Antisemitism: German Society and the Persecution of the Jews, 1933–1941* (New York, 2000).

gument on the demonization of the Jews as playing a significant role in their barbarous treatment by individual Germans, as well as in legitimizing their persecution and ultimate mass murder for much of the German population.[14]

Unfortunately, Goldhagen's book does not give due credit to the many studies that have probed the political radicalization and ideological indoctrination of several important sectors of German society, such as the youth, the army, the veterans of the First World War, and the *Freikorps* paramilitary units of the 1920s, that is, those elements of society in the interwar years which provided the bulk of Hitler's perpetrators.[15] By referring to other studies which have similarly stressed the importance of ideological motivation and the mobilization of prejudice by the Nazi regime, not least among the soldiers of the Wehrmacht, Goldhagen might have had to surrender his claim of originality, but his book would have gained a great deal in subtlety of argument.[16]

Conceived as a wholesale revision of the history of the Holocaust, Goldhagen's book devotes the first part (about one hundred pages) to a survey of European and German antisemitism before and during the early years following Hitler's "seizure of power."[17] These chapters do not add much to our knowledge of antisemitism, nor do they do much justice to the subject. Reading them, one might believe that the historical process of Jewish emancipation and assimilation into European culture never took place; that the great cultural surge within Jewish communities throughout Europe, and particularly in Germany, in the nineteenth century and the early part of the twentieth century, is a myth, and that the Holocaust was already on the minds of the majority of Europeans, or at least Germans, since 1848 at the very latest. If we are to accept Goldhagen's version, German Jews were either blind or downright stupid, since the writing was on the wall for one hundred years, and their whole existence was founded on an illusion.[18]

---

[14] On "redemptive antisemitism," see S. Friedländer, *Nazi Germany and the Jews*, vol. 1 (New York, 1997), chap. 3.

[15] G. Rempel, *Hitler's Children: The Hitler Youth and the SS* (Chapel Hill, 1989); James M. Diehl, *Paramilitary Politics in Weimar Germany* (Bloomington, 1977); K. Theweleit, *Male Fantasies*, 2 vols. (Minneapolis, 1987–1989); F. L. Carsten, *The Reichswehr and Politics 1918–1933* (Oxford, 1966).

[16] J. Förster, "The German Army and the Ideological War against the Soviet Union," in *The Policies of Genocide: Jews and Soviet Prisoners of War in Nazi Germany*, ed. G. Hirschfeld (London, 1986), 15–29; O. Bartov, *Hitler's Army: Soldiers, Nazis, and War in the Third Reich* (New York, 1991).

[17] Goldhagen, *Willing Executioners*, 27–128.

[18] J. Katz, *Out of the Ghetto: The Social Background of Jewish Emancipation, 1770–1870*

This view of the past also confronts us with serious problems about the present, since what Goldhagen calls "eliminationist antisemitism," the forerunner of its exterminationist version, appears to have totally vanished from Germany after 1945.[19]

To say that this is the first study of the perpetrators is, to use the term that Goldhagen applies to most of the historical interpretations criticized in his book, simply false.[20] Indeed, as with his chapters on antisemitism, Goldhagen himself refers to several studies that have devoted a great deal of work to the perpetrators on all levels of the Nazi murder regime.[21] Curiously, Götz Aly's *"Final Solution"* (discussed in chapter 3, above), published in Germany shortly before Goldhagen's book, makes precisely the same claim, although its interpretation of the Holocaust is almost exactly the opposite of *Hitler's Willing Executioners*, presenting as it does a rather sophisticated and complex version of the functionalist thesis, based on a mass of hitherto unknown documents.[22] Whether we accept Aly's or Goldhagen's interpretations (and both of them are problematic and far too polarized), neither is justified in his claim of originality.

Yet Goldhagen's dilemma is greater than Aly's, since the latter has identified one group of perpetrators about whom relatively little was known until he turned his attention to them, namely, the middle-ranking Nazi bureaucrats who were involved in planning the massive resettlement of ethnic Germans (*Volksdeutsche*) in western Poland and who simultaneously organized the expulsion, concentration, and finally murder of the Jews from those same areas, along with large

---

(Cambridge, Mass., 1973); D. Sorkin, *The Transformation of German Jewry, 1780–1840* (New York, 1987); U. Tal, *Christians and Jews in Germany: Religion, Politics, and Ideology in the Second Reich, 1870–1914* (Ithaca, 1975); P. Birnbaum and I. Katznelson, eds., *Paths of Emancipation: Jews, States, and Citizenship* (Princeton, 1995).

[19] On the complexities of postwar Jewish life in Germany, see M. Brenner, *After the Holocaust: Rebuilding Jewish Lives in Postwar Germany* (Princeton, 1997); J. Borneman and J. M. Peck, *Sojourners: The Return of German Jews and the Question of Identity* (Lincoln, Neb., 1995); S. L. Gilman, *Jews in Today's German Culture* (Bloomington, 1995).

[20] See, most prominently, R. Hilberg, *The Destruction of the European Jews*, 3 vols., rev. ed. (New York, 1985). See also G. Sereny, *Into That Darkness: An Examination of Conscience* (New York, 1983); E. Klee, W. Dressen, and V. Riess, eds., *"The Good Old Days": The Holocaust as Seen by Its Perpetrators and Bystanders* (New York, 1991).

[21] Most striking is, of course, Browning, *Ordinary Men*. See also Browning, *The Final Solution and the German Foreign Office: A Study of Referat D III of Abteilung Deutschland, 1940–43* (New York, 1978).

[22] Aly, *"Final Solution"* (1995), 1, 246.

numbers of non-Jewish Poles (who were, however, not slated for extermination).[23] Goldhagen, by contrast, is concerned with a type of perpetrator about whom one of the foremost historians of the Holocaust, Christopher Browning, has already published an important study.[24] It is no coincidence, in fact, that Browning's book is called *Ordinary Men* and Goldhagen's is called *Ordinary Germans*.

On the most basic level, Goldhagen's book is a reply to, and an attempt to refute, Browning's thesis, using to a large extent the same documentation but drawing different conclusions from it.[25] There is nothing unusual in two scholars reaching different conclusions from the same sources. What is disturbing is not only that Goldhagen asserts repeatedly the originality of his sources, but that at the same time he makes unwarranted and unfair attacks on Browning, insinuating that for some reason or another Browning had not used certain documents which did not sustain his thesis, documents which, had they been cited, irrefutably show Goldhagen's view to be the only possible one. Goldhagen launches not merely a debate over interpretation, but also an attack on the scholarly integrity of another historian of the Holocaust, made in countless notes throughout the text and hinting at some unspoken fault, some illicit sympathy.[26]

THE DEBATE

And what is the debate all about? Browning has investigated the police battalions used by the Nazi regime to perpetrate mass killing on Jewish communities in Poland between 1941 and 1943. His research concentrated especially on the Hamburg Reserve Police Battalion 101, which was composed of relatively old men who had been exposed only to a minimal degree of Nazi indoctrination and showed no signs of being enthusiastic supporters of Hitler. This was not a unit normally associated with the death-squads or *Einsatzgruppen* of the SS and the SD. At least at the beginning of its murder activities, moreover, the men were given the option not to take an active part in the killing. And yet

[23] See G. Aly and S. Heim, *Vordenker der Vernichtung: Auschwitz und die deutschen Pläne für eine neue europäische Ordnung* (Hamburg, 1991) for an earlier study of this group.

[24] Browning, *Ordinary Men.*

[25] See also Goldhagen's review of *Ordinary Men* in *TNR* (July 13, 1992): 49–52.

[26] See Goldhagen, *Willing Executioners*, 531 note 36, 534 note 1, 536–37 note 19, 551 note 65, 579 note 17.

they became mass murderers. Browning's explanation of this phenomenon is that these "ordinary men" became acclimatized to mass killing during the first few murder operations and ended up (with few exceptions) viewing them as part of a job, distasteful as it might have been to some of them, which they had to carry out. In Browning's account, it was not beliefs but circumstances which made ordinary men into killers.[27]

Goldhagen has also studied Reserve Police Battalion 101, along with some other units for which there apparently exists less documentation. Employing the same evidence regarding the manpower composition of this unit, he claims that these perpetrators, precisely because they were spared massive indoctrination owing to their age, are the best illustration of the fact that they were not ordinary men but ordinary Germans. That is, that they were representative of German society, which had internalized "eliminationist" and therefore potentially exterminationist antisemitism long before Hitler came to power. Goldhagen stresses that its members could avoid participation in the killing, and so they killed, in his view, not because of their circumstances but because of their hatred of Jews. Most of them not only enjoyed killing, as Goldhagen shows, they also tortured their victims horribly before finally murdering them.[28]

It is quite possible, of course, to stake out a third position, one which stresses a crucial factor neglected both by Browning's circumstantial interpretation and by Goldhagen's essentialist view, namely the powerful impact of ideology and indoctrination on the perpetrators. I agree with Goldhagen that it is more than likely that many of these killers were motivated by antisemitic sentiments and truly believed that it was necessary to kill Jews. Yet to say that they represented all Germans in the Third Reich, and, even more radically, that they were representative of widespread German sentiments even before Hitler's regime, is a judgment that is impossible to prove and too farfetched to be of any analytical or historical value. I have myself disagreed with Browning's diminishment of ideological motivation among the perpetrators (and have stressed its importance in my own work on German soldiers); yet as his meticulous research demonstrates (and as my own work on the brutalization of soldiers also indicates), one cannot dis-

---

[27] Browning, *Ordinary Men*, 159–89.
[28] Goldhagen, *Willing Executioners*, 203–80.

miss the reality of acclimatization to murder by repeated involvement in it.[29]

Goldhagen does not present sufficient evidence to refute this claim, and his argument that we cannot believe the perpetrators' assertions about their initial reluctance to kill in testimonies given twenty years later is highly problematic for the simple reason that his own study is based almost exclusively on those same testimonies.[30] There is a great deal of evidence to show that a dehumanized view of Jews (and Russians, Bolsheviks, Gypsies, Poles, and others) did play an important role in motivating Hitler's murderers. But Goldhagen's own evidence suggests (along with much more documentation that he does not cite) that this view was internalized largely during the Third Reich. Even if the perpetrators on whom Goldhagen has chosen to focus were in their late thirties, they had nevertheless spent many years under Hitler's rule and were exposed to massive propaganda before they set out to kill Jews (as Robert Gellately has shown in his work on the Gestapo).[31] To be sure, Nazi ideology was most successful where it made use of existing prejudices; antisemitism, as well as fear of Slavs and Bolsheviks, was widespread before 1933, although how widespread is difficult to gauge, and whether it differed from such sentiments, say, in Poland, is doubtful.[32] But it was only in the Third Reich that these sentiments were given the sanction of the regime and could be provided with the impetus of a sophisticated propaganda machine wielded by a modern state.

Moreover, it would have been useful to contextualize the case of the police battalions by reference to regular army soldiers who massacred vast numbers of non-Jewish Russians, along with Poles, Serbs, Greeks, Italians, and so forth.[33] This is important precisely because of Goldha-

[29] O. Bartov, *The Eastern Front, 1941–1945*, 2d ed. (New York, 2001), chaps. 3–4; Bartov, *Hitler's Army*, chap. 4; and chaps. 1–2, above.

[30] Goldhagen, *Willing Executioners*, 466–67, 601 note 11.

[31] R. Gellately, *The Gestapo and German Society: Enforcing Racial Policy, 1933–1945* (Oxford, 1990). See also Gellately, *Backing Hitler: Consent and Coercion in Nazi Germany* (Oxford, 2001); E. A. Johnson, *Nazi Terror: The Gestapo, Jews, and Ordinary Germans* (New York, 1999); and note 16, above.

[32] J. Weiss, *The Ideology of Death: Why the Holocaust Happened in Germany* (Chicago, 1996); W. W. Hagen, "Before the 'Final Solution': Toward a Comparative Analysis of Political Anti-Semitism in Interwar Germany and Poland," *JMH* 68/2 (1996).

[33] Note 29, above; H. Heer and K. Naumann, eds., *War of Extermination: The German Military in World War II, 1941–1944* (1995; New York, 2000).; C. Gerlach, *Kalkulierte Morde* (Hamburg, 1999) ; essays by U. Herbert, W. Manoschek, C. Gerlach and C.

gen's insistence on the disproportionate attention paid to the death camps in Holocaust scholarship and the need to focus more closely on murder units such as the police battalions that he has studied (a problematic assertion to which I will return). The soldiers carried out their "tasks" efficiently and often willingly. At the same time, as Mark Mazower has shown, there were also complaints about the demoralizing effects of massacring, especially the massacring of women and children.[34]

This does not mean that the troops were not motivated by powerful prejudices, reinforced by years of ideological indoctrination and brutalization by image and deed. It does mean, however, that antisemitism is not sufficient as a single factor in explaining the conduct of individual German soldiers, policemen, SS or SD men, or anyone involved in murder during that period. It is much more convincing to argue that such actions were the result of a cluster of conditions, some ideological and some existential, some reality and others rooted in a distorted perception of it. No single element can explain this terrible phenomenon. We wish that it could, on the assumption that by doing away with that element we could eliminate the possibility of such brutality altogether. But much that has happened since the end of the Holocaust demonstrates that massacres and genocides can find many reasons to occur.

In order to further substantiate his case that "ordinary" Germans were imbued with a blind hatred of Jews and were therefore all potential torturers and murderers simply waiting for the opportunity to vent their wild passions on the victims, Goldhagen devotes several chapters to the labor camps and the death marches during the last months and weeks of the Nazi regime. Dismissing a whole body of literature on the relationship between Nazi demographic policies, forced labor, and extermination as "false," he proceeds to demonstrate that labor camps were only one more example of the Germans' desire to humiliate, to torture, and to kill Jews.[35] He provides some horrifying and

---

Dieckmann in *National Socialist Extermination Policies: Contemporary German Perspectives and Controversies*, ed. U. Herbert (New York, 2000); W. Manoschek, *"Serbien ist judenfrei." Militärische Besatzungspolitik und Judenvernichtung in Serbien 1941/42* (Munich, 1995); Browning, *Fateful Months: Essays on the Emergence of the Final Solution* (New York, 1985), 39–56.

[34] M. Mazower, "Military Violence and the National Socialist Consensus: The Wehrmacht in Greece, 1941–44," in Heer and Naumann, 146–74.

[35] W. Benz and B. Distel, eds., "Sklavenarbeit im KZ," *Dachauer Hefte* 2 (Munich,

hitherto unknown information on a number of labor camps and makes a strong case for the barbarity of the guards. And he provides disturbing and (to my knowledge) previously unpublished information on some specific death marches at the end of the war, mostly culled from testimonies by perpetrators given in the 1960s, and shows that even when left to their own devices, even when ordered by Himmler himself (for his own selfish reasons) no longer to mistreat Jews, the guards of these senseless marches behaved in the most atrocious manner.[36]

And yet it is not at all clear that these cases actually sustain Goldhagen's thesis. His repeated question—why did the Nazis treat the Jews so terribly?—sounds strangely naive and out of place. The men and women about whom he writes were involved in a genocidal undertaking, unprecedented in its ferocity and its scale. They were obviously under the influence of a good measure of Nazi ideology, exposure to endless barbarities, and circumstances which brought out in them the most base instincts, while facing victims who had been reduced to a condition in which they appeared to resemble precisely the kind of *Untermenschen* that Nazi propaganda had always claimed them to be.

Moreover, there are serious contradictions within Goldhagen's accounts. While arguing that these brutal killers were merely "ordinary Germans," he presents not a few killers who were either ethnic Germans, that is, men and women who had been raised and educated far from the culture he claims to have been imbued with a unique brand of "eliminationist antisemitism," or non-Germans, Ukrainians, Lithuanians, and so forth.[37] To be sure, these perpetrators were probably at

---

1993); U. Herbert, *Hitler's Foreign Workers: Enforced Foreign Labor in Germany under the Third Reich* (Cambridge, 1997); U. Herbert, "Labour and Extermination: Economic Interest and the Primacy of *Weltanschauung* in National Socialism," *P&P* 138 (1993); U. Herbert, K. Orth, and C. Dieckmann, eds., *Die nationalsozialistischen Konzentrationslager: Entwicklung und Struktur*, 2 vols. (Göttingen, 1998), vol. 2, sec. 4; N. Frei et al., eds., *Darstellungen und Quellen zur Geschichte von Auschwitz*, vols. 3–4. (Munich, 2000).

[36] His claim to be the first to write on the death marches is, however, false. See K. Orth, *Das System der nationalsozialistischen Konzentrationslager: Eine politische Organisationsgeschichte* (Hamburg, 1999) 270–336; essays by D. Blatman, A. Strzelecki, I. Sprenger, and E. Kolb in Herbert, Orth, and Dieckmann, 2 vols. (Göttingen, 1998) 2:1063–1138; S. Krakowski, "The Death Marches at the Phase of the Camp Clearance," in Y. Gutman et al., eds., *The Nazi Concentration Camps: Structure and Aims. The Image of the Prisoner. The Jews in the Camps* (Jerusalem, 1984), 373–84, in Hebrew; R. H. Abzug, *Inside the Vicious Heart: Americans and the Liberation of Nazi Concentration Camps* (New York, 1985); J. Reilly, *Belsen: The Liberation of a Concentration Camp* (New York, 1998); J. Bridgman, *The End of the Holocaust: The Liberation of the Camps* (Portland, Ore., 1990).

[37] Goldhagen, *Willing Executioners*, 299, 335.

least as antisemitic as the Germans. But then what are we to do with Goldhagen's argument about the specificity of German antisemitism?

Even more problematic, perhaps, is the fact that, in his zeal to show the inhumanity of all Germans, Goldhagen notes that the guards of the death marches refused to allow the starving Jews to eat food thrown to them by the inhabitants of the towns through which they passed. He does not remark upon the rather obvious fact that the people who threw that food to the Jews were also "ordinary" Germans. Such acts of kindness were probably rare occurrences, though Goldhagen cites a surprisingly high number of such cases; but they do indicate that some Germans, even as late as 1945, recognized Jewish victims to be human beings.[38]

THE SINGULARITY OF THE HOLOCAUST

The most troubling aspect of Goldhagen's book is its contention that "ordinary" Germans belonged to an entirely extraordinary people, a people unlike any other, which had been that way for the better part of a century. He cites the *Sonderweg* thesis approvingly as still further proof of his thesis, but in fact his argument differs greatly from the German original: the proponents of the "special path" had stressed structural factors, while he rejects those out of hand and emphasizes the mental makeup of the German psyche, an argument entirely foreign to the body of scholarship to which he refers.[39] Goldhagen's view of Germany cannot be sustained by evidence, and like all essentialist views it does not require evidence; it is inimical to strictly historical analysis. People may well act as they do because of what they are; but tautology rarely makes for good history.

And what are the implications of such a notion that there exists a nation of ingrained murderers? How useful is this assumption for explaining a historical phenomenon? To what extent is this a bizarre inversion of the Nazi view of the Jews as an insidious, inherently evil nation? At one point Goldhagen himself seems to recognize the danger in his argument. He remarks in a footnote that the Germans since 1945 are different, having somehow gone through a rapid process of democratization and denazification which transformed them almost overnight into normal (ordinary?) men and women.[40] But this is only a footnote. We are left with the thesis that the Germans were normally

---

[38] Ibid., 348–49. See also Horwitz, chap. 7.
[39] See notes 4–5, above.
[40] Ibid., 593–94, note 53.

monsters, and that the only role of the Nazi regime was to furnish them with the opportunity to act on their evil desires. This is not a new idea. It was, quite naturally, entertained by many of their victims. But as an historical explanation of a specific event it is useless, and not really historical at all.

In this sense, although Goldhagen has attempted to combine a long-term context for his thesis with what he claims to be a "thick" description of the perpetrators' actions, his book is in fact an entirely decontextualized interpretation of the Holocaust. It fails to confront the central question of the Nazi genocide, with which those very scholars he dismisses so nonchalantly have tried (with varying degrees of success) to grapple for so long—namely, what was it that made the Holocaust a wholly unprecedented event in human history *and* an event which was part and parcel of the specific historical conditions from which it evolved? For genocides are anything but a new phenomenon. Brutality, mass killings, torture, sadism, and everything which Goldhagen is at pains to describe in gory detail, are as old as humanity itself. And as new: it suffices to recall the recent butcheries in Rwanda and Bosnia to see that these particular aspects of the Holocaust are anything but unique. What was—and remains—unprecedented about the Holocaust is a wholly different matter, one which Goldhagen avoids treating: the industrial killing of millions of human beings in factories of death, ordered by a modern state, organized by a conscientious bureaucracy, and supported by a law-abiding, patriotic, "civilized" society.[41]

Never before, or after, has a state decided to devote so many of its technological, organizational, and intellectual resources to the sole purpose of murdering every single member of a certain category of people in a process that combined the knowledge acquired in mass industrial production with the experience of waging total war. This was a novel phenomenon: striving to produce corpses with the same methods employed to produce goods. In this case, however, destruction was the *goal* of production, not its opposite.

In circumstances of mass murder, sadism flourishes; but sadism is not unique to the Holocaust. Antisemitism is a pernicious phenomenon with long historical roots, but the question remains as to how was it employed in creating and legitimating death camps rather than expressed in savage pogroms. We need to probe much deeper into the

---

[41] For the origins of industrial killing, see Bartov, *Murder*, chap. 2.

culture that produced genocide in the heart of European civilization. What was it that induced Nobel Prize-winning scientists, internationally respected legal scholars, physicians known throughout the world for their research into the human body and their desire to ameliorate the lot of humanity, to become not merely opportunistic accomplices, but in many ways the initiators and promoters of this attempt to subject the human race to a vast surgical operation by means of mass extermination of whole categories of human beings? What was there (or is there) in our culture that made the concept of transforming humanity by means of eugenic and racial cleansing seem so practical and rational? And how was all this related to the immense advances in science over the preceding century, the widespread disenchantment with some aspects of modernity, and, not least, the mass slaughter of Europeans on the battlefields of the Great War in 1914–18?[42]

These are all critical questions that Goldhagen fails to treat, and so his book cannot claim by any stretch of the imagination to be a new interpretation of the Holocaust. It is a useful study of some aspects of the genocide of the Jews, aspects which have many common features with other genocides throughout history. Indeed, by focusing on these events, Goldhagen undermines his own claim regarding the uniqueness of the Holocaust, for his book completely misses precisely those aspects of the genocide which have made it stand out as unprecedented even in the bloodiest century humanity has seen; and by doing so it fails to demonstrate any understanding for the profound and continuing relevance of the industrial killing perfected by the Nazis for our own societies.

Goldhagen believes that he has cut straight through the tortuous and often contradictory arguments of a vast amount of scholarship and given us the clear, simple, strangely comforting answer for which we had all been longing. He is wrong. By eschewing subtlety and nuance, and by mistaking passion for an impatience with complexity, Goldhagen is actually appealing to a public that wants to hear what it already believes. By doing so, he obscures the fact that the Holocaust was too murky and too horrible to be reduced to simplistic interpretations that rob it of its pertinence to our own time.

[42] See further in D. Pick, *War Machine: The Rationalisation of Slaughter in the Modern Age* (New Haven, 1993); P. Weindling, *Health, Race and German Politics between National Unification and Nazism, 1870–1945* (Cambridge, 1989); R. Proctor, *Racial Hygiene: Medicine Under the Nazis* (Cambridge, Mass., 1988).

[6]

Germans as Nazis

GOLDHAGEN'S HOLOCAUST

AND THE WORLD

Whether it generated enthusiasm or wrath, *Schaden-freude* or indifference, the "Goldhagen phenomenon" provides us with an opportunity to investigate the impact of Nazism and the Holocaust on the redefinition of national and group identities at the end of the millennium. While chapter 5 considered some of the merits and limitations of *Hitler's Willing Executioners*, the goal of this chapter is to view the book's reception as a kind of measuring-rod for the changing and differing perceptions of the Holocaust in several national contexts.[1] While a number of previous commercially successful representations of Jewish persecution under the Third Reich have similarly both reflected and molded public attitudes, the crucial distinction here is that Goldhagen's book was the first scholarly study of the Shoah to have gained the status of an international best seller.[2] Hence, this chapter will be also concerned with the gap (more obvious in some countries than in others) between the book's critical reception by the scholarly community and its unprecedented popularity among otherwise very different reading publics. These different reactions to the book arguably reveal a lack of communication between self-enclosed academic discourses and popular opinions on an issue that remains central to individual, group, and national self-definition throughout much of the Western hemisphere.

In the following pages I thus discuss American, German, French,

[1] For reviews of the book, see J. H. Schoeps, ed., *Ein Volk von Mördern? Die Dokumentation zur Goldhagen-Kontroverse um die Rolle der Deutschen im Holocaust* (Hamburg, 1996); R. R. Shandley, ed., *Unwilling Germans? The Goldhagen Debate* (Minneapolis, 1998); N. G. Finkelstein and R. B. Birn, *A Nation on Trial: The Goldhagen Thesis and Historical Truth* (New York, 1998).

[2] On the most recent cinematic equivalent, see Y. Loshitzky, ed., *Spielberg's Holocaust: Critical Perspectives on Schindler's List* (Bloomington, 1997).

and Israeli reactions to Goldhagen's book. What interests me in each case is the extent to which the controversy over the book was integrated into, changed the terms of, or remained peripheral to other major public, intellectual and academic debates. Depending on the specific national context, such debates concern the relationship between history and memory, tensions between group and national identity, distinctions between complicity and resistance, generational conflicts, and, not least, the links between past and present atrocity. Clearly, this controversy touches on a question that should concern all scholars. To what extent can we mold public opinion without compromising our professional principles and reputation? And conversely, can we remain entirely aloof from the influence of our environment, its politics, prejudices, and seductions? In order to illustrate the complexities of this issue, I demonstrate, by way of conclusion, that Stanley Milgram's behaviorist theories, frequently cited during the Goldhagen debate as an example of an ideologically neutral explanation of human conduct in extreme situations, were in fact strongly influenced by his own class, gender, and ethnic prejudices.[3] This only reinforces my conviction that even the most careful and balanced scholarly interpretations of human conduct are invariably implicated in the conventions of their time.

HOLOCAUST IDENTITY: MULTICULTURALISM
AND THE POLITICS OF VICTIMHOOD

Even before it became available in bookstores, Goldhagen's book began drawing massive media attention in the United States, much of it ranging from positive to wildly enthusiastic.[4] Indeed, one is hard put

[3] S. Milgram, *Obedience to Authority: An Experimental View* (New York, 1974).

[4] For a sampling of positive and critical early reviews, see J. Heilbrunn, "Jolting, Flawed Account of Germany and the Holocaust," *WT* (March 17, 1996); P. Johnson, "An Epidemic of Hatred," *WP* (March 24, 1996); L. Begley, "Just Plain Volk," *LAT* (March 24, 1996); D. Pryce-Jones, "The University of Evil," *WSJ* (March 26, 1996); R. Bernstein, "Was Slaughter of the Jews Embraced by Germans?" *NYT* (March 27, 1996); E. K. Coughlin, "'Willing Executioners,'" *CHE* (March 29, 1996); J. Elson, "What Did They Know?" *Time* (April 1, 1996): 73; A. M. Rosenthal, "Some Ordinary Germans," *NYT* (April 2, 1996); M. Kenney, "The Germans' New Accuser," *BG* (April 9, 1996); V. R. Berghahn, "The Road to Extermination," *NYTBR* (April 14, 1996); G. A. Craig, "How Hell Worked," *NYRB* (April 18, 1996): 4–8; C. James, "Blaming the Germans," *TNY* (April 22, 1996): 44–50; R. Andersen, "Extraordinary Evil," *CT* (April 21, 1996); J. Adler, "History Lesson," *Newsweek* (April 29, 1996); S. Hoffmann, "Recent Books on International Relations," *FA* (May/June, 1996): 144; R. S. Wistrich, "Helping Hitler," *Commentary* 102, no. 1 (July 1996): 27–31.

to think of another scholarly book, even of smaller dimensions and less heavily burdened by academic jargon, that has met with such a barrage of reviews, commentary, and interviews in the print and electronic media. The unprecedented excitement surrounding the book has been attributed by some to a cleverly managed public relations campaign by the publisher, combined with the media savvy of the author and, not least, his assertion that he had come up with a definitive answer to one of the century's most troubling questions, namely, why did the Holocaust happen? But while these explanations cannot be wholly dismissed, I would argue that from the perspective of the present they do not sufficiently clarify the larger context of this phenomenon.

The most striking aspect of the book's reception in the United States was the difference between the media's all out enthusiasm and the far more cautious and often highly critical reaction of the scholarly community.[5] In the meantime, of course, thanks to the media's short attention span, the book has been relegated to the status of "history" on those rare occasions that it is still referred to at all. As for specialists, Goldhagen's study has become a kind of "unmentionable presence," alluded to in numerous academic lectures, conference papers, articles and book reviews, but rarely discussed in detail. While many American scholars are now inclined to see it as an example of "bad scholarship," not a few would concede that it has some inherent merits and would even more readily accept that it has had an impact (whether positive or negative) both on future scholarship and on the lay public.[6]

[5] For a sampling, see C. R. Browning, "Human Nature, Culture, and the Holocaust," *CHE* (October 18, 1996); Browning, "Daniel Goldhagen's *Willing Executioners*," *H&M* 8 (1996): 88–108; F. Stern, "The Goldhagen Controversy: One Nation, One People, One Theory?" *FA* 75 (1996): 128–38; S. E. Aschheim, "Archetypes and the German-Jewish Dialogue: Reflections Occasioned by the Goldhagen Affair," *GH* 15 (1997): 240–50; A. Shatz, "Browning's Version," *LF* (February 1997): 48–57; R. Gellately, review, *JMH* 69 (1997): 187–91; L. Douglas, "The Goldhagen Riddle," *Commonweal* (May 9, 1997): 18–21; I. Deák, "Holocaust Views: The Goldhagen Controversy in Retrospect," *CEH* 30 (1997): 295–307; F.H. Littell, ed., *Hyping the Holocaust: Scholars Answer Goldhagen* (East Rockaway, N.Y., 1997). See Goldhagen's response in "Motives, Causes, and Alibis," *TNR* (December 23, 1996): 37–45. See the exchange between Goldhagen, Browning, and Bartov in *TNR* (February 10, 1997): 4–5.

[6] See G. Eley, ed., *The "Goldhagen Effect": History, Memory, Nazism—Facing the German Past* (Ann Arbor, 2000). British reviews, available to Americans via the Internet, included R. Harris, "The Awful Truth," *ST* (March 24, 1996); G. Sereny, "The Complexities of Complicity," *LT* (March 28, 1996); H. Pick, "Your Neighbour the Murderer," *Guardian* (March 29, 1996); E. Wiesel, "Little Hitlers," *Observer* (March 31, 1996); J. Morris, "The Hate of the Common People," *Independent* (March 30, 1996); "If All Were

Thus we find that from a condition of extreme divergence between media enthusiasm and scholarly rejection, Goldhagen's book came to be treated with relative media indifference and somewhat greater scholarly interest or even partial recognition of its potentially positive achievements. What, then, can this process tell us about the book's role in American perceptions of the Holocaust, and how did preconceived notions about the genocide of the Jews influence the reception of the book? What have we learned about the gap between scholarly and public opinion? Finally, what is the relationship between the book's reception and the American politics of identity, discourses on victimhood, and the quest for identifiable enemies?

There is little doubt that in the past couple of decades the Holocaust has moved from a marginal place in American political conversation and scholarly activity to a highly prominent position.[7] While no single cause can account for this "Americanization" of the Holocaust, it can only be understood as part of the emergence of multiculturalism, namely, the shift from the politics of the "melting pot" to a growing emphasis on the distinct cultural identities and historical roots of the many immigrant communities that make up the United States. And while each ethnic group will assert its own unique history, what has surfaced as a particularly potent symbol of identity has been a consciousness of (past, and often also present) victimhood among those groups that still feel threatened or are still burdened by the memories of past suffering, either in the United States or in their countries of origin (or both).[8] To be sure, this focus on victimhood is often also linked

Guilty, None Were," *Economist* (April 27, 1996): 91–92; J. D. Noakes, "No Ordinary People," *TLS* (June 7, 1996); M. Mazower, "Fighting Demonization with Demonization," *PP* 30 (1996): 73–75; P. Pulzer, "Psychopaths and Conformists, Adventurers and Moral Cowards," *LRB* (January 23, 1997): 20–21; R. B. Birn and V. Riess, "Revising the Holocaust," *HJ* 40/1 (1997): 195–215. Goldhagen's response: "The Fictions of Ruth Bettina Birn," *GPS* 15, no. 3 (Fall 1997): 119–65. A disturbing anti-American antisemitic diatribe is Taki, "Book Burning Lights Up In the Big Bagel," *ST* (April 7, 1996).

[7] P. Novick, *The Holocaust in American Life* (Boston, 1999); M. Marrus, "The Use and Misuse of the Holocaust," in *Lessons and Legacies: The Meaning of the Holocaust in a Changing World*, ed. Peter Hayes (Evanston, Ill., 1991), 106–19; J. Shandler, *While America Watches: Televising the Holocaust* (New York, 1999). On an alleged Jewish financial conspiracy, see N. G. Finkelstein, *The Holocaust Industry: Reflections on the Exploitation of Jewish Suffering* (London, 2000); E. Piper, ed., *Gibt es wirklich eine Holocaust-Industrie? Zur Auseinandersetzung um Norman Finkelstein* (Zurich, 2001).

[8] A powerful rejection of the term *race* in P. Gilroy, *Against Race: Imagining Political Culture Beyond the Color Line* (Cambridge, Mass., 2000). The German context in U. Linke, *German Bodies: Race and Representation after Hitler* (New York, 1999).

to a sense of pride and self-esteem, related to the ability of such groups to survive persecution and maintain or even further develop their distinct culture. But precisely for this reason, even the assertion of accomplishment derives much of its force from the narrative (historical or mythical) and memory (personal or collective) of prior victimization and persecution.

The rise of "Holocaust consciousness" (a rather unsavory term) must thus be understood in the context of American identity politics, even while it is obviously also related to the impact, most especially, of the Eichmann trial and the 1967 Six Day War, both on American Jewry and, albeit to a lesser extent, on the rest of the American public. Conversely, once the Holocaust moved to the fore of Jewish consciousness, it gradually acquired the status of the ultimate paradigm of victimhood (and evil) in the United States and subsequently in much of Europe. Consequently, assertions of identity by other minorities are often accompanied by claims of having experienced a Holocaust of their own. There is something grotesque about this process, of course, since the Holocaust was all about annihilating the physical identity and erasing the memory of a whole people. Yet having come to be seen as an historical episode which galvanized Jewish identity through a consciousness of common victimhood, it (or its near equivalents) became a much sought-after commodity for other minorities seeking to establish and fortify their own common fate and unique characteristics. Moreover, the Holocaust has great appeal for the media, since it contains precisely those "powerful" visual and emotional components that draw audiences and increase ratings, and because it can easily be simplified into a tale of good and evil, innocence and monstrosity, which culminated in a triumphal happy end whereby the (American) values of liberty and democracy defeated the forces of (German) darkness.[9]

This is where the very different trends in scholarship got in the way. Just as the lay public began to think of the Holocaust as one of the core events of the century, caused primarily by German antisemitism, increasing numbers of scholars shifted the emphasis to other factors in

---

[9] Further in O. Bartov, *Murder in Our Midst: The Holocaust, Industrial Killing, and Representation* (New York, 1996), chaps. 3, 5, 8. The legal and historical context of the Eichmann trial in H. Yablonka, *The State of Israel vs. Adolf Eichmann* (Tel Aviv, 2001), in Hebrew; L. Douglas, *The Memory of Judgment: Making Law and History in the Trials of the Holocaust* (New Haven, 2001), 97–182.

German and European society. In the United States, this was most clearly demonstrated by the growing attention paid to Raul Hilberg's work of 1961, reissued in a much expanded and revised edition in 1985, as well as to studies by such scholars as Karl Schleunes and Christopher Browning.[10] Unlike the case of Germany, this *did not* mean that antisemitism was ever totally dismissed as an important motivating factor, as illustrated, for instance, by the respect in which the work of Saul Friedländer has always been held.[11] It did mean, however, that monocausal interpretations of the kind favored by the general public and the media were no longer considered sufficient by the majority of scholars. Moreover, even the growing preoccupation of scholars with questions of identity and the impact of cultural studies by no means led to a revival of teleological historical interpretations of the kind popularized by A. J. P. Taylor in the immediate aftermath of World War II.[12] Earlier studies on the precursors of Nazism by American scholars of European origin such as Fritz Stern, George Mosse, and Walter Laqueur, were complemented by works that investigated both the complex roots of German antisemitism and the numerous attempts to create a German-Jewish symbiosis throughout the latter part of the nineteenth century and the early decades of the twentieth century.[13]

Consequently, while the historical literature on Nazism and the Holocaust rapidly expanded, its interpretation of that period increas-

[10] R. Hilberg, *The Destruction of the European Jews*, 3 vols., rev. ed. (New York, 1985); K. A. Schleunes, *The Twisted Road to Auschwitz: Nazi Policy Toward German Jews, 1933–1939*, 2d ed. (Urbana, 1990); C. R. Browning, *Fateful Months: Essays on the Emergence of the Final Solution* (New York 1985) and *The Path to Genocide: Essays on Launching the Final Solution* (New York, 1992).

[11] S. Friedländer, *Nazi Germany and the Jews*, vol. 1 (New York, 1997); Friedländer, *Memory, History, and the Extermination of the Jews of Europe* (Bloomington, 1993), and "The Extermination of the European Jews in Historiography: Fifty Years Later," in O. Bartov, *The Holocaust: Origins, Implementation, Aftermath* (London, 2000).

[12] A. J. P. Taylor, *The Course of German History: A Survey of the Development of Germany since 1815* (London, 1945). Further in I. Kershaw, *The Nazi Dictatorship*, 3d ed. (London, 1993), 1–16.

[13] F. Stern, *The Politics of Cultural Despair: A Study in the Rise of the Germanic Ideology* (Berkeley, 1961); G. L. Mosse, *The Crisis of German Ideology: Intellectual Origins of the Third Reich* (New York, 1964); W. Laqueur, *Young Germany: A History of the German Youth Movement* (New York, 1962); J. Weiss, *The Ideology of Death: Why the Holocaust Happened in Germany* (Chicago, 1996); J. Reinharz and W. Schatzberg, eds., *The Jewish Response to German Culture: From the Enlightenment to the Second World War* (Hanover, 1985); S. E. Aschheim, *Culture and Catastrophe: German and Jewish Confrontations with National Socialism and Other Crises* (New York, 1996); A. Rabinbach, *In the Shadow of Catastrophe: German Intellectuals between Apocalypse and Enlightenment* (Berkeley, 1997).

ingly differed from the popular—in part media-generated—consensus on the genocide of the Jews. The triumphal note that accompanied many early works was replaced by an awareness of the troubling similarities between Germany and other modern societies. Although a few scholars had pointed in that direction many decades before,[14] it was only in the 1980s that the role of the bureaucracy, the professions (especially physicians and lawyers), and, more generally, the European nation-state's crisis of modernity took center stage in the scholarly debate.[15] The progressively complex, at times rather jargon-ridden scholarly literature, appeared all the more inaccessible to the person "on the street." If the politics of identity demanded clearly etched victims and perpetrators, academic discourse seemed to prefer moral relativism, radical skepticism, and convoluted, self-centered argumentation.[16]

It was at this point that Goldhagen's book exploded on the scene. Here was a scholarly text that finally proposed to clear the air from all academic obfuscation and ambivalence and to provide a clear and definitive answer to a question that had, over the previous couple of decades, become of major concern to large sectors of the public, a question that had moved to the fore of the political debate and was therefore of great commercial interest to the media. Goldhagen did not "merely" propose to tell the public why the Holocaust had happened and who was guilty of it; he also led a frontal attack against all those scholars who had apparently become completely incapable of seeing what the general public had intuitively known all along, that it was "the Germans" who had done it, that they had always wanted to do it, that they did it because they hated Jews, and that once called upon to do it, they did it with great enthusiasm and much pleasure. This kind of argumentation played both on the anti-German sentiments of some sectors in the American public and on a growing frustration with aca-

[14] E. Fraenkel, *The Dual State* (New York, 1941); F. Neumann, *Behemoth: The Structure and Practice of National Socialism* (London, 1942); H. Arendt, *The Origins of Totalitarianism* (New York, 1951); J. L. Talmon, *The Origins of Totalitarian Democracy* (London, 1952).

[15] M. Kater, *Doctors under Hitler* (Chapel Hill, 1989); I. Müller, *Hitler's Justice: The Courts of the Third Reich* (Cambridge, Mass., 1991); J. Herf, *Reactionary Modernism: Technology, Culture, and Politics in Weimar and the Third Reich* (Cambridge, 1984); D. J. K. Peukert, *The Weimar Republic: The Crisis of Classical Modernity* (New York, 1992); Z. Bauman, *Modernity and the Holocaust* (Ithaca, 1989).

[16] See application of literary theory and psychological models to interpretations of the Holocaust by Hayden White and Dominick LaCapra in *Probing the Limits of Representation: Nazism and the "Final Solution,"* ed. S. Friedländer (Cambridge, Mass., 1992).

demic discourse. It also came along with an important safety valve, since it not only steadfastly ignored all other antisemitic traditions, but also insisted on the absence of this sentiment in postwar Germany, America's loyal ally.

Presented by a young scholar endowed with the credentials of a Harvard degree and the moral authority of being the son of a survivor, Goldhagen's thesis had the strength of being so obvious that one just had to wonder how nobody had thought of it before. Indeed, here was an answer that had all the qualities of an Agatha Christie murder mystery—the smoking gun was right there for all to see, yet precisely because it was so obviously placed, everyone had missed it. (For the more literary-minded, this book's exercise in unveiling the obvious might be reminiscent of Edgar Allan Poe's *The Purloined Letter*, which Jacques Lacan and Jacques Derrida have made into a major trope in psychoanalysis and literary criticism).[17] Criticism by seasoned scholars of the young rebel's thesis only enhanced his reputation in the public domain, confirming his status as a lone fighter against an established and self-satisfied academic elite. Goldhagen's appearances in the media, his constant repetition of the "simple truth" which any lay person could grasp, were far more convincing than the seemingly convoluted assertions and qualifications made by his "rivals." Conversely, his own book's size, its hundreds of footnotes, and jargon-ridden language, all seemed to prove that this was indeed a most serious scholarly undertaking.

Media hypes have a notoriously short life expectancy. The long-term consequences of the American debate are more difficult to predict. To some extent, the situation was confused by the fact that while Goldhagen directed his initial attacks against American scholars, they were much more to the point regarding the German historiography of the Holocaust. As noted above, in the United States the issue of antisemitism never entirely disappeared from the scholarly debate as one of the important factors leading to the Nazi genocide of the Jews. Moreover, the very size and diversity of American academe has allowed for the existence of widely differing opinions and has hindered the hegemony—at least for more than a brief period—of any conven-

---

[17] See *The Great Tales and Poems of Edgar Allan Poe* (New York, 1951); J. Lacan, *Écrits* (Paris, 1966); J. Derrida, "Le Facteur de la Vérité," *Poétique* 21 (1975); B. Johnson, "The Frame of Reference: Poe, Lacan, Derrida," in *Literature and Psychoanalysis: The Question of Reading: Otherwise*, ed. S. Felman (Baltimore, 1982), 457–505.

tion of interpretation or the dominance of any group of scholarly gurus. Nevertheless, it would appear that even in the United States Goldhagen contributed to an increased preoccupation with antisemitism and Jewish-German relations. To be sure, Goldhagen's book itself was the product of a certain *Zeitgeist*, but it doubtlessly further legitimized this renewed interest. Initial worries that Goldhagen's sweeping generalizations and inflated rhetoric would undermine the reorientation of scholarship toward a greater emphasis on ideological motivation and traditional prejudice (a reorientation for which some historians, including myself, had been calling since the mid-1980s) have been greatly exaggerated.[18]

Since public debates tend to present polarized views, the argument over the book was constructed as a confrontation between Goldhagen's insistence on the primacy of German antisemitism and Christopher Browning's emphasis on the dynamics of peer pressure.[19] In retrospect, however, we can say that neither of these explanatory models can be fully accepted at the cost of entirely dismissing the other. Rather, only a more nuanced analysis of the social-cultural environment, and of the relationship between ideological and circumstantial factors, can bring us closer to an understanding of the perpetrators' motivation and conduct. As a recently published study of another police battalion has convincingly demonstrated, for instance, the members of this unit were neither "ordinary men" nor "ordinary Germans," thanks to a selection and indoctrination process that set them apart from the German population as a whole.[20] In this case, at least, it appears that one needs to take into account the Third Reich's educational and political climate, the specific ideological training of the men in question, and the brutalizing effects of the fighting in the East, in order to gain a full picture of how these policemen were transformed into murderers.

To sum up, while Goldhagen's book both reflected and enhanced the American public's interest in, if not fascination with, the Holocaust, its long-term impact on the scholarship of the period has not been particularly significant. As the smoke of the dispute clears, we find the

[18] O. Bartov, *The Eastern Front, 1941–1945*, 2d ed. (New York, 2001).

[19] C. R. Browning, *Ordinary Men: Reserve Police Battalion 101 and the Final Solution in Poland* (New York, 1992).

[20] E. B. Westermann, "'Ordinary Men' or 'Ideological Soldiers'? Police Battalion 310 in Russia, 1942," *GSR* 21 (February 1998): 41–68.

camps more or less where they had been before. Goldhagen increasingly speaks about his book to public audiences, mostly non-academic Jewish groups, who are glad to hear him confirm what they had always believed; meanwhile, scholars continue to pursue the central questions raised by the Holocaust: the balance between ideology and circumstances, age-old prejudices and the impact of mass politics and modern science, state-organized genocide and individual complicity, resistance and collaboration, historical uniqueness and comparability.

In the public sphere, by focusing on pre-1945 German antisemitism, the Goldhagen debate has unfortunately obscured those aspects of Nazi genocidal policies that should be of concern to all citizens of modern, bureaucratic, technological states. This may be heartening to some and disturbing to others. But the argument that after the fall of Nazism the Germans became "just like us," and that therefore they are as unlikely to perpetrate genocide again as "we" are, can produce an excessive sense of complacency not merely about postwar Germany but about the rest of "us." The danger is that instead of perceiving the Holocaust as an event that should warn us about the potentials of our civilization, we would relegate it to a no longer relevant past. This may be one of the more comforting conclusions of Goldhagen's book and one reason for its commercial success, but it unfortunately does not reflect the reality of our world, whose last fifty years have witnessed the perpetuation of genocide and atrocity on a scale that belies the erroneous impression that following the Holocaust the worst is behind us.

LIBERATING ATROCITIES: POLICEMEN, SOLDIERS,
AND ORDINARY GERMANS

Even before the publication of the German translation, Goldhagen's book was met with a tremendous wave of media interest in Germany. Unlike reactions in the United States, however, initial German reactions tended to be either dismissive or hostile.[21] It should be noted that

---

[21] American reports of early German reactions include R. Atkinson, "In Germany, A Collective 'Howl of Protest,'" *WP* (April 25, 1996); A. Cowel, "Germans, Jews and Blame: New Book, New Pain," *NYT* (April 25, 1996); J. Adler et al., "Why Did They Do It? Angry Reaction to a New Book Asserting That When It Came to Jews, All Germans Were Fanatics," *Newsweek* (April 29, 1996): 42; T. Petty, "Germans Denounce Holocaust Theory," *LAT* (April 28, 1996). For early German press reactions see M. Niroumand, "Little Historians," *TAZ* (April 13 / 14, 1996); T. Henegahn, "German Critics Slam New U.S. Book on Holocaust," *Reuter* (April 15, 1996); Augstein in Schoeps, 106–9; W. Birkenmaier, "Ein ganzes Volk auf der Anklagebank?" *StZ* (April 17, 1996); P. De Thier,

the German "middlebrow" and "highbrow" print and electronic media provide a much larger forum for scholarly opinion than their American equivalents. Hence we cannot speak of a clear-cut distinction between media and scholarly reactions in the German case. Indeed, some early scholarly views about the book could be encapsulated in the statement of one prominent historian, Eberhard Jäckel, who stated that Goldhagen's study was "simply a bad book."[22] Other contributions, however, tended to be far more cautious, reflecting, among other things, disagreements within the German scholarly community about the place of the Third Reich in the larger context of German history and the centrality of the Holocaust for the history of Nazism.[23]

Once the translation of the book was published in Germany, and especially following Goldhagen's lecture tour there, which was described by one commentator as a "triumphal procession," media and scholarly opinion underwent a remarkable transformation, drawing far closer to the lay German public's unexpectedly enthusiastic reception of both the book and its author.[24] This can be traced at least in part to the situation that repeated itself over and over again in the packed

---

"Deutsche als Hitlers willige Henker? Experten zerpflücken das Buch eines US-Historikers über den Holocaust," *BZ* (April 23, 1996); G. Koch, "Eine Welt aus Willen und Vorstellung," *FR* (April 30/May 1, 1996). Compilations include Schoeps; V. Ullrich, ed., *Die Goldhagen-Kontroverse* (*Die Zeit:* Dokument 1, 1996); M. Heyl, "Die Goldhagen-Debatte im Spiegel der englisch- und deutschsprachigen Rezensionen von Februar bis Juli 1996. Ein Überblick," *Mittelweg 36* 4 (1996): 41–56. And see Goldhagen's response, "Das Versagen der Kritiker," *Die Zeit* (August 2, 1996): 9–14.

[22] In Schoeps, 187–92.

[23] See especially essays by H.-U. Wehler and U. Herbert in Schoeps, 193–209, 214–24, respectively.

[24] *Hitlers willige Vollstrecker: Ganz normale Deutsche und der Holocaust* was published in August 1996. E. Roll, "Goldhagens Diskussionsreise," writes that "the more his critics press him, the more the public leans toward the scholar: here is someone who asks the right questions about the perpetrators," *SZ* (September 9, 1996); V. Ullrich, "Daniel J. Goldhagen in Deutschland," writes that "the book tour became a triumphal procession. The historians criticize *Hitler's Willing Executioners:* the public finds the book liberating," *Die Zeit* 38 (September 13, 1996). R. Augstein was transformed into a Goldhagen fan: *Der Spiegel* 33 (August 12, 1996): 40–55. See also W. Birkenmaier, "Ein zorniges, moralisches Buch," *StZ* 189 (August 16, 1996). More critical views in W. Sofsky, "Normale Massenmörder," *NZZ* 10 (August 11, 1996); D. Pohl, "Die Holocaust-Forschung und Goldhagens Thesen," *VfZ* 1 (1997): 1–48. Overviews in J. Joffe, "Goldhagen in Germany," *NYRB* (November 28, 1996): 18–21; A. Elon, "The Antagonist as Liberator," *NYTM* (January 26, 1997): 40–44; M. Ash, "American and German Perspectives on the Goldhagen Debate: History, Identity, and the Media," *HGS* 11 (1997): 396–411.

lecture halls where older professors who attacked Goldhagen with some vehemence were in turn confronted by clear expressions of hostility from audiences of third generation Germans who preferred to embrace the beleaguered young (Jewish) American scholar precisely because they felt that for once they were being told the "truth" that their teachers had always refused to admit.

Of course, there was clearly something troubling about early German reactions to the book. Anti-American and anti-Jewish sentiments were reflected in broad hints that the book's success in the United States was linked to the predominance of Jews in the media.[25] The quality of American universities was questioned, the underlying assumption being that Goldhagen's obviously flawed Ph.D. dissertation, which served as the basis for his book, would never have been accepted at a German university.[26] Conversely, one could detect a visible degree of defensiveness regarding the central claim of Goldhagen's study, namely, that all (or at least most) Germans in the Third Reich were willing executioners (whether they actually perpetrated murder or would have been happy to do so if asked). Goldhagen's self-presentation as the son of a survivor served some German critics to question his ability to write an objective historical account (while of course expressing sympathy with his own and his father's predicament).[27] This was an interesting development, since while in the United States Goldhagen's family history was seen as adding moral authority to his text and hence validating it, in Germany the curious assumption was made that Germans could somehow maintain greater "scientific" detachment from the horrors of the Holocaust than Jews, who, unlike their German counterparts, would never be liberated from their "understandable" mystifying predilections and emotional involvement.

None of this should have been surprising to anyone who could remember similar arguments made during the *Historikerstreit* of the mid-1980s.[28] Much more striking was the change of attitudes not only

---

[25] See Augstein in Schoeps, 106, where he dismisses the "mostly Jewish American non-historian columnists."

[26] H.-U. Wehler in Schoeps, 206–207. But also Y. Bauer's April 8, 1996, lecture at the United States Holocaust Memorial Museum in Washington, D.C., cited in M. Mitchell, H-German listserv, german@h-net.msu.edu, April 11, 1996.

[27] A. Geldner, "Porträt der Woche: Daniel Goldhagen," *StZ* 184 (August 10, 1996); F. Schirrmacher, "Hitler's Code: Holocaust aus faustischem Streben? Daniel John [sic] Goldhagens Remythisierung der Deutschen," *FAZ* (April 15, 1996).

[28] See M. Broszat and S. Friedländer, "A Controversy about the Historicization of National Socialism," in *Reworking the Past*, ed. P. Baldwin (Boston, 1990), 106.

toward Goldhagen's book—criticism of which by no means entirely disappeared—but, much more significantly, with respect to the need to recognize the centrality of the Holocaust, if not the need to change the research methodologies concerning it. Of course, this trend did not begin with the publication of the book; rather, the debate surrounding it seems to have provided those involved in a reorientation of German scholarship on the Third Reich with an opportunity to air and promote their views. It had been assumed in some quarters that following reunification the Nazi period would finally recede into the historical past and no longer feature as prominently as it once had in public debates. Reactions to Goldhagen's book, however, along with several other cases mentioned below, demonstrated that Nazism has remained a crucial issue in German political, intellectual, and scholarly discourse.[29]

We can thus conclude that German reactions to Goldhagen's book shifted quite quickly from outright media rejection to a more balanced, and in some cases even very positive, evaluation. Academic opinion, initially either very cautious or wholly negative, has by now similarly evolved to a more positive stance, despite the usual scholarly qualifications. Moreover, since history books have a longer shelf life in Germany than in the United States, and because scholars are more closely involved in the media, the debate has not been completely relegated to the status of "history." This, of course, has to do also with the greater centrality of the Nazi past to questions of German identity and politics. Indeed, the somewhat more positive evaluation of the book by German scholars today—as compared with their American colleagues—concerns their appreciation of its political impact rather than its inherent qualities, a point clearly made by the sociologist Jürgen Habermas in his speech on the occasion of giving Goldhagen the Democracy Prize for his book (a somewhat controversial decision, as far as German historians were concerned).[30] Generally, then, it would

---

[29] U. Herbert, "Der Judenmord war das Kernereignis des Jahrhunderts," *Die Welt* (March 16, 1998), argues that on average 85 percent of the text of all major works on the Nazi period published until 1990 was devoted to the pre-1939 period and only 15 percent to the war, of which a mere 5 percent was on the Holocaust.

[30] J. Habermas, "Über den öffentlichen Gebrauch der Historie: Warum ein 'Demokratiepreis' für Daniel J. Goldhagen? Eine Laudatio," *Die Zeit* 12 (March 14, 1997): 13–14; J. P. Reemtsma, "Abkehr vom Wunsch nach Verleugnung: Über 'Hitlers willige Vollstrecker' als Gegenstück zur 'historischen Erklärung,'" *BDIP* (April 1997): 417–23; U. Raulff, "Der lange Schrecken: Goldhagen, Habermas, Reemtsma: Ein Preis, drei Reden," *FAZ* (May 12, 1997).

appear that by now a degree of consensus has been reached among German scholars regarding the book's political contribution and potential long-term effects on the changing focus of German research on, and perceptions of, Nazism and the Holocaust, all of this despite a commonly held view regarding the untenable nature of Goldhagen's thesis as a whole.

It has been noted that among Goldhagen's most enthusiastic German audiences were numerous members of the third generation, namely, young people whose own parents were either born after the war or were still children during the waning years of the Third Reich. For these men and women, most of whom were apparently middle-class university students, the book was said to have produced a "liberating experience."[31] How are we to understand this seemingly curious formulation, whereby a study asserting that the vast majority of Germans during the Third Reich were either actual or potential murderers was somehow perceived by Germans born in the 1970s as liberating? It should first be realized that as far as these young crowds were concerned, the Holocaust was an event that occurred when their grandparents were about their own age. Unlike their parents, whose complex relationship with the "perpetrator generation" was often expressed in long silences, outbursts of rage, and occasional use of distorted Holocaust imagery for their own political agendas, the third generation has a more detached view of the Nazi past.[32] Interestingly, some have noted that members of the third generation communicate more easily with their grandparents (not an uncommon phenomenon in generational relations) and have more sympathy for their predicament under Nazism.[33] Conversely, or perhaps precisely for this very reason, they can also afford to take up a more accusatory stance vis-à-vis that generation as a whole, since whatever they might say about it has little direct bearing either on their own life experiences and self-perception, or on that of their grandparents.

[31] Ullrich, "Goldhagen in Deutschland"; Joffe, "Goldhagen."

[32] D. Herzog, "'Pleasure, Sex, and Politics Belong Together': Post-Holocaust Memory and the Sexual Revolution in West Germany," *CI* 24 (Winter 1998): 393–444; U. Linke, "Murderous Fantasies: Violence, Memory, and Selfhood in Germany," *NGC* 64 (Winter 1995): 37–59.

[33] A. Cowel, "After 50 Years, Europe Revisits Its War Stories: History Has Become New as a Younger Generation Casts Aside Its Parents' Comforting National Myths," *NYT* (July 6, 1997). On the impact of victimhood on later generations, see R. Moses, ed., *Persistent Shadows of the Holocaust: The Meaning to Those Not Directly Affected* (Madison, Conn., 1993).

Second, but also related to generational relations, young German students seem to be increasingly impatient with the complex and often highly theoretical and detached (not to say bloodless) interpretations of Nazism offered by their professors.[34] As has been pointed out by some younger scholars,[35] academics of the older generation were rarely capable of confronting the reality of mass murder head-on and preferred to integrate it into a larger, somewhat abstract theoretical framework, in which conceptualizations of totalitarianism, bureaucratic rule, and a fragmented decision-making process largely left out both the blood and gore of genocide and the still troubling question of guilt and responsibility. Goldhagen's rhetoric during his visit to Germany managed both to reintroduce such issues to the debate and, at the same time, to distance the younger generation from the event and its ostensible primary cause, by emphasizing—much more than he had done in his book—that postwar Germany had gone through a complete metamorphosis and was therefore no longer plagued by that unique brand of antisemitism that had previously made it essentially different from "us." In this manner, the twenty-year-olds who applauded his lectures and booed his critics were liberated both from the seemingly obfuscating interpretations of their often authoritarian professors and from any sense of collective guilt or otherness, all by a young (Jewish) American maverick who dared to challenge the conventional interpretation and confront the old establishment on its own territory.

This does not mean, of course, that young German students of Nazism accepted Goldhagen's arguments at face value. Quite to the contrary, the impression is that they share much of their older colleagues' criticism of his simplistic thesis. But they do seem to have felt liberated also in the sense that they could think about the period in moral terms viewed previously as irrelevant or even detrimental to scholarly work. They could also now turn their attention to individual brutality and ideological conviction without needing to justify them-

---

[34] *National Socialist Extermination Policies: Contemporary German Perspectives and Controversies*, ed. U. Herbert (New York 2000); D. Pohl, *Nationalsozialistische Judenverfolgung in Ostgalizien 1941–1944: Organisation und Durchführung eines staatlichen Massenverbrechens* (Munich, 1996); T. Sandkühler, *"Endlösung" in Galizien: Der Judenmord in Ostpolen und die Rettungsinitiativen von Berthold Beitz 1941–1944* (Bonn, 1996); W. Manoschek,*"Serbien ist judenfrei." Militärische Besatzungspolitik und Judenvernichtung in Serbien 1941/42* (Munich, 1995).

[35] Herbert, *Extermination*, chap. 1; Herbert, *"Eine 'Führerentscheidung' zur 'Endlösung'? Neue Ansätze in einer alten Diskussion," NZZ* (March 14/15, 1998).

selves to their scholarly mentors against accusations of being diverted to marginal issues of little explanatory value. The fact is that while Goldhagen's attack on his American colleagues was hardly justified, there was much to criticize about the German historiography of the Third Reich and especially its marginalization of the Holocaust.

From this perspective, we can say that Goldhagen's book had a beneficial effect in Germany, since it helped legitimize a new focus on the role of antisemitism in the Holocaust, asserted the centrality of the Holocaust for the history of Nazi Germany—previously denied by a number of prominent older scholars—and focused interest on recently published or forthcoming works by younger scholars heading in precisely that direction. Indeed, until recently very little serious research on the actual perpetration of genocide had been undertaken by German historians, not so much for lack of documentation (although recently opened archives in former communist countries have significantly expanded the source base), but due to the insistence of older historians, in what is still a very hierarchical "guild," on "functionalist" theories that largely ignored empirical research and desisted from historical reconstructions of the realities of mass murder.

Approaches to the study of Nazism have always been related to politics and self-perception. As initial interpretations of Hitler's dictatorship as either a takeover by a criminal clique or the culmination of a militaristic tradition led by a traditional elite unrepresentative of the mass of the population were finally rejected in the 1960s, they were replaced by a complex mechanistic explanatory model that portrayed an elaborate process of "cumulative radicalization" within the context of a "polycratic" regime as the main engine of genocide.[36] Not only was ideology seen as largely irrelevant, human agency and motivation was also described as marginal. To be sure, there was no denying that the killing itself might have been carried out in part by sadists or even antisemites, but this was not perceived as the fundamental facet of the phenomenon, but at most as its symptom and ultimate consequence. And since the functioning of the cogs did not explain the machine as a

---

[36] F. Meinecke, *Die deutsche Katastrophe* (Wiesbaden, 1946); G. Ritter, *Europa und die deutsche Frage* (Munich, 1948); M. Broszat, "Hitler and the Genesis of the 'Final Solution': An Assessment of David Irving's Theses," in *Aspects of the Third Reich*, ed. H. W. Koch (London, 1985); H. Mommsen, "The Realization of the Unthinkable: The 'Final Solution of the Jewish Question' in the Third Reich," in H. Mommsen, *From Weimar to Auschwitz* (Princeton, 1991).

whole, once the bureaucratic and decision-making apparatus was analyzed, there seemed little need to examine its low-level operators.[37] Historical explanations could thus be constructed that left the majority of the perpetrators, as well as their relationship to the mass of German society, out of the picture. Conversely, Goldhagen's book dramatized precisely the opposite end of the process and thereby underlined the necessity of returning to the face-to-face killing and providing a satisfactory explanation for the manner in which it was perpetrated. Even if one rejected the book's argument regarding the psychology and motivation of the killers, and the extent to which they represented their society, it certainly demonstrated that avoiding this question altogether was no longer possible.

The extent to which German society has found it difficult to come to terms with the individual, human aspects of the Holocaust, concerning both the perpetrators' motivation and conduct and the victims' identity and fate, is illustrated by the fact that the public was compelled to confront the realities of mass murder mainly as a result of outside interventions. This process began with the Allies' insistence on exposing residents of communities next to concentration camps to the horrors perpetrated in close proximity to their homes; it went on to the screening of documentaries to Germans under military occupation and the holding of the Nuremberg trials; and it has continued with the periodic arrival in Germany of Holocaust representations written or produced elsewhere, ranging from Anne Frank's diary to the television mini-series *Holocaust* to Steven Spielberg's *Schindler's List.*

It may be recalled that the *Historikerstreit* of the 1980s, in which one group of scholars came out against another for allegedly trivializing the crimes of the Third Reich, in fact did not bring with it any new work on the realities of genocide but was focused on questions of German national identity and its relationship to the past.[38] It was rather the impact of imported products, even when their inherent quality was at times rather questionable, that enhanced the public's sensibility to the past, unleashed public debates over the role of the Holocaust in the German present, and, despite initial criticism of their political, his-

---

[37] This is also H. Arendt's conclusion in *Eichmann in Jerusalem: A Report on the Banality of Evil* (New York, 1963).

[38] See, chap. 1, note 13, above.

torical, and aesthetic merits by the intelligentsia and the academic community, eventually influenced trends in German writing and research, representation and rhetoric. Goldhagen's book can be seen as yet another link in this chain of foreign interventions that have compelled, or allowed, a shift from an often mute and ignorant *Betroffenheit* (roughly meaning a speechless sense of shock and shame that facilitates absolution) to an integration of genocide as an inseparable part of German self-perception.[39]

In this context, it is also interesting to note the different reactions to Browning's study *Ordinary Men* in the United States and Germany. Although it did not achieve the status of an international bestseller, Browning's book did reach a relatively wide readership for an academic work and was revisited during the Goldhagen debate. American scholars were often convinced by Browning's emphasis on peer pressure, and his application and extension of Stanley Milgram's theory on obedience to authority as playing a cardinal role in instigating atrocity. This thesis, moreover, seemed to confirm previous interpretations, which relegated ideological motivation to a secondary place, such as Raul Hilberg's and Hannah Arendt's studies. It was also related to early sociological theories, such as the concept of "primary groups" propounded by Morris Janowitz and Edward Shils.[40] Browning's work, however, did not have a comparable effect on the American media and lay public, not least, perhaps, since there was nothing particularly sensational about it, peer pressure being a rather familiar and generally accepted notion within American educational, sports, and military institutions. Conversely, as far as American, and especially Jewish American, perceptions of Germany were concerned, it appears that the popular notion that Germans and Nazis were synonymous during the war was not about to be abandoned merely because an historical study had demonstrated the role of peer pressure in motivating a group of perpetrators.

German reactions to Browning's book reflected very different sensibilities and conventions. While his close-up view of a small group of perpetrators heralded Goldhagen's better-publicized study, Brown-

---

[39] For a comparison of strategies to come to terms with the past, see I. Buruma, *The Wages of Guilt: Memories of War in Germany and Japan* (New York, 1994). For a discussion of the term *Betroffenheit* in this context, see ibid., 21.

[40] Further in O. Bartov, *Hitler's Army: Soldiers, Nazis, and War in the Third Reich* (New York, 1991), 29–58.

ing's directly opposite conclusions tended to confirm the consensus in German scholarship and public opinion that discipline, authority, and peer group pressure had played a much greater role than antisemitism and ideological motivation. To be sure, this view had been under attack at least since the mid-1980s, when research on the Wehrmacht had shown the impact of indoctrination on the conduct of regular soldiers in the field.[41] But Browning's well-argued test case, and his use of an apparently dispassionate (albeit, as I will argue below, problematic) behaviorist theory taken from another discipline, was especially welcomed by those German students of the period who could now say that "even" a well-known American Holocaust scholar had dismissed the role of prejudice and ideology. For this very reason, *Ordinary Men* gained public prominence in Germany only after the publication of *Hitler's Willing Executioners*, since it could be cited as a seemingly foolproof refutation of Goldhagen's thesis.[42]

Moreover, while Goldhagen's study was ultimately received with a good deal of approval by significant sectors in academe and the media, other arguments regarding the impact of antisemitism on pro-Nazi sentiments in the Third Reich and the involvement of "ordinary Germans" in criminal policies elicited strongly negative reactions from some of the public and the political establishment and were met with a fair amount of scholarly skepticism. This was especially the case with the exhibition "War of Extermination: The Crimes of the Wehrmacht, 1941–44," which toured Germany and Austria between 1995 and 1999.[43] The reception of this exhibition, produced by German rather than foreign scholars—who were, however, not members of the historical "guild" but rather of the privately financed Institute for Social Research in Hamburg—sheds some more light on the manner in which Goldhagen's book was read and understood by the German public. For what most analyses of Goldhagen's reception in Germany seem to have missed is that for all its insistence on the lack of distinction between Germans and Nazis, his book focuses primarily on the

[41] Further in O. Bartov, ed., *The Holocaust: Origins, Implementation, Aftermath* (London, 2000), 162–84.

[42] See T. Sandkühler, "Böse menschen, böse Taten, und die Normale Holocaust-Forschung: Der Historiker Christopher Browning über Goldhagen und Genozid," *FAZ* (February 6, 1997).

[43] Introduction, note 4, above; *Besucher einer Ausstellung: Die Ausstellung* "Vernichtungskrieg. Verbrechen der Wehrmacht 1941 bis 1944" in *Interview und Gespräch*, ed. Hamburger Institut für Sozialforschung (Hamburg, 1998).

conduct of policemen, who cannot, by any stretch of the imagination, be said to represent German society.

German policemen were about as representative of their society as police forces anywhere else in the world, and probably even less so, given the emphasis on ideological instruction and the ideological selection procedures in these units. But even those unaware of the specific differences between the recruitment and training of policemen and regular soldiers could not think of the former as "ordinary Germans." People anywhere may feel proud about their fathers' or grandfathers' wartime service, but even Germans are unlikely to boast of the glorious deeds of ancestors who wore police uniforms. Goldhagen might claim that the members of the police battalions he investigated were "regular folk," but the vast majority of Germans remembered their own or their relatives' experiences *as soldiers.* Hence the much greater discomfort with the Wehrmacht exhibition, since, being a mass conscript army, the Wehrmacht did indeed represent German society: saying that it perpetrated mass crimes was tantamount to a collective charge against German society (or at least its adult male population).

The Holocaust may not have been a "national project," as Goldhagen has asserted, but the war definitely was. The assertion that the war was a criminal undertaking that also facilitated the genocide of the Jews meant that the millions of soldiers who had served in the ranks of the Wehrmacht could not escape blame for the Holocaust. Such a statement was obviously seen by conservative circles as an attempt to besmirch the army's "shield of honor" and slander a whole generation of young men who had returned from the battlefield to rebuild both Germanys. It also threatened to reverse the process of rehabilitating the Wehrmacht and normalizing the past begun during former President Ronald Reagan's notorious visit to the Bitburg military cemetery in 1985.[44] No wonder that, to cite just one example, the organization of former Wehrmacht soldiers in the Austrian city of Salzburg, whose membership consists by now mostly of the veterans' sons and daughters, warned their fellow citizens to protect their children from the Wehrmacht exhibition lest it poison their minds and undermine their love for family and (the German) fatherland.[45]

---

[44] G. Hartman, ed., *Bitburg in Moral and Political Perspective* (Bloomington, 1986).

[45] "Eltern, schützt Eure Kinder! Landesschulrat: Keine Empfehlung zum Besuch der Reemtsma-Ausstellung," *KA* 1, no. 2 (January/February 1998); "'Wehrmachtsausstellung': Fälschung empört Salzburg," "Ein Sturm der Entrüstung gegen die un-

One final point on the German case. Goldhagen's book is explicitly about the perpetrators and as such is similar to the bulk of German scholarship on the Holocaust, in which the victims appear only as the final product of the process to be reconstructed and explained. What distinguishes this book, however, is that the author's empathy is given exclusively to the victims rather than the perpetrators. In demonizing the perpetrators, Goldhagen makes no attempt to understand them; his focus is on portraying them as sadistic murderers who enjoy their "work" of torturing and killing Jews. The bulk of German scholarship, as well as for that matter Browning's book, is devoted to understanding what made these men behave as they did. Goldhagen, for his part, calls forth sympathy, pity, and compassion for the victims, and anger and frustration vis-à-vis the killers. This is a new perspective in German scholarship, although some such examples do exist in English-language works.[46] This is not to say that German scholars have ever shown any sympathy for the killers, but rather that they concentrate on figuring out how their minds worked, not on how their actions were experienced by those they murdered.[47]

Indeed, empathy with the victims has always appeared impossible for German scholars; even new research being written and published in Germany now has yet to overcome this obstacle.[48] This may have to do both with the perceived "otherness" of the victims and with the psychological burden such an approach would entail for scholars who still believe in the need for detachment. This, I would argue, also partly explains the commercial success and widespread impact of Victor Klemperer's recently published diaries, which finally made it possible for the German public to read an account of German society under Nazism from the perspective of one who was both a complete insider, a patriot who saw the Nazis as "un-German," and yet was made into a total outsider, increasingly shunned by his environment, while remaining throughout Hitler's twelve-year rule in the midst of German

---

selige 'Wehrmachtsausstellung' in Salzburg: 'Mein Vater war kein Mörder!'" and other articles, all in *SK* 13,573 (February 24, 1998).

[46] This issue is discussed in I. Deák, "Memories of Hell," *NYRB* (June 26, 1997): 38–43; U. Herbert, "Hitlers Wut und das Weggucken der Deutschen," *SZ* 70 (March 24, 1998).

[47] See my discussion of W. Sofsky, *The Order of Terror: The Concentration Camp* (1993; Princeton, 1997), in chap. 4, above.

[48] See Pohl, *Ostgalizien*, 15.

society.[49] One would hope that in the future German scholars will find it possible to write a history of Germany's victims, rather than of its perpetrators. Perhaps one merit of Goldhagen's book in Germany is that by launching a debate over the practice of face-to-face murder, it will in the long-run motivate German scholars to study these same situations also from the perspective of the victimized.

DIVERSIONARY TACTICS: CAMPS, GENOCIDES,
AND FRANCE'S SHOAH SYNDROME

Both in France and Israel, Goldhagen's book met with less commercial success and aroused only limited intellectual interest, mostly generated by its reception in the United States and Germany, rather than by local concerns. The main cause of this cooler reaction is that debates over Nazism and the Holocaust in both countries at the time of the book's publication were focused on issues that had little to do with the main thrust of Goldhagen's thesis. Hence, despite a fair amount of publicity, the book cannot be said to have had a major effect on public opinion or scholarly debate in France and Israel. A closer examination of the book's reception, however, indicates that the relative indifference observed in these two countries can be traced back to almost diametrically opposed reasons.

In France, after a few reviews in the daily print media, some more positive than others, the book was vehemently attacked by several scholars and intellectuals writing in a couple of special issues of academic journals devoted to the debate.[50] One young French scholar used the opportunity to publish a small book that provided the background and outlined the main arguments of the debate in the United States and

---

[49] V. Klemperer, *I Will Bear Witness: A Diary of the Nazi Years* (1995; New York, 1998–1999). See my analysis in chap. 7, below.

[50] For a sampling, see D. Vernet, "Les Allemands et la culpabilité collective de la Shoah," *Le Monde* (April 26, 1996); F. Schlosser, "Une nation d'assassins?" *NO* (November 28–December 4, 1996): 136–38; N. Weill, "Le meurtre antisémite, une maladie d'Allemagne?" and "Succès populaire, réserve des historiens," both in *MdL* (January 1997); E. Husson, "Le phénomène Goldhagen," and P. Burrin, "Il n'y a pas de peuple assassin!" both in "Génocide: Les Allemands tous coupables?" *L'Histoire* 206 (January 1997): 80–85; essays by O. Bartov, J. Joffe, F. Stern, R. Wistrich, and Goldhagen's response, *Le Débat* 93 (January-February 1997): 122–88; essays by P. Bouretz, P.-Y. Gaudard, R. Hilberg, L. Kandel, and C. Lanzmann, *LTM* 52, no. 592 (February-March 1997): 1–61; D. Bechtel, "Un Livre en débat," *VS* 54 (April-June 1997): 138–40. *Les Bourreaux volontaires de Hitler: Les Allemands ordinaires et l'Holocauste* was published in January 1997.

especially in Germany for the benefit of French readers who had little knowledge of these developments.[51] Following this, "le phénomène Goldhagen" quickly blew over, and there is little likelihood that it will be resurrected in the future.

French scholarship on the Holocaust is anything but impressive, and apart from a few major works, even translations of foreign studies are hard to come by.[52] This is not to say that French scholars and intellectuals, as well as the media, are not concerned with questions related to World War II. But in France the main focus is not on the genocide of the Jews, but rather on collaboration and resistance during the German occupation, on the one hand, and on the general question of totalitarianism and political repression, including the phenomenon of concentration camps, on the other.[53] Both the Francocentric perspective and the political-theoretical discussion do, of course, take the Holocaust into account, but rarely as a topic in its own right. In fact, whenever the Holocaust is mentioned, one often detects a tendency to relativize, marginalize, or generalize it. Moreover, for much of the 1990s France was preoccupied or, as some would have it, obsessed, with a reexamination of the Occupation, collaboration with the Nazi regime, and what the historian Henry Rousso has called the "Vichy Syndrome," namely, the manner in which the Fourth and Fifth Republics had long refused to come to terms with those "somber years."[54] Yet for all that, scholarship on and knowledge about Nazism and the Holocaust remain remarkably sparse.

This is one major reason why Goldhagen's book has had very little

---

[51] E. Housson, *Une culpabilité ordinaire? Hitler, Les Allemands et la Shoah: Les enjeux de la Controverse Goldhagen* (Paris, 1997).

[52] R. Hilberg's *The Destruction of the European Jews* appeared in French twenty-seven years after its original publication in English. The appearance in 1994 of the annual publication, *Les cahiers de la Shoah*, indicated the beginning of a new trend; but translations of foreign scholarship are still rare.

[53] Recent literature on Vichy is surveyed in O. Bartov, "The Proof of Ignominy: Vichy France's Past and Present," *CoEH* 7, no.1 (1998) and S. Fishman et al., eds., *France at War: Vichy and the Historians* (Oxford, 2000). The debate on the camps and totalitarianism is summarized in E. Traverso, *L'Histoire déchirée: Essai sur Auschwitz et les intellectuels* (Paris, 1997), 71–99. Most recently, see J. Kotek and P. Rigoulot, *Le siècle des camps: Détention, concentration, extermination* (Paris, 2000).

[54] H. Rousso, *The Vichy Syndrome: History and Memory in France since 1944* (Cambridge, Mass., 1991); E. Conan and H. Rousso, *Vichy: An Ever-Present Past* (Hanover, 1998). Recent exceptions include A. Kaspi, *Les Juifs pendant l'Occupation* (Paris, 1991), and A. Cohen, *Persécutions et sauvetages: Juifs et Français sous l'Occupation et sous Vichy* (Paris, 1993).

bearing on contemporary French debates about the past. The argument that the Germans were mostly Nazi came as no surprise to the French and could not have conceivably been a cause for any sort of sensation. Compared with the various scandals surrounding the Klaus Barbie trial, the Bousquet, Touvier, and Papon affairs, and, not least, the revelations regarding former President Mitterrand's affiliation with the extreme Right in the 1930s and his service for the Pétain regime before he finally opted for the Resistance, Goldhagen's book appeared to be merely stating the obvious.[55]

The book's ponderous style, repetitive arguments, moralistic tone, and obsession with the perpetrators' brutality were certainly not the right ingredients to provoke an intellectual debate in France. Moreover, Goldhagen's focus on the genocide of the Jews and his lack of interest in the murder of any other categories of people either by the Nazi regime and its collaborators or by other regimes in the course of the century meant that his book could not fit into the debate over totalitarianism and genocide that was taking shape in France at precisely the same time.[56] Conversely, the book's insistence on the uniqueness of German antisemitism, and its adamant refusal to compare it with either East or West European manifestations, could not but be quietly welcomed in a nation whose own antisemitic record, from Dreyfus to the 1930s, let alone under Vichy, had been obscured for many years thanks in part to the far greater ferocity of the Nazi regime.[57]

It is, of course, perfectly reasonable to argue that the links between the two current debates in France, and the lacunae that characterize both sets of arguments, could be identified with greater ease if more

[55] E. Paris, *Unhealed Wounds: France and the Klaus Barbie Affair* (New York, 1985); A. Finkielkraut, *Remembering in Vain: The Klaus Barbie Trial and Crimes Against Humanity* (New York, 1992); R. J. Golsan, ed., *Memory, the Holocaust, and French Justice: The Bousquet and Touvier Affairs* (Hanover, 1996); N. Wood, *Vectors of Memory: Legacies of Trauma in Postwar Europe* (Oxford, 1999), chap. 5; P. Péan, *Une jeunesse française: François Mitterrand 1934–1947* (Paris, 1994).

[56] F. Furet, *The Passing of an Illusion: The Idea of Communism in the Twentieth Century* (1995; Chicago, 1999); K. Pomian, "Totalitarisme," *VS* 47 (July-September, 1995): 4–23; I. Kershaw, "Nazisme et stalinisme: Limites d'une comparaison," *Le Débat* 89 (March-April 1996): 177–89.

[57] P. Birnbaum, *Le moment antisémite: Un tour de la France en 1898* (Paris, 1998); Birnbaum, *Anti-Semitism in France: A Political History from Léon Blum to the Present* (Cambridge, Mass., 1992); V. Caron, *Uneasy Asylum: France and the Jewish Refugee Crisis, 1933–1942* (Stanford, 1999); P.-A. Taguieff, ed., *L'antisémitisme de plume 1940–1944: Études et documents* (Paris, 1999).

attention were paid to the Holocaust. For what has remained most troubling about France under the Germans has been the collaboration of the Vichy regime, as well as much of the French administrative apparatus in the Occupied Zone, in the genocide of the Jews.[58] And what distinguishes most clearly between types of modern dictatorships, oppressive regimes, and totalitarian systems is the extent to which they resort to genocidal policies. Thus the main difference between Stalinist Russia and Nazi Germany, much debated in France, is that the former did not carry out genocide on the basis of race, and the latter did. And yet these distinctions and observations are rarely made in contemporary French debates, and Goldhagen's book has had remarkably little effect on them.[59]

The roots of both debates stretch back to the early postwar period; in fact, the dispute over pacifism, fascism, and communism, ultimately presented as compelling a choice between Hitler or Stalin, goes back to the 1930s and must be seen as one of the causes for French conduct during the Occupation.[60] And while French writers, filmmakers, and philosophers made a lasting contribution to the portrayal of political prisoners' lives in the Nazi "concentrationary universe," the ambiguities of complicity and resistance, and the role of antisemitism in European civilization,[61] France also served as an early staging ground for a "negationist" literature determined to deny the genocide of the Jews or at least to diminish its scope and significance.[62] Nor was this an

[58] P. Burrin, *France under the Germans: Collaboration and Compromise* (New York, 1996); M. O. Baruch, *Servir l'État français: L'administration en France de 1940 à 1944* (Paris, 1997).

[59] This is most evident in S. Courtois, et al., *The Black Book of Communism: Crimes, Terror, Repression* (Cambridge, Mass., 1999). Compare to T. Martin, "The Origins of Soviet Ethnic Cleansing," *JMH* 70 (December 1998): 813–61.

[60] C. Jelen, *Hitler ou Staline: Le prix de la paix* (Paris, 1988); N. Ingram, *The Politics of Dissent: Pacifism in France 1919–1939* (Oxford, 1991); E. Weber, *The Hollow Years: France in the 1930s* (New York, 1994); P. Burrin, *La Dérive fasciste: Doriot, Déat, Bergery 1933–1945* (Paris, 1986); O. Bartov, "Martyrs' Vengeance: Memory, Trauma, and Fear of War in France, 1918–1940," in *The French Defeat of 1940: Reassessments*, ed. J. Blatt (Providence, 1998), 54–84.

[61] D. Rousset, *The Other Kingdom* (New York, 1982); this was originally published as *L'Univers concentrationnaire* in 1946; R. Antelme, *The Human Race* (1947; Marlboro, VT, 1992); C. Delbo, *Auschwitz and After* (1970; New Haven, 1995); J.-P. Sartre, *Anti-Semite and Jew* (1946; New York, 1976); L. Poliakov, *The History of Anti-Semitism* (1955; New York, 1965). Filmmakers include Alain Resnais, Marcel Ophuls, René Clément, Louis Malle, and Claude Lanzmann.

[62] P. Vidal-Naquet, *Assassins of Memory: Essays on the Denial of the Holocaust* (New

ephemeral phenomenon that could be relegated to a fanatic, pro-fascist fringe. "Negationist" arguments have been produced by both the Right and the Left and have been made by people with university degrees and often impressive intellectual credentials. By now this seems to have become an established trend, whereby the more vociferous deniers of the genocide of the Jews seem to be only the extreme manifestation of a much more pervasive, albeit more moderate, relativizing assertion which rejects the distinction between Himmler's death camps and the Soviet gulags, usually accompanied by the moralizing claim that the overemphasis on Jewish victimhood has led to the repression of the memory of other victims and to indifference to current atrocities. This acute discomfort with the centrality of the Holocaust for the European experience has been most powerfully expressed recently by Alain Brossat, professor of philosophy at the Sorbonne, whose latest book avers that the Jewish insistence on "their" Holocaust actually facilitated the continuation of genocide after 1945, as illustrated, to his mind, by the direct link between the "Final Solution" and the Palestinian refugee camps.[63]

In this atmosphere, it is interesting to note that even Henry Rousso, whose book on the "Vichy Syndrome" heralded the French reexamination of the past, subsequently became uneasy with the tendency of some Jewish French intellectuals to focus attention on the fate of the Jews under German occupation, at the expense of the previous concentration on the Resistance.[64] It should be noted that in French representations of the Occupation in the early postwar decades, the victims of Nazism—or at least those victims who mattered and deserved commemoration—seemed to have been almost exclusively members of the Resistance.[65] It is only relatively recently, and not least due to the trials of French collaborators and the political scandals they generated, that much of the public has come to view French Jewry and Jews who had taken refuge in France but were denied citizenship or stripped of it by the late Third Republic and Vichy, as the main victims of both the German occupiers and the French authori-

York, 1992). See also D. Lipstadt, *Denying the Holocaust: The Growing Assault on Truth and Memory* (New York, 1993); R. J. Evans, *Lying About Hitler: History, Holocaust, and the David Irving Trial* (New York, 2001).

[63] A. Brossat, *L'épreuve du désastre: Le xxᵉ siècle et les camps* (Paris, 1996), 20, 23.

[64] Conan and Rousso, 1, 15.

[65] A. Wieviorka, *Déportation et génocide: Entre la mémoire et l'oublie* (Paris, 1992).

ties. This process of coming to terms with the victimization of French men and women by their own compatriots—all under the mantle of foreign occupation—has been long in the making and has produced a great deal of recrimination and denial. It can be traced back to Marcel Ophuls's remarkable 1969 film, *The Sorrow and the Pity,* which announced the crumbling of Charles de Gaulle's "myth of the resistance." But it is still possible that one reason for the success of Claude Lanzmann's no less extraordinary 1985 film *Shoah* (whose title has subsequently become the name commonly used in France for the Holocaust) was that it had avoided any mention of French collaboration and instead concentrated on Polish brutality and indifference. Indeed, despite claims of overemphasis on the Holocaust in recent public debates, the lack of systematic knowledge of its realities and the obvious reluctance of educational institutions to include it on their curricula is indicated by the fact that an extremely limited number of French university-level courses are devoted entirely to the study of the genocide of the Jews.[66]

It is the discussion on totalitarianism that seems to satisfy the French need for a more comprehensive view of inhumanity and to cast *la grande nation* in the role of an intellectual center for universalist values rather than to corner it into an apologetic or negationist stance. Hence also the current fascination with camps and genocides, consciously evoked in the plural form so as to stress their universal implications.[67] To be sure, the term *totalitarianism* has always retained an ambivalent quality, burdened as it was with political and ideological implications for both those who proudly applied it to their own regimes and those who attributed it as a derogatory term to others or merely sought to analyze it.[68] Similarly, by speaking of camps in the plural, one is always in danger of confusing or making false connotations between, for instance, concentration and extermination camps, on the one hand, and camps for prisoners of war, refugees, or displaced persons, on the other. There is little doubt that the camp phenomenon, just like totalitarianism, is inherent to our century (since the Spanish repression of

[66] Such as the "Seminaire sur l'histoire de la Shoah" at L'Université de Paris I (Sorbonne), and a research seminar at the École des Hautes Études en Sciences Sociales.

[67] C. Coquio, ed., *Parler des camps, penser les génocides* (Paris, 1999); Kotek and Rigoulot. But see also the focused study, A. Grynberg, *Les camps de la honte: Les internés Juifs des camps français 1939–1944* (Paris, 1999).

[68] A. Gleason, *Totalitarianism: The Inner History of the Cold War* (New York, 1995).

Cuba in 1896),[69] but precisely for this reason one must resist its political misrepresentation and abuse.

Finally, and perhaps most perniciously, while the term *genocide* has served to describe a whole range of forms of annihilation, from physical extermination to cultural assimilation, using its plural form only further enhances the confusion and ultimately renders it wholly useless as a description of a prevalent and yet very specific type of event. The excessive use and loose application of this terminology may of course create an awareness of the breadth and depth of inhumanity in the world and motivate people into action against repressive regimes, criminal organizations, and unjust wars. Conversely, however, this may also have the effect of making for such an open-ended definition of evil that one would no longer be able to distinguish between types and degrees of violence, victimhood, and resistance, indeed, between humanity and inhumanity, to the extent of producing a fatal combination of self-righteousness and moral paralysis. In other words, since action against evil often entails violence, that is, choosing the lesser evil rather than waiting for utopia, radical relativism and absolute morality may end up by legitimizing a total abdication of responsibility and accommodation with the powers that be: it is this latter stance, after all, that characterized the majority of the French during the Occupation.

In a recent debate conducted on the pages of the French daily *Le Monde*, the writer Henri Raczymow protested the assertion by the historian Stéphane Courtois, in his introduction to the *Black Book of Communism*, that "the deliberate starvation of a child of a Ukrainian kulak as a result of the famine caused by Stalin's regime 'is equal to' the starvation of a Jewish child in the Warsaw ghetto as a result of the famine caused by the Nazi regime."[70] Raczymow argued that this statement represented an "ever more prevalent trend of thinking, an historical, literary, and moral trend, which considers that any crime is equal to another, any victim is equal to another." For Raczymow, "this current is not made up of negationists (those who negate the reality of the gas chambers), but much more, it appears, of people who are exacerbated by the claim—made by Jews—of the absolute uniqueness of the

[69] Kotek and Rigoulot, 45–59.

[70] H. Raczymow, "D'un 'détail' qui masque le tableau," *Le Monde* (January 21, 1998), referring to Courtois, 9 (19 in the original). Raczymow is the author, inter al., of *Writing the Book of Esther* (1985; New York, 1995).

Shoah, its incommensurability, its incomparability." This argument was answered in turn by Catherine Coquio, professor of comparative literature at the Sorbonne, who accused Raczymow of failing to understand the implications of his own assertion: "He says that the life of a child in one place is not equal to [the life of a child] in another." Thereby, she writes, he does not see that "all life is incomparable, and its value is incalculable." For Coquio, "that a writer would, at this point, be unaware of the meaning of his own words, that is to say, be unaware of the value of words and phrases, just as much as of the value of every human face, is an overwhelming defeat for all of us who employ words and phrases."[71] Another response, this time by the Bulgarian-born French critic Tzvetan Todorov, whose book *The Abuse of Memory* was also attacked by Raczymow, rejected the notion of uniqueness. Citing the original *Black Book* on the Nazi crimes in the Soviet Union, he noted that Vassili Grossman, coeditor of the book with Ilya Ehrenburg, had written the following lines: "The Germans say: The Jews are not human beings. That's what Lenin and Stalin say: The Kulaks are not human beings." For Todorov, "every human being has the same price"; hence one can never say that one crime is "worth" more than another. What he finds identical in all genocides is not the historical details, but that on the "moral plane" they are "'worth' . . . absolute condemnation." Pursuing this logic, Todorov goes on to express admiration for all those who fought against the Nazis or the Soviets, against torture in Algeria or massacres in the former Yugoslavia, and claims that the debate is neither about comparison nor about uniqueness, but about the use and abuse of memory and its capacity either to facilitate atrocity or to motivate people to resist it.[72]

None of those who took part in the debate were historians of the Holocaust, including the writers of the books criticized by Raczymow, among whom is also the Belgian sociologist Jean-Michel Chaumont, author of *The Competition of Victims*.[73] Indeed, this debate was not at all about the Holocaust, but rather about the meaning, memory, and po-

[71] C. Coquio, "'Valeur' des vies, 'valeurs' des mots," *Le Monde* (January 27, 1998).

[72] T. Todorov, "Je conspire, Hannah Arendt conspirait, Raymond Aron aussi . . ." *Le Monde* (January 31, 1998); Todorov, *Les Abus de mémoires* (Paris, 1995). The definitive French edition of the original *Black Book* is I. Ehrenbourg and V. Grossman, *Le Livre noir: Textes et témoignages* (Paris, 1995). See also H. Asher, "The *Black Book* and the Holocaust," *JGR* 1 (1999): 401–16.

[73] J.-M. Chaumont, *La Concurrence des victimes* (Paris, 1997).

litical use of crimes against humanity. Raczymow's insistence on the uniqueness of the Holocaust, of course, had nothing to do with a lack of awareness on his part of the suffering endured by millions of people in numerous other mass crimes. His was an argument about the reluctance of French intellectuals to focus on the Holocaust as an event in its own right, especially since France itself—including many of its intellectuals at the time—had played a much greater role in that very specific event than they wish to concede. And the arguments leveled against him merely proved his point. The rhetorical question about the suffering of children was precisely the kind of abuse of memory against which Todorov himself had rightly warned. For the individual suffering of innocents under any regime and in any historical context does not tell us enough about the nature of the regime and the meaning of the event; but it can serve as a device to relativize or normalize the past, as the example of the German *Historikerstreit* in the mid-1980s had already shown.

Suffering is never relative, but its assertion does not suffice to distinguish one historical event from another, does not make one "better" or "worse." Todorov, whose earlier book *Facing the Extreme* valiantly tries to recover the existence of what he calls "moral life in the concentration camps," makes no effort to distinguish between Hitler's and Stalin's camps.[74] This is anything but a coincidence in the French context. François Furet, former member of the Communist Party and renowned historian of the French Revolution, passed away just before writing what would have been the original introduction to the *Black Book of Communism*. Furet had only recently published his own massive monograph, in which he berated intellectuals in the West, and especially in France, for their long love affair with communism and their blindness to its crimes, rooted both in the anti-fascist ethos of the 1930s and 1940s, and in the inability to lead an intellectual existence without a utopian vision.[75] It was as part of this trend of criticizing long-held loyalties to a bankrupt ideology following the collapse of communist regimes throughout Europe that France became preoccupied with the *Black Book of Communism*. Intentionally echoing the original book on

[74] T. Todorov, *Facing the Extreme: Moral Life in the Concentration Camps* (New York, 1996). More detailed discussion in O. Bartov, *Mirrors of Destruction: War, Genocide, and Modern Identity* (New York, 2000), 165–85.

[75] Furet. Rousset heralded this criticism as early as 1946. See also T. Judt, *Past Imperfect: French Intellectuals, 1944–1956* (Berkeley, 1992).

the genocide of the Jews, this dense collection of book-length essays was preceded by an introduction that set the tone of the debate by asserting that the only difference between Nazi and communist crimes was that the scale of the latter was far greater (conveniently ignoring the fact that Nazism was destroyed by Soviet Russia rather than by the French intelligentsia).[76]

Thus France remains torn between trying to come to terms with its own ignominious legacy and asserting its status as the center of European civilization and the conscience of humanity. In the process, the Holocaust is either shoved aside and ignored, or is presented as an obstacle to humanizing contemporary politics. It should be pointed out that while the "syndrome of Vichy" was identified by a Frenchman (of Jewish origin), the history of Vichy as a willing collaborationist regime was uncovered by the American historian Robert Paxton, and the extraordinary extent of French accommodation with the German occupation was finally exposed by the Swiss historian Philippe Burrin.[77] It is thus difficult to see how Goldhagen's book could have had any impact on these debates; at the most, it served to divert attention once more from France's active involvement in the genocide of the Jews. For, reading Goldhagen, it appears that only the Germans had done it.

In their recent book *Vichy: An Ever-Present Past*, Éric Conan and Henry Rousso argue that it would be an error to accuse the French of failing to come to terms with the past.[78] Robert Paxton, in his foreword to the English translation of the book, wholeheartedly embraces this assertion.[79] Indeed, over the past fifteen years, France has experienced a series of scandals, revelations, trials, confessions, and recriminations, all concerned with the "somber years" of 1940–44; one could say that Rousso's "Vichy syndrome" has come to haunt the nation with a vengeance. Conan and Rousso believe that the effects of this preoccupation with the past, especially because of the manner in which this

[76] However, two major contributors to the volume publicly dissociated themselves from Courtois's introductory essay. See N. Werth and J.-L. Margolin, "Communisme: Le retour à l'histoire," *Le Monde* (November 14, 1997), and the response by S. Courtois, "Comprendre la tragédie communiste," *Le Monde* (December 20, 1997). For the historiographical context, see M. Malia, "Foreword," in Courtois, ix-xx; H. Rousso, "La légitimité d'une comparaison empirique," in *Stalinisme et nazisme: Histoire et mémoire comparées*, ed. H. Rousso (Brussels, 1999), 11–36.

[77] R. O. Paxton, *Vichy France* (New York, 1972); Burrin, *France*.

[78] Conan and Rousso.

[79] Robert O. Paxton, "Foreword," in Conan and Rousso, ix-xiii.

French version of *Vergangenheitsbewältigung* has been practiced, have by now become largely counter-productive. The slogan about the "duty to remember," they claim, has made it impossible for the nation to face up to the future; rather than facilitating action against contemporary problems and injustices, the obsession with the past merely obstructs one's view of the present. Moreover, as Conan and Rousso rightly argue, remembering is not the same as knowing; references to the past are all too often made by people who are quite ignorant of its realities. Hence memory must be replaced, or at least enhanced, by historical knowledge, whose production is the task of the historian. This "duty to know" must be accompanied, the authors claim, by the "right to forget," so as to be able to get on with life in the present.

The problem is, of course, that one cannot forget what one does not remember, and that knowledge about the past, which is indeed still scarce in France precisely because the process of coming to terms with it began so late, is fragmented, biased, and selective. This is not only a French problem. Even in Germany, where important scholarly work on Nazism has been carried on for years, some crucial aspects of that past were left untouched, couched in clichés and expressions of grief rather than studied and analyzed. Both in Germany and in France, what has been lacking is an understanding of how a nation turns against a part of its own population, and this hiatus in historical knowledge, this national amnesia camouflaged by euphemisms of distance and strangeness, is also at the root of current German and French xenophobia and definitions of national identity. That past refuses to go away because it is still happening in the present, and it happens in the present because its roots had never been sufficiently uncovered. It is also the case that in both nations there has been a tremendous amount of resistance to facing up to the fact that the genocide of the Jews, more than anything else, made those "dark years" unique in their own national history, and that therefore this specific episode must, indeed, be studied in much greater depth and not merely be confined to forgetting through mechanisms of remembrance and commemoration.

But precisely because France's past is more ambivalent than Germany's, because France initiated antisemitic policies but not the murder itself, and because its actions were mostly carried out under German occupation, resistance to this realization has been all the greater. This was the cause for the remarkable success of de Gaulle's "myth of the Resistance," and this is why "negationism" and "revisionism" have taken root among respectable intellectual and academic circles. For the Holocaust is stuck in the throat of all those who wish to present France as still charged with a "civilizing mission" and as the cradle of humanism. That Jewish fate is the obstacle to reasserting French national identity, and that its history and memory are now reflected in new waves of anti-foreign sentiments, cannot but make for deep, perhaps often unconscious resentment. Hence the bizarre contemporary argument that the genocide of the Jews diverts attention from "human" suffering and victimhood, which has replaced the previous focus on the fate of the "truly" French victims, the political resisters, at the expense of the allegedly passive, partly foreign Jewish victims.

To be sure, an obsessive preoccupation with remembering can obscure both the realities of the past and the problems of the present. It seems, however, that France still has a long way to go to before it will internalize a knowledge of its role in genocide, not through scandals and television shows, but by much more research, study, and teaching. The past never goes away before it becomes known; as long as it remains a dark secret it will keep haunting the present. The assertion of the German "revisionists" in the 1980s that the burden of the past made it impossible for Germany to forge a new national identity was ultimately answered by an increased effort to learn about that past rather than to put it aside. So too in France, only an enhanced learning process will enable it to forge for itself a national identity rooted in knowledge and understanding, not in empty rhetoric and recriminations.

OVEREXPOSURE: HOLOCAUST FATIGUE
AND ISRAEL'S BANALITY OF HORROR

The publication of the Hebrew translation of Goldhagen's book was originally planned as a joint undertaking by Yad Vashem, the Holocaust Memorial and Research Institute in Jerusalem, and the publishing house of *Yediot Ahronot*, a mass circulation daily. But growing scholarly criticism of the book seems to have convinced Yad Vashem, which has published numerous important studies of the Holocaust over the past four decades, to pull out of the project. Moreover, despite a media blitz by the remaining commercial publisher, Israeli reactions to the book, both in the media and by the scholarly community, were largely unenthusiastic, and in several cases downright dismissive. The book did make the non-fiction best-seller list for a few weeks, but since in Israel even the most popular among such works rarely reach a wide audience, it seems unlikely that its sales figures were particularly impressive. To be sure, a relatively positive review by Yisrael Gutman, a respected Holocaust expert and former director of Yad Vashem's Research Institute, was published in an Israeli daily even before the book appeared in Hebrew.[80] It was this review that Goldhagen cited in his response to criticism by German scholars, just as in his preface to the paperback American edition he cited the positive reception of the German translation as confirming the importance of his book and the unfairness of American criticism. But Gutman's review was hardly representative of the Israeli reception.[81] Moreover, if one takes the trouble to read Gutman's essay in full, it becomes clear that it was mainly focused on the specific Israeli context and thus had much more to do with what some local scholars perceive as the distortion of the Holocaust by the so-called new historians in Israel, on the one hand, and with perceptions of contemporary Germany, on the other, than with the inherent merits of the study itself. Indicatively, when Yad Vashem held a symposium with Goldhagen during his visit to Israel, the organizers insisted on it being a closed forum to which only a select group of scholars was invited. Apparently, researchers and administrators at Yad Vashem were beset by a certain sense of embarrassment and discomfort about a book that, at least from their perspective, had been the occasion for a commercialization of the Holocaust entirely foreign to their own approach and predilections.[82]

While Israeli reviews of the book were by and large negative, some

---

[80] Y. Gutman, "Daniel Goldhagen and the Inconceivable Cruelty of the Germans," *Ha'aretz* (July 12, 1996), in Hebrew. Unless otherwise indicated, all translations from Hebrew are mine. Early critical reviews include O. Heilbrunner, "How Antisemitic were the Nazis?" *Ha'aretz* (July 26, 1996), in Hebrew; G. Ne'eman Arad, "The Unbearable Simplification of Interpretation," *Sefarim* (May 8, 1996): 4, 13, in Hebrew; M. Zimmermann, "Germany and the Goldhagen Festival," *Ha'aretz* (October 18, 1996), in Hebrew. The book was published in 1998 as *Talyanim me-ratson be-sherut Hitler: Germanim regilim veha-Shoah*.

[81] For critical reviews by scholars following the book's publication in Hebrew, see A. Shapira, "A Sermon on Ordinary Germans," *Sefarim* (February 4, 1998): 1, 12, 14, in Hebrew; Y. Bauer and Y. Gutman, "The Crucial Point is Ideology," *Ha'aretz* (April 16, 1998), in Hebrew.

[82] R. Meiberg, "Goldhagen Is Worth Gold," *Ma'ariv* (November 21, 1997): 5, in Hebrew. Goldhagen is described as "the Schwarzenegger of the Holocaust," and Y. Bauer, then director of the Research Institute at Yad Vashem, is cited as saying that he "would not have been willing to publish the book."

observers pointed out its potential utility for others, and especially for Germans, since it was felt that even though Goldhagen had not discovered anything that was unknown to the Israeli public, such knowledge was lacking in Germany.[83] By now, on those infrequent occasions that the book is mentioned in the media, it is normally described as a "typical" product of American commercialism whose success was derived from a combination of simplistic arguments with sophisticated sales and publicity techniques. Apart from revealing a degree of anti-American sentiment, especially among Israeli academics and intellectuals, it should also be noted that Goldhagen's personal style failed to appeal to the lay public, which seems to prefer older, more traditional scholars, and is wary of young, well-groomed foreigners who come to tell Israelis what they believe they know best.

Indeed, precisely Goldhagen's claim that he offered a "final" and definitive interpretation of the Holocaust—an assertion which made for much of his book's appeal in the United States and Germany—seems to have repelled numerous Israeli critics and readers. Israelis have been exposed for many years to a veritable flood of information, imagery, and demagogy on the Holocaust: newspaper articles and scholarly publications; educational and political rhetoric; cinematic, theatrical, artistic, and musical representation; commemorative sites and gatherings; and, not least, a highly intimate contact with the realities and memories of the Holocaust through personal accounts in the family circle or among close friends. In this context, a book with such far-reaching claims as Goldhagen's could not but be viewed with a skeptical, even resentful eye. The tone, the rhetoric, and the self-righteous indignation, rather than specific findings of the study, were rejected. Hence the question, "What can he tell us about the Holocaust—as a whole, rather than the actions of this or that murder squad—that we don't know already?" Moreover, since the book's main thesis was so familiar to Israelis, it could not but appear banal; people simply could not understand what was innovative about an ar-

---

[83] S. Volkov, "The Germans were Shaken," *Ma'ariv* (January 22, 1998), in Hebrew. M. Zimmermann, "Goldhagen or Kornfein," Ha'aretz (April 16, 1998), in Hebrew, reports on a poll by the Institute for German History at the Hebrew University in March 1998, according to which 83.3 percent of respondents had never heard of Goldhagen's book, 11.3 percent had heard of the book but had no opinion, and of the 5.4 percent who had an opinion 3.5 agreed with Goldhagen. Kornfein, the goalkeeper of a local soccer team, is thus said to be vastly more popular than Goldhagen.

gument that presented the Germans as antisemitic murderers of Jews. This was what they learned in school, read in books, were told on the radio, watched on television, and heard from relatives. Israelis might be curious about German reactions to this statement; but as for the person on the street, this was simply obvious. Hence, the public showed interest mainly in the book's impact abroad, that is, in the phenomenon rather than the text.[84]

One might indeed say that Goldhagen's book appeared in Israel at a time when overexposure to documentation, representation, and rhetoric had produced what I would call "Holocaust fatigue." Since people now "know" what it was all about, and since they all too often expect the Holocaust to be used for contemporary political purposes, they tend to seek shelter from this barrage of information and misinformation. Some simply refuse to hear any more about the Shoah. Thus, for instance, while in Germany public lectures on the Holocaust are very well attended by young people, in Israel audiences consist mainly of scholars and the elderly (although there is some renewed interest now, especially among those entering middle age).

A second, more sophisticated technique of "sheltering" from conventional Holocaust rhetoric is to turn it on its head. This obviously does not remove the Holocaust from the public agenda, since it stimulates new, and often highly acrimonious debates. Yet what is at stake in these controversies is not German complicity, but rather the role of the Holocaust in the creation and consolidation of Israeli national identity. This is not an issue to which Goldhagen's book has much to contribute. But because his book appeared on the Israeli scene just as the local debate over the Holocaust was intensifying, elements of Goldhagen's arguments were mobilized by both sides in the controversy. For some he served as a tool against the "new historians" who were attempting to rewrite the conventional Zionist narrative of the Holocaust. For others, Goldhagen provided proof for the brutalizing effects of a dehumanizing ideology and military occupation. At the same time, however, it was argued that in the Israeli context it was precisely the kind of rhetoric of Jewish victimization offered by Goldhagen, the insistence to remember what had not been experienced and could not

---

[84] For the larger context of Israeli perceptions of the Holocaust, see Segev; Yablonka; R. Stauber, *Lesson for this Generation: Holocaust and Heroism in Israeli Public Discourse in the 1950s* (Jerusalem, 2000), in Hebrew.

be reversed, and the inability to take revenge against the real perpetrators, that was having a pernicious effect on young Israelis, something that was especially troubling in the case of soldiers occupying a
hostile population. The danger lay, therefore, in a double reversal of
roles whereby Jews were transformed from victims to occupiers, and
the Palestinians were perceived not as an occupied people but as potential murderers.[85]

Israeli national identity is grounded in two events: the Holocaust
and the conflict with the Arabs. While the former is in the past, it retains a strong presence in personal and collective memory and anxieties. And while the circumstances of the latter have greatly changed
over the decades, it remains a central preoccupation, both as memory
and as reality, and maintains a hold over people's perceptions of the
future. These two components of Israeli identity are so strongly bound
to each other historically and ideologically that by now it has become
very difficult to speak or write on one without constantly referring to
the other. It is for this reason that attempts to seek shelter from overexposure to Holocaust rhetoric in Israel are so closely related, though
in different ways, to the Arab-Israeli conflict. Thus, for instance, Israelis will justify their reluctance to hear any more about the Holocaust
by saying that they have more urgent matters on their minds, invariably related to issues of security ranging from military service to the
demands of an economy straining under the pressure of enormous
army budgets. In a rather different vein, those scholars engaged in
rewriting the history and memory of Israel, a project described by
some as an attempt to "slaughter the sacred cows" of traditional
national symbolism and myth, often combine an accusatory rhetoric
about Zionist policies vis-à-vis the Arabs with a no less accusatory
rhetoric concerning the policies of the Yishuv toward the Diaspora
during the Holocaust and the reception of the survivors by the Jewish
state.

Indeed, most "new historians" in Israel, whether their research focuses on the Arab-Israeli conflict or on Israel and the Holocaust, have
expressed themselves in various forums on both issues and have
drawn a variety of links between them. This should come as little sur-

---

[85] On the Holocaust and occupation, see Y. Elkana, "In Favor of Forgetting,"
Ha'aretz (March 2, 1988) 13, in Hebrew; M. Zuckermann, *Shoah in the Sealed Room: The
"Holocaust" in Israeli Press During the Gulf War* (Tel Aviv, 1993), 17–31, in Hebrew.

prise, of course, since these scholars are primarily engaged in delineating the making of Israeli national identity, and such an undertaking must consider the relationship between the trauma of the Holocaust and the struggle for Jewish nationhood.[86]

All this is to say that Israeli attitudes toward the Holocaust are complicated by a variety of factors. These include Zionist anti-Diaspora rhetoric, but also frustration over the Yishuv's inability to save the Diaspora; deep feelings of guilt combined with accusations concerning the callous treatment of the survivors; the long-term effects of individual and national trauma along with the political and demographic role of the Holocaust in the creation of the state; and, finally, the exploitation of the Holocaust for political purposes, not least of which is the legitimization of what some consider indefensible occupation policies, and the disconcerting fact that Israel itself has undergone a process of brutalization in its treatment of an increasingly rebellious occupied population.

From this perspective, simplistic theses such as that offered by Goldhagen struck the wrong chord among his potential readership, most of whom belong to an academic and intellectual elite involved in a dispute over their nation's history. For the Left, his book seemed to provide ammunition for those who have always claimed that "the world is against us," that Israel is still facing potential extinction, and that therefore it is justified in pursuing any policies that would ensure its security, and that it must not heed the advice or bow to the pressure of anyone else. But even for the Right, Goldhagen's book could present a threat, because while it portrays the Jews as helpless victims, its focus on the effects of a dehumanizing ideology and on the brutalization of armed men confronted with an innocent civilian population, provokes comparisons of a disturbing nature. The assertion by a senior army officer cited in a major Israeli daily in January 2002, that in order to prepare for the next campaign, he must draw lessons from all previous battles, including the manner in which the German army operated in

---

[86] For a comprehensive introduction, see Y. Weitz, ed., *From Vision to Revision: A Hundred Years of Historiography of Zionism* (Tel Aviv, 1997), in Hebrew. Further, see G. Ne'eman Arad, ed., *Israeli Historiography Revisited*, special issue of *H&M* 7 (Spring/Summer 1995); J. Mahler, "Uprooting the Past: Israel's New Historians Take a Hard Look at their Nation's Origins," *LF* 7 (August 1997): 24–32; A. Elon, "Israel and the End of Zionism," *NYRB* 43/20 (December 19, 1996): 22–30. For a fascinating comparison, see J. Brunner, "Pride and Memory: Nationalism, Narcissism and the Historians' Debates in Germany and Israel," *H&M* 9 (Fall 1997): 256–300.

putting down the uprising in the Warsaw ghetto, gives one an inkling of the perverse manner in which the genocide of the Jews is being translated into allegedly rational policies toward the Palestinians in the present conflict.[87]

Consequently, the Israeli public is interested mainly in such studies on Nazism and the Holocaust that touch on topics relevant to contemporary debates, question the consensus, and problematize conventions. A good example is Tom Segev's *The Seventh Million*, a pioneering analysis of changing Israeli attitudes toward the Holocaust since the foundation of the state.[88] Although he came in for a great deal of criticism, Segev succeeded in establishing this very question as a legitimate and important field of inquiry. Other works have reevaluated the absorption of Holocaust survivors into a society that felt great affinity and sympathy for them but at the same time had raised its children on an ideology of "shelilat ha'galut" (negation of the Diaspora).[89] These young Sabras were taught to despise the Jews who "went like sheep to the slaughter" and were determined to correct this "shameful" episode in Jewish history by emulating the mythical Hebrew heroes of antiquity, to the point of describing death in battle for the national cause as the supreme virtue.[90]

Also related to this issue was a recent work by Idith Zertal, which unleashed yet another public debate. Zertal argues that the Yishuv's efforts to bring the "she'erit ha'pleta" (surviving remnants) of the Holocaust to Palestine involved a great deal of Zionist indoctrination,

---

[87] A. Oren, "At the Gates of Yasirgrad," *Ha'aretz* (January 29, 2002), in Hebrew. For the larger context, see now M. Gilbert, *Israel: A History* (London, 1998); A. Dowty, *The Jewish State: A Century Later* (Berkeley, 1998); B. Morris, *Righteous Victims: A History of the Zionist-Arab Conflict, 1881–1999* (New York, 1999); A. Shlaim, *The Iron Wall: Israel and the Arab World* (New York, 2000).

[88] Segev. Israel's difficulties with certain interpretations of the Holocaust are reflected in the fact that Hanna Arendt's *Eichmann in Jerusalem* (1963) was published in Hebrew only in 2000, while Raul Hilberg's *The Destruction of the European Jews* (1961) has still not been translated. See also *Hannah Arendt and Eichmann in Jerusalem*, special issue of *H&M* 8 (Fall/Winter 1996); Bartov, *Mirrors*, 127–35.

[89] I. Keynan, *Holocaust Survivors and the Emissaries from Eretz-Israel: Germany, 1945–1948* (Tel Aviv, 1996), in Hebrew; H. Yablonka, *Survivors of the Holocaust: Israel After the War* (Houndmills, UK, 1999).

[90] Y. Zerubavel, *Recovered Roots: Collective Memory and the Making of Israeli National Tradition* (Chicago, 1995); N. Ben-Yehudah, *The Massada Myth: Collective Memory and Mythmaking in Israel* (Madison, Wis., 1995); O. Almog, *The Sabra: The Creation of the New Jew* (Berkeley, 2000); N. Gertz, *Myths in Israeli Culture: Captives of a Dream* (London, 2000).

arm-twisting, and attempts to deny the survivors access to any other path out of the DP (displaced persons) camps. She also insists that these policies were motivated primarily by the desire to expand rapidly the manpower resources of the future state, not least because of the expectation of imminent war.[91] Conversely, the Hebrew translation of Saul Friedländer's *Nazi Germany and the Jews* was welcomed in Israel, because it portrays, in a complex manner, the gradual process of disassociation between German Jewry and its gentile environment. Rather than demonizing the Germans and mocking the Jews for having refused to read the handwriting on the wall, Friedländer forcefully demonstrates the "betrayal of the intellectuals" that characterized the German elites, and the bewilderment and confusion that beset German Jewry during the early years of the Third Reich. He thus undermines several conventions that are still particularly strong in Israel, and may have also stuck a chord with those who are aware of the Israeli intelligentsia's own complex—and not always admirable—relationship with the politically powerful, the military elite, and the Arab minority.[92] Similarly, the publication in Hebrew of my own *Hitler's Army* also aroused a fair amount of interest, because it tries to reconstruct the manner in which a variety of factors—existing prejudices and pre-army schooling, military indoctrination and punitive discipline, hardship at the front and criminal orders—led to the brutalization of German troops in World War II and distorted their perception of the very reality they had helped to create. Once more, it appears, this study both provided a more complex picture of German society under Nazism than was commonly known in Israel and was associated with domestic issues regarding the conduct of Israeli troops in their daily clashes with the Palestinian population.[93]

---

[91] I. Zertal, *From Catastrophe to Power: Holocaust Survivors and the Emergence of Israel* (Berkeley, 1998). Other works on Zionist policies include D. Ofer, *Escaping the Holocaust: Illegal Immigration to the Land of Israel, 1939–1944* (New York, 1990); D. Porat, *The Blue and the Yellow Stars of David: The Zionist Leadership in Palestine and the Holocaust, 1939–1945* (Cambridge, Mass., 1990); Y. Bauer, *Jews for Sale? Nazi-Jewish Negotiations, 1933–1945* (New Haven, 1994).

[92] Friedländer, *Nazi Germany*, published in Hebrew in 1997. See also I. Hammermann, "The Shoah and Best Sellers," *Ha'aretz* (December, 26, 1997), in Hebrew; O. Heilbrunner, "German Antisemitism and the Question of its Continuity in German History," *Ha'aretz* (January 23, 1998), in Hebrew; D. Porat, "Where Is 'the Dustbin of History'?" *Ha'aretz* (February 6, 1998), in Hebrew.

[93] Bartov, *Hitler's Army*, appeared in Hebrew in 1998. See R. Rosental, "Stupid Soldiers," *Ma'ariv* (April 24, 1998), in Hebrew; B. Gur, review, *Ha'aretz* (May 7, 1998), in Hebrew.

Thus while Goldhagen's book was seen as controversial in the United States and Germany, and as largely irrelevant in France, within the Israeli context it both stated the obvious and underlined themes that were crucial components of the early Israeli national myth; hence in Israel the book came under attack from left-leaning academic and intellectual circles. The demonization of the Germans, who were often seen as representative of most other European gentiles—whose obverse side, namely, the state's official recognition of "righteous gentiles" at Yad Vashem merely highlights the alleged essential characteristics of the majority—has always served as a fundamental legitimization for Israeli policies, indeed for the very existence of the state. One should point out, however, that criticism of the book did not come only from the Left. Indeed, many of those who perceive the "new historians" as anti-Zionists engaged in undermining the legitimacy of the state, dismissed the book on scholarly and intellectual grounds. Thus Shlomo Aronson, who has often attacked the "post-Zionist" trend in new Israeli historiography, criticized the book severely. In the same article, he also comments on the reason for the different reception of the book in other countries:

> Goldhagen's book . . . has given rise to a huge storm, especially in Germany. . . . But in Israel, the book has not drawn much public attention, perhaps because the attitude toward Germany here has changed and become much more moderate than it is in the United States, where many praised the book, and many condemned it. Many will agree with Goldhagen a priori that Nazi Germany carried out what generations of Germans had been born into, had absorbed at home, in school, in church and in bars. That violent antisemitism prepared the path to extermination.[94]

This is a telling statement, since it contains an interesting contradiction. The Israeli public has indeed greatly moderated its attitudes toward Germany. On the one hand, unlike during the 1950s and 1960s, Israelis now make no apologies for driving German cars or traveling on vacation to Austria and the Federal Republic. On the other hand, most Israelis continue to view the Holocaust primarily as a product of antisemitism. Thus while Israelis may be less anti-German than Americans, they are more convinced of the overwhelming role that antisemitism played in the Nazi genocide of the Jews. But for most Israelis,

[94] S. Aronson, "Hatred in the Blood," *Ma'ariv* (November 22, 1996), in Hebrew.

acknowledging German or gentile antisemitism, then as now, merely serves the function of legitimizing the existence of their state and their decision to live in it. It thus plays a positive, constructive role in Israeli self-perception and the consolidation of national identity. Conversely, American Jews, proportionately probably Goldhagen's most avid consumers in the United States, perceive antisemitism as remaining a potential threat for their national identity as Americans; and precisely because antisemitism is a contemporary worry, it is both easier to accept its centrality for Nazism, and, at the same time, to feel relieved at seeing it confined geographically and chronologically to pre-1945 Germany and the Holocaust. Hence the anxieties evoked and reflected by the book (and its author) are much more in line with American than with Israeli conditions and sensibilities.[95]

One final point on the Israeli reception. It has been said that Goldhagen's focus on the horrors of the killing had a voyeuristic element that appealed to certain readers. There is no doubt that some elements in his text seem to reflect his own fantasies—themselves most probably the product of (over)exposure to media representations of the Holocaust and other massacres—rather than the information culled from the documents he cites. Goldhagen wants us to imagine with him the thoughts that went through the minds of a German policeman and the little girl he shot; he wants us to imagine what the shooting actually looked like; he even urges us to imagine conversations between SS men and women after they made love following a day of sadistic torture; in short, he demands that we fantasize atrocity (and its sexual titillations) and be morally outraged by the horrors conjured up in our minds. This kind of prose may have appeared innovative, or even morbidly fascinating, to certain American and German readers who were dissatisfied with the drier, more detached depictions and interpretations of conventional Holocaust scholarship. Especially in the United States, this insistence on the most explicit aspects of horror must have, at the same time, been quite familiar to readers exposed to a tremendous amount of real and staged representations of violence in the media. But precisely because of their association with the media, that is, with entertainment, Goldhagen's images of horror remained sufficiently distant to prevent alienation through anxiety and disgust.

[95] Compare Y. Gorny, *The State of Israel in Jewish Public Thought: The Quest for Collective Identity* (New York, 1994), and *Israel at Fifty: A Compassionately Critical Analysis*, special issue of *Tikkun* (March/April 1998).

In Israel, however, this type of prose failed to have the same effect on the public, because Israelis are ceaselessly reminded of the horrors of the Holocaust and have never developed a detached attitude to it, even while some do their best to avoid this flood of horrifying images. Long before television came in the late 1960s, young Israelis who had been spared the Holocaust (and we should stress that at the time the population still included a large number of survivors) were exposed to memoir and fiction literature on the Holocaust that provided sufficient graphic horror to last a lifetime.[96] For many Israelis, it seems, Goldhagen's explicit descriptions seemed dangerously close to kitsch. Moreover, as always, for Israelis the horrors of the past are intimately linked with those of the present. Daily exposure to the brutalities of the conflict with the Arabs, be they bombings by terrorists or beatings and random killing by the security forces, means that Goldhagen's type of voyeurism hits too close to home to have the same riveting effect it appears to have had in the United States and Germany. All of this should explain why Goldhagen's book fell flat in the Jewish State.

CONCLUSION: PREJUDICED BEHAVIORISM

Debates over Goldhagen's book were thus clearly framed within the national and historical contexts in which they took place. All four nations examined in this chapter had been preoccupied with certain aspects of Nazism and the Holocaust long before the appearance of *Hitler's Willing Executioners,* and in all cases this involved a wider discussion of national and group identities. Thus the reception of Goldhagen's book serves to illustrate the different ways in which the genocide of the Jews has come to play an important role in self-perception and self-definition, in understanding the past, facing up to the present, and preparing for the future.

On another level, however, these debates were clearly concerned just as much with the abstract as well as the concrete implications of genocide for our understanding of human nature. This is one reason why Christopher Browning's very different interpretation of perpetrator motivation was frequently brought into the debate, quite apart from the more obvious proximity in publication dates, similarity of sources, and Goldhagen's vehement attacks on Browning both in his book and in later disputes. As is well known, in the final chapter of his

---

[96] Bartov, *Mirrors,* 185–212.

Ordinary Men, Browning cites the theory developed in Stanley Milgram's 1974 book *Obedience to Authority* as an important tool in elucidating the motivation of German policemen who perpetrated murder. Curiously, to the best of my knowledge, not one of the innumerable contributions to this debate in all four countries took the trouble to go back to Milgram's text and analyze it on its own terms rather than merely through the prism provided by Browning.[97] Yet this is a worthwhile exercise.

By way of conclusion, I would like to shed some light on one feature of Milgram's study, which seems to undermine both the objective nature of the experiment it describes and the fundamental assumption made by its author. Without wishing thereby either to wholly reject Browning's thesis, or to adopt Goldhagen's ideas, I hope that this brief discussion will demonstrate that we are still very far from having a sufficient explanation for how "ordinary men" are transformed into serial killers. Moreover, I believe that the example of Milgram reminds us once more that none of us comes to this debate as a tabula rasa, and that not even the most careful scholarly assertion can ever be accepted at face value.

Milgram's is a behaviorist interpretation par excellence, based on an experiment in which a group of volunteers was ordered to apply ever more powerful electric shocks to a man tied to a chair as part of what was described to them as an experiment in learning under threat of physical punishment. While in reality no electric shock was involved, the actor in the chair convinced most volunteers that he was suffering increasing pain, by physical contortions, pleas, cries, and feigned fainting, unable as he was to release himself from his seat. In a significant majority of cases the volunteers obeyed the instructor's directions to go on applying shocks, even as the dial clearly indicated that they could have lethal consequences.

Milgram interpreted his experiment as proving that "the essence of obedience consists in the fact that a person comes to view himself as the instrument for carrying out another person's wishes, and he therefore no longer regards himself as responsible for his actions. Once this crucial shift of viewpoint has occurred in the person, all of the essen-

---

[97] For a recent analysis of debates over the "Nazi personality," see J. Brunner, "'Oh Those Crazy Cards Again': A History of the Debate on the Nazi Rorschachs, 1946–2001," *PS* 22, no. 2 (2001): 233–61.

tial features of obedience follow."[98] Consequently, "obedience is the psychological mechanism that links individual action to political purpose."[99] According to Milgram, "it is the extreme willingness of adults to go to almost any length on the command of an authority that constitutes the chief finding of the study."[100] Milgram assumes—without producing any evidence—that "the Nazi extermination of European Jews is the most extreme instance of abhorrent immoral acts carried out by thousands of people *in the name of obedience*"[101] (my italics). And since he asserts that the participants in his experiment were not "monsters, the sadistic fringe of society," but rather "represented *ordinary people* drawn from working, managerial, and professional classes" (my italics), he concludes "that Arendt's conception of the *banality of evil* comes closer to the truth than one might dare imagine. The ordinary person who shocked the victim did so out of a sense of obligation—a conception of his duties as a subject—and not from any peculiarly aggressive tendencies." Hence, he writes, "the most fundamental lesson of our study" is that "ordinary people, simply doing their jobs, and without any particular hostility on their part, can become agents in a terrible destructive process."[102]

Milgram concedes the limits of his experiment. He notes that "at least one essential feature of the situation in Germany was not studied here—namely, the intense devaluation of the victim prior to action against him." He asserts that "in all likelihood, our subjects would have experienced greater ease in shocking the victim had he been convincingly portrayed as a brutal criminal or a pervert." Yet he adds that "many subjects harshly devalue the victim *as a consequence* of acting against him." Moreover, while "many of the people studied in the experiment were in some sense against what they did to the learner, and many protested even while they obeyed," what they lacked was "the capacity for transforming beliefs and values into action. Some were totally convinced of the wrongness of what they were doing but could not bring themselves to make an open break with authority. Some derived satisfaction from their thoughts and felt that—within themselves, at least—they had been on the side of the angels." Nevertheless,

---

[98] Milgram, xii.
[99] Ibid., 1.
[100] Ibid., 5.
[101] Ibid., 2.
[102] Ibid., 5–6.

Milgram insists that "subjective feelings are largely irrelevant to the moral issue at hand so long as they are not transformed into action. The attitudes of the guards at a concentration camp are of no consequence when in fact they are allowing the slaughter of innocent men to take place before them."[103]

Thus we are left to conclude that most people, if put into a situation similar to that created by Milgram, would act in the same manner. A few unique individuals might resist authority and refuse to obey; others, who had internalized some prejudice against the victim, would cause pain with even less compunction. But generally speaking, the makeup of human psychology and the structure of human society should lead us to expect most people to be the willing executioners of their fellow human beings when told to do so by a recognizable authority. Unlike Goldhagen, Milgram does not believe in choice, since "a person does not get to see the whole situation but only a small part of it, and is thus unable to act without some kind of overall direction. He yields to authority but in doing so is alienated from his own actions."[104] Browning reaches similar conclusions:

> Everywhere society conditions people to respect and defer to authority . . . Everywhere people seek career advancement . . . bureaucratization and specialization attenuate the sense of personal responsibility. Within virtually every social collective, the peer group exerts tremendous pressures on behavior and sets moral norms. If the men of Reserve Police Battalion 101 could become killers under such circumstances, what group of men cannot?[105]

Conversely, Goldhagen adamantly asserts that "any explanation that fails to acknowledge the actors' capacity to know and to judge, namely to understand and to have views about the significance and morality of their actions, that fails to hold the actors' beliefs and values as central, that fails to emphasize the autonomous motivating force of Nazi ideology, particularly its central component of antisemitism, cannot possibly succeed in telling us much about why the perpetrators acted as they did."[106]

[103] Ibid., 9–10.
[104] Ibid., 11.
[105] Browning, *Ordinary Men*, 189.
[106] D. J. Goldhagen, *Hitler's Willing Executioners: Ordinary Germans and the Holocaust* (New York, 1996), 13.

There is obviously no simple answer to this central question of human psychology and society. In the present context I will not attempt to articulate my own position, which in any case I have tried to clarify elsewhere.[107] Suffice it to say that to my mind, motivation and obedience—especially to questionable or seemingly illegal orders—are the result of a combination of factors, such as education, cultural environment, ideological input, as well as the social and material context in which an individual is placed. Yet what deserves mention here—and has hitherto escaped notice—is a striking aspect of Milgram's study, namely, that his carefully balanced, apparently objective and scientific conclusions were reached on the basis of an experiment in which his own biases were clearly exhibited and cannot but have influenced his observations. By following Milgram's account of several cases, with special attention to the links he makes between class, "race," and gender, on the one hand, and the subjects' physical features, moral conduct, and most crucially their capacity to withstand malevolent authority, on the other hand, we find that this objective scientist brings to the experiment a baggage of preconceived notions and ideas that belie his assertion that all people are fundamentally the same and would act similarly under identical conditions. It appears, then, that even the most clinical and scientific behaviorist theory is informed precisely by those internalized prejudices whose importance it seeks to diminish.

Let us take a brief look at some of these examples:

1. Mr. Bruno Batta, thirty-seven, a welder born in New Haven to Italian parents, has "a rough-hewn face that conveys a conspicuous lack of alertness. His overall appearance is somewhat brutish. An observer described him as a 'crude mesomorph of obviously limited intelligence.' But this is not fully adequate, for he relates to the experimenter with a submissive and deferential sweetness." Mr. Batta, a blue-collar worker of south European, Mediterranean extraction, whose vulgar features and primitive muscularity betray his moral character, acts with "total indifference" to the victim, derives "quiet satisfaction at doing his job properly," and professes that he "got disgusted" when the man he tortured refused to cooperate.

2. A professor, "a somewhat gaunt, ascetic man," who "could be taken

---

[107] See, especially, Bartov, *Eastern Front*, chap. 3; Bartov, *Hitler's Army*, chap. 2; O. Bartov, "Daily Life and Motivation in War: The Wehrmacht in the Soviet Union," *JSS* 12 (1989): 200–214; Bartov, "Indoctrination and Motivation in the Wehrmacht: The Importance of the Unquantifiable," *JSS* (1986): 16–34.

for a New England Minister" but in fact "teaches Old Testament liturgy at a major divinity school." This elderly and educated man of religion, obviously of a good north European family, naturally balks after administering only 150 volts, asserting ethical reasons, since, he says, "if one has as one's ultimate authority God, then it trivializes human authority."

3. Jack Washington, drill press operator, thirty-five, "a black subject," born in South Carolina, "is a soft man, a bit heavy and balding, older-looking than his years. His pace is slow and his manner impassive; his speech is tinged with Southern and black accents." An obviously primitive blue-collar worker, this dull-minded and morally insensitive African American from the South casually delivers a lethal charge of 450 volts when instructed to do so and later explains that he was simply "following orders."

4. Jan Rensaleer, thirty-two, industrial engineer, "sporting blond hair and a mustache . . . self-contained and speaks with a trace of a foreign accent . . . neatly dressed." Having "emigrated from Holland after the Second World War," he "is a member of the Dutch Reform Church . . . mild-mannered and intelligent." A member of the professional middle-class, an elegant north European and God-fearing man, Rensaleer has the requisite moral qualities to withstand malevolent authority. He refuses to continue beyond 255 volts, and reacts to the standard statement that he has no choice but to continue by emphatically declaring, "I *do* have a choice." Subsequently, he accepts responsibility for shocking the victim. Described as being "hard on himself," he remarks that "on the basis of his experience in Nazi-occupied Europe, he would predict a high level of compliance to orders." His own conduct, however, is close to exemplary.[108]

5. Fred Prozi, about fifty, unemployed, "dressed in a jacket but no tie; he has a good-natured, if slightly dissolute, appearance. He employs working-class grammar and strikes one as a rather ordinary fellow." This blue-collar worker, apparently kind but clearly a simple and stupid man, probably of Italian origin, obviously lacks the moral qualities required to withstand authority. Hence he continues giving a lethal electric shock to the victim—who for all intents and purposes appears dead—as long as he is ordered to do so.

6. Karen Dontz, forty, a "housewife who for the past six years has worked part time as a registered nurse. Her husband is a plumber. She is Catholic and her mother was born in Czechoslovakia. Mrs.

---

[108] Milgram, 45–52, for description of these experiments.

Dontz has an unusually casual, slow-paced way of speaking, and
her tone expresses constant humility. . . . Throughout the experiment she is nervous." This working class woman of East European
origin betrays the lack of intelligence and nervous disposition typical of her sex and class. She clearly lacks true moral fiber. Consequently she continues administering the lethal 450 volts to a victim,
who appears to have been permanently silenced, until told to stop.
She knows as a nurse that she could have killed the victim but is
satisfied that she did what an authority figure told her to perform.

7. Elinor Rosenblum, a housewife, "takes pleasure in describing her
background: She graduated from the University of Wisconsin . . .
her husband, a film distributor, attended Dartmouth. She does volunteer work with juvenile delinquents . . . has been active on the local Girl Scout organization and the PTA. She is fluent and garrulous
and projects herself strongly, with many references to her social
achievements. She displays a pleasant though excessively talkative
charm." This middle-class, obviously Jewish woman (although Milgram shies away from stating this outright), displays all the stereo-
typical characteristics of her sex and ethnicity, and all the
mannerisms of an outsider newly arrived at a respectable social status. She had the intelligence to climb up the social ladder but still
lacks the moral fiber that comes with self-assurance. She is thus
hypocritical and self-centered: "Mrs. Rosenblum, even as she ad-
ministers increasingly more painful shocks to the victim, constantly
complains: 'Must I go on? Oh, I'm so worried about him . . . I'm
shaking. I'm shaking. Do I have to go up there [on the dial]?'" But
she delivers the lethal 450-volt shock three times. Milgram explains
that "she was nervous not because the man was being hurt but because *she* was performing the action . . . she asserts her own distress
. . . A self-centered quality permeates her remarks . . . she is not
against punishment per se but only against her active infliction of it.
If it just 'happens,' it is acceptable." Milgram concludes that "Mrs.
Rosenblum is a person whose psychic life lacks integration. She has
not been able to find life purposes consistent with her needs for esteem and success. Her goals, thinking, and emotions are fragmented. She carries out her experimental role as teacher showing
great outward conviction, while at the same time she displays another side of herself to the experimenter, behaving meekly and sub-
missively. It is not surprising that she failed to mobilize the psychic
resources needed to translate her compassion for the learner into
the disobedient act. Her feelings, goals, and thoughts were too di-
verse and unintegrated. All evidence indicates that at the time of

her performance she believed the learner was being shocked. But it is not difficult for a woman of hysterical tendencies to adjust her thinking in a manner consistent with a positive self-image. In a questionnaire returned to us a few months later, she states that during the experiment her 'mature and well-educated brain' had not believed the learner was getting shocks. Through a post-facto adjustment of thought, she protects her cherished—if unrealistic—picture of her own nature." Milgram obviously despises this woman.

8. Gretchen Brandt, thirty-five, a "medical technician who works at the University Medical School. She had emigrated from Germany five years before and speaks with a thick German accent." This cultivated, elegant north European, is a model of exemplary conduct: calm and composed, completely sure of herself, combining intelligence with an unwavering moral compass. Milgram's admiration is all the greater because being a woman and a German he might expect very different behavior from her, yet she seems both attractive and of the appropriate social and cultural background. After administering 210 volts, "she turns to the experimenter, remarking firmly, 'Well, I'm sorry, I don't think we should continue.'" The experiment is stopped. Milgram comments that she is "firm and resolute throughout. She indicates in the interview that she was in no way tense or nervous, and this corresponds to her controlled appearance throughout." Indeed, "the woman's straightforward, courteous behavior in the experiment, lack of tension, a total control of her own action seems to make disobedience a simple and rational deed. Her behavior is the very embodiment of what I had initially envisioned would be true for almost all subjects." Milgram concludes: "Ironically, Gretchen Brandt grew to adolescence in Hitler's Germany and was for the great part of her youth exposed to Nazi propaganda. When asked about the possible influence of her background, she remarks slowly, 'Perhaps we have seen too much pain.'"[109] One can almost see the scientist falling in love with his subject.

Although Milgram introduces the detailed exposition of his experiment by claiming that people from different professions and classes behaved similarly, his examples do not confirm this assertion and reveal his own biases. If we were to sketch a portrait of the typical perpetrator based on the findings of this experiment, he would be working class, crude, muscular, lacking in education and intelligence,

---

[109] Ibid., 73–85, for description of these experiments.

possibly lethargic, badly dressed and speaking ungrammatical English, originating in southern Europe or the American South, probably black or Italian. Women supporters would belong to the working class, possibly of East European origin, or be hysterical, hypocritical, arriviste Jews. Conversely, those most unlikely to become perpetrators would be middle-class academics, professionals, the clergy or at least men of faith, intelligent, elegant, probably blonds of north European, most likely Protestant background. Those exposed in the past to war, atrocity, and complicity would be unlikely to comply.

The problem is, of course, that the typical supporter of Nazism came from the north German, middle-class, Protestant milieu.[110] We know that the commanders of the Nazi death squads, the elite of the SS and the Police, were men with university degrees, often with a Ph.D. in law.[111] We know that the medical and legal professions collaborated happily with Nazism and facilitated many of its crimes; that the clergy, Protestant and Catholic, did little to oppose the genocide of the Jews and much to popularize prejudice.[112] We know that the brutalizing effects of World War I played a major role in the success of Nazism.[113] That is, those most unlikely to comply with malevolent authority supported Hitler. We also know that inside Germany it was first and foremost members of the working class who opposed the regime.[114] We know that Nazism's victims came mainly from Eastern Europe and European Jewry, from among the handicapped, the Gypsies, the homo-

[110] R. F. Hamilton, *Who Voted for Hitler?* (Princeton, 1982); M. Kater, *The Nazi Party: A Social Profile of Members and Leaders, 1919–1945* (Oxford, 1983).

[111] U. Herbert, *Best: Biographische Studien über Radikalismus, Weltanschauung und Vernunft 1903–1989* (Bonn, 1996), pts. 1-2; H. Krausnick and H.-H. Wilhelm, *Die Truppe des Weltanschauungskrieges* (Stuttgart, 1981); L. Hachmeister, *Der Gegnerforscher: Die Karriere des SS-Führers Franz Alfred Six* (Munich, 1998); Y. Lozowick, *Hitler's Bureaucrats: The Nazi Security Police and the Banality of Evil* (Jerusalem, 2001), 55–83, in Hebrew.

[112] See note 15, above; R. J. Lifton, *The Nazi Doctors: Medical Killing and the Psychology of Genocide* (New York, 1986); D. L. Bergen, *Twisted Cross: The German Christian Movement* (Chapel Hill, 1996); R. P. Ericksen and S. Heschel, "The German Churches Face Hitler: Assessment of the Historiography," *TAJ* 23 (1994): 433–59; O. Bartov and P. Mack, eds., *In God's Name: Genocide and Religion in the Twentieth Century* (New York, 2001), chaps. 2–5.

[113] K. Theweleit, *Male Fantasies*, 2 vols. (Minneapolis, 1987–1989); J. W. Baird, *To Die for Germany: Heroes in the Nazi Pantheon* (Bloomington, 1990); P. H. Merkl, *Political Violence under the Swastika: 581 Early Nazis* (Princeton, 1975); Bartov, *Murder*, pt. 1.

[114] T. Mason, *Social Policy in the Third Reich: The Working Class and the "National Community"* (Providence, 1993); and Mason, *Nazism, Fascism and the Working Class*, ed. J. Caplan (Cambridge, 1995), chaps. 2, 4, 7, 9.

sexuals.[115] We know that Italians tried to hinder crimes perpetrated by Germans in Europe (although in Ethiopia they practiced habitual colonial mass killing).[116]

This does not mean that Milgram is necessarily wrong in his psychological portrait, but rather that he got his history wrong. Had these men and women acted merely out of a sense of obedience to authority, the results of the experiment could not possibly conform to the reality in Nazi Germany. Hence we are left to conclude that the opposite is the case, namely, that middle-class professional Germans supported Hitler for what appeared to them intellectually and morally sound reasons and that Gretchen Brandt, for instance, might have joined the Nazi Women's Organization with the same calm self-assurance that made her refuse to follow an order she did not agree with. It means that, for a while at least, people had a choice and what they chose indicated their beliefs.

At the same time, Milgram's experiment indicates that what we believe to be an objective reality and sound rational arguments are often so strongly influenced by our biases as to wholly distort our findings. Milgram obviously would never have considered himself a racist, a misogynist, an antisemite, or a social elitist. Yet his descriptions of his subjects' physical, intellectual, and moral qualities are so clearly related to their ethnicity, gender, and social background that one must ask how is it that those who have used the results of his experiment over the years have never noticed his prejudices. One is tempted to argue that a sociopsychological experiment so deeply imbued with bias cannot possibly be taken seriously as anything but a reflection of the prejudices of the experimenter and his time (merely a generation ago). I would not go that far, since some of Milgram's insights seem to me of paramount importance. But I would stress, nevertheless, that what this experiment proves above all is that obedience to authority is not at all merely about a person coming to see himself "as the instrument

[115] G. Aly, *"Endlösung": Völkerverschiebung und der Mord an den europäischen Juden* (Frankfurt/M., 1995); L. Yahil, *The Holocaust: The Fate of European Jewry* (New York, 1990); M. Burleigh, *Death and Deliverance: "Euthanasia" in Germany, 1900–1945* (Cambridge, 1994); H. Friedlander, *The Origins of Nazi Genocide: From Euthanasia to the Final Solution* (Chapel Hill, 1995); M. Zimmermann, *Rassenutopie und Genozid: Die nationalsozialistische "Lösung der Zigeunerfrage"* (Hamburg, 1996); B. Jellonnek, *Homosexuelle unter dem Hakenkreuz: Die Verfolgung von Homosexuellen im Dritten Reich* (Paderborn, 1990).

[116] J. Steinberg, *All or Nothing: The Axis and the Holocaust 1941–43* (London, 1990).

for carrying out another person's wishes," who "therefore no longer regards himself as responsible for his actions." Rather, I would argue that obedience to authority among those whose collaboration is most necessary, the educated professional elites, men and women of religion and faith, teachers and technicians, generals and professors, comes from accepting the fundamental ideas that guide that authority and wishing to help realize them in practice; and that this becomes possible only if both the authority and those who obey it share the same prejudices, the same view of the world, the same fundamental perception of reality.

What then are we to conclude from this brief analysis of Milgram's experiment, his social, ethnic, and gender biases? What does this tell us about the relationship between the reception of interpretations of atrocity by different societies in different periods? All we can say at this juncture, I believe, is that while atrocity is the product of numerous factors, some historical, political, and ideological, others psychological and sociological, so too is the interpretation of such events in the past and the present. If we can and must learn from the study of inhumanity, so too can we learn a great deal about our own societies by evaluating the manner in which they react to theories and interpretations of past atrocities. From this perspective, the greatest long-term merit of Goldhagen's study is not to be found in his interpretation of the Holocaust, but rather in the manner with which it was received and what that reception tells us about the world in which we live.

7

Jews as Germans
VICTOR KLEMPERER
BEARS WITNESS

THE PRESENCE OF THE PAST

More than fifty years have passed since the final defeat of Nazism, and yet its presence in our minds seems to be stronger than ever. This demands explanation. After all, public interest in events of the past normally diminishes as they recede in time. Younger generations have other, more pressing concerns; even the memories of those who experienced the past will fade and lose their pertinence to a world busily rushing forward into the future and unwilling to waste time on history. But the case of Nazism, and especially of the Holocaust, is different.

There are episodes in history whose centrality can only be recognized from a chronological distance. The mass of inexplicable, often horrifying details is endowed with sense and meaning only retrospectively, after it has passed. Gradually such events come to cast a shadow over all that had previously seemed of greater significance, reaching backward and forward, until they finally touch our normal lives, reminding us with ever growing urgency that we are the survivors of cataclysms and catastrophes that we never experienced. The Holocaust is such an event.

The presence of the past is felt in many ways. It may be expressed in works of historical scholarship, such as the current avalanche of studies on Adolf Hitler;[1] in the growing stream of publications on Nazism

---

[1] B. Hamann, *Hitler's Vienna: A Dictator's Apprenticeship* (New York, 1999); H. A. Turner, Jr., *Hitler's Thirty Days to Power: January 1933* (Reading, Mass., 1996); J. Lukacs, *The Hitler of History* (New York, 1997); M. Steinert, *Hitler: A Biography* (New York, 1997); R. Rosenbaum, *Explaining Hitler: A Search for the Origins of His Evil* (New York, 1998); I Kershaw, *Hitler*, 2 vols. (New York, 1999–2000).

and the Holocaust by American, European, and Israeli scholars;[2] and in such commotions as the *Historikerstreit* of the mid-1980s and the recent controversy about Daniel Goldhagen's book.[3] Moreover, the presence of the past may be expressed and promoted by more popular forms of representation, from television documentaries such as the BBC's *The Nazis* to films such as *Schindler's List* and *Life Is Beautiful.*[4] It may provoke political abuse as well as deep understanding, commercial exploitation as well as empathy and compassion.

It has been fifty years, and the survivors are disappearing. Hence, too, the innumerable memoirs of survivors published over the last few years, and the growing overlap between them and the memoirs and fictions of the second generation.[5] We are living at the edge of memory. Soon we will be all alone, staring into the darkness of the past without anything to guide us but the written and photographic traces left by those who had been there. Hence, finally, the urgency with which survivors' testimonies are now being recorded on videotape around the world.

The void of direct experience is gradually being filled with vicarious memories. Indeed, the phenomenon of vicarious memory seems to be one of the hallmarks of our time. Writers do not only "feel" themselves into the past, they actually "remember" a past that they never experienced, not merely as a literary device or an aesthetic exercise, but also as an attempt to acquire an identity barred to them, mercifully, by time and by biology: to become the victims they never were. This seems to

[2] C. R. Browning, *Ordinary Men: Reserve Police Battalion 101 and the Final Solution in Poland* (New York, 1992); H. Friedlander, *The Origins of Nazi Genocide: From Euthanasia to the Final Solution* (Chapel Hill, 1995); D. J. Goldhagen, *Hitler's Willing Executioners: Ordinary Germans and the Holocaust* (New York, 1996); S. Friedländer, *Nazi Germany and the Jews,* vol. 1 (New York, 1997); G. Aly, *"Final Solution": Nazi Population Policy and the Murder of the European Jews* (1995; New York, 1999); M. Burleigh, *The Third Reich: A New History* (New York, 2000); R. Gellately, *Backing Hitler: Consent and Coercion in Nazi Germany* (Oxford, 2001).

[3] On the *Historikerstreit* see chap. 1, note 13, above. On Goldhagen, see chap. 6, note 1, above.

[4] Further in E. L. Santner, *Stranded Objects: Mourning, Memory, and Film in Postwar Germany* (Ithaca, N.Y., 1990); A. Kaes, *From Hitler to Heimat: The Return of History as Film* (Cambridge, Mass., 1989); O. Bartov, *Murder in Our Midst: The Holocaust, Industrial Killing, and Representation* (New York, 1996), pt 3; Y. Loshitzky, ed., *Spielberg's Holocaust: Critical Perspectives on Schindler's List* (Bloomington, 1997).

[5] On the latter, see J. M. Rymkiewicz, *The Final Station: Umschlagplatz* (New York, 1994); B. Schlink, *The Reader* (New York, 1997); H. Raczymow, *Writing the Book of Esther* (New York, 1995).

have been the case with Binjamin Wilkomirski's *Fragments*, the most striking recent example of writing oneself into a new identity—into the identity of the ultimate victim, a Jewish child during the Holocaust.[6] Be that as it may, the growing number of works of fiction by second-generation writers striving to enter a chronologically impenetrable past that is nevertheless as present as an exposed nerve, as unbearably painful as an amputated limb, must indicate the centrality of the Holocaust for the mind of the current moment.

Beyond fantasy and imagination, or at the root of it, is testimony. Yet testimony is never an unambiguous historical source: it can clarify and shed light on the past, and it can obscure and repress it. Both Christopher Browning and Daniel Goldhagen used testimonies of perpetrators in their studies of the killers' motivation, but they reached diametrically opposed conclusions from the same material. Those particular testimonies were given long after the event, under conditions of a police inquiry whose results would have served to determine the fate of the witnesses. Survivors' testimonies have also often been collected at a great distance of time from the catastrophe; and they, too, are influenced by the representation of the event in the intervening years, by the mind's facility in remembering and forgetting, and by the refusal or the inability of witnesses to recall the worst things. Such interviews are also molded in part by the interests and the prejudices the interviewers.

For Jorge Semprun, the Spanish-born, French-educated writer who was incarcerated in Buchenwald as a political prisoner, the question after his liberation was "writing or life." Many decades later he articulated this dilemma in his memoir. Writing about his camp experience in the immediate aftermath of the war would have made life unbearable; but living with the memory of those months of torture was also unbearable. Writing was liberation, but writing about the camp perpetuated the reality of imprisonment and its hopelessness. One was liberated by returning to the camp, only to find oneself once more imprisoned within the barbed wire of trauma.[7]

---

[6] B. Wilkomirski, *Fragments: Memoirs of a Wartime Childhood* (New York, 1996). Further in P. Gourevitch, "The Memory Thief," *TNY* (June 14, 1999): 48–68; E. Lappin, "The Man with Two Heads," *Granta* (summer 1999): 9–65; O. Bartov, *Mirrors of Destruction: War, Genocide, and Modern Identity* (New York, 2000), 213–30.

[7] J. Semprun, *L'écriture ou la vie* (Paris, 1994), misleadingly translated as *Literature or Life* (New York, 1997).

Primo Levi wrote about the *Lager* soon after his liberation; but as the temporal distance from the event increased, the pain increased. The memory of hell made life after hell all the more insupportable. As Levi observed shortly before his presumed suicide, the realization that his reconstruction of the camp experience had failed accurately to reflect its reality, and that it could not be transmitted to younger generations, was all the more acute because he felt a need, like many others, to justify his survival by telling and retelling the story of the millions who did not survive with him.[8]

Charlotte Delbo wrote the first volume of her trilogy on Auschwitz in 1946, but did not publish it until 1965.[9] Paul Celan, who created the greatest poetic monument to the disaster, moved increasingly away from early articulations of pain and atrocity, loss and meaninglessness, to a language that seems finally to have disintegrated along with his own personality, culminating in his suicide in 1970.[10] Thus bearing witness may lead to personal freedom and reveal hidden truths; but it may also provoke despair, disillusionment, and confusion. For how can we tell the truth of an event that our minds could not then, and cannot now, encompass?

THE INSIDER AS OUTSIDER

Victor Klemperer did not see a contradiction between writing and life. He wrote *for* life, in an effort to maintain his own existence in a world that had turned against him and threatened to undermine all his beliefs. He also wrote in order to leave a record for those who would come after him, for the life after the disaster. As he observed in his journal on May 27, 1942: "But I shall go on writing. This is *my* heroism. I will bear witness, precise witness!"[11] He increasingly doubted that he would survive, but he never wavered in his conviction that Nazism would be defeated, that there would be life after Hitler.

Klemperer's diary has the immediacy and poignancy of unedited notes written in the thick of experience. Unlike us, his readers, he does

---

[8] P. Levi, *The Drowned and the Saved* (New York, 1988), 83–84.

[9] L. L. Langer, "Introduction" to C. Delbo, *Auschwitz and After* (1970; New Haven, 1995), x.

[10] J. Felstiner, *Paul Celan: Poet, Survivor, Jew* (New Haven, 1995).

[11] V. Klemperer, *I Will Bear Witness: A Diary of the Nazi Years* (1995; New York, 1998–1999), 2:61. Originally published as *Ich will Zeugnis ablegen bis zum letzten*, 2 vols., ed. W. Nowojski (Berlin, 1995).

not know what will happen, and his grim foreboding is always qualified by expressions of hope, by encouraging signs that the German population may turn against Hitler. Written only for himself, this vast diary contains all the petty complaints and worries of a middle-aged scholar, an often self-centered and occasionally ungracious husband, a conservative, pedantic, and sometimes irritatingly bourgeois member of the German academic elite. Klemperer is a very normal human being, indeed, a man of his time, his class, and his culture. It is for this reason that his memoirs are so revealing.

Yet he is much more than that. Not only is he an extremely perceptive observer of events in Germany, he is also increasingly made into a pariah in his own homeland. What we have in this extraordinary book, then, is a view of German society under Nazism by the perfect insider who is rapidly transformed by the regime's ideology and its internalization by the population into the ultimate outsider, a Jew in a racist, violently antisemitic land that succeeds in bringing about the social death of its Jewish citizens even before it condemns them to physical annihilation.

I have already noted (in chapters 3 and 5, above) the curious similarity between the German historian Götz Aly's argument that "the retrospective interpretation of National Socialism as a rule follows the perspective of the victim,"[12] and the American scholar Daniel Goldhagen's assertion that "until now the perpetrators . . . have received little concerted attention."[13] Both scholars thus insisted on the need to understand the killers rather than the killed. Despite appearances, this was hardly a drastic departure from the traditional focus of Holocaust scholarship. As Marion Kaplan has rightly pointed out, "the emphasis [in the historiography] has been on the killers [and] on Nazi policies toward the Jews."[14] Historians find it easier to write on the perpetrators because they can refer to official documentation, which is generally seen as more reliable and less subjective than the kind of material on which one must rely for the study of the victims, such as diaries, memoirs, letters, and interviews.

Still, one must be careful when making such frozen distinctions between perpetrators and victims. As we learn from Klemperer, the

[12] Aly, *"Final Solution,"* 246.
[13] Goldhagen, *Willing Executioners,* 5.
[14] M. Kaplan, *Between Dignity and Despair: Jewish Life in Nazi Germany* (New York, 1998), 4.

transformation in the status of both Jewish and gentile Germans was gradual, and in the early stages of the nightmare almost imperceptible. Klemperer does not perceive himself right away as a victim, nor does he view his German environment as made up entirely of perpetrators. Goldhagen's well-known picture of German society as more or less monolithically antisemitic—eighty million willing executioners—is not confirmed by Klemperer. Conversely, the argument made by many German and American reviewers of Klemperer's diaries, according to which they illustrate the extent to which German society did not turn against the Jews, is also based on a highly selective reading of the text.

The world we see through Klemperer's eyes is a world in which most (though not all) Germans gradually turned their backs on the Jews, excluding them from their midst partly out of prejudice or conviction, partly because of fear and opportunism, and partly out of indifference and moral callousness. In some ways, moreover, the complicated picture is the most frightening picture. It serves as a reminder that none of us is immune from ignoring the fate of a minority as long as our own lot is not threatened.

Klemperer's is also a curious case. For this vivid document of its time was not published until long after his death in 1960, at the age of 78. Thus his life exemplified in several ways the extraordinary relationship between Jews and non-Jews in Germany, and the fate of his diary can be seen as representative of Germany's tortuous postwar confrontation with the memory of Nazism and the often repressed transformation of German Jews into their fellow-citizens' victims.

Klemperer was born in 1881 in Landsberg an der Warthe (today Gorzów Wielkopolski in Poland), the son of a Reform rabbi. He studied philosophy and philology in Germany and abroad, and converted to Protestantism when he was thirty-one years old.[15] He worked as a journalist, and finally completed his doctorate and his *Habilitation* on the eve of World War I. After serving at the front and as a military censor, he was appointed a professor of Romance languages at the Tech-

---

[15] Klemperer actually converted for the first time in 1903 so as to qualify as a reserve officer in the military, a decision he later regretted. Following his second conversion in 1912 he considered himself a German Protestant of Jewish ancestry. See N. H. Donahue, "At the Heart of the Matter: Deliberations on Crisis in the Diaries of Victor Klemperer, 1933–1945," in *Literarisches Kriegsbewusstsein: Ein Perzeptions- und Produktionsmuster im 20. Jahrhundert*, ed. K. Bullivant and B. Spies (Munich, 2001), 110–11.

nical University of Dresden in 1920, a position that he held until he was forced by the Nazis to retire in 1935.[16]

It was not Klemperer's commitment to his homeland that saved his life under the Nazi dictatorship. He was saved, rather, by the fact that his wife Eva Schlemmer, a pianist and musicologist whom he married in 1906, was considered an "Aryan" by the regime. Moreover, as his diary reveals, it was their intense devotion to each other that sustained them through long years of abuse and humiliation, social isolation and material deprivation.[17]

Klemperer published several scholarly works before and after World War II, on Montesquieu, Corneille, the history of ideas, and the history of French literature and lyric since the eighteenth century. Until recently he was known only to scholars in his field and to some specialists in the history of the Third Reich, thanks to a book he wrote shortly after the war. It was only in 1989, with the publication of his memoirs, *Curriculum vitae*, and especially with the appearance of the German original of *I Will Bear Witness* in 1995, that Klemperer emerged from obscurity as one of the shrewdest and most meticulous observers of life under the Nazi dictatorship.

WAITING FOR THE GERMANS

I first encountered Klemperer in 1980, when Tim Mason, my doctoral advisor at the time, proposed that I read Klemperer's book *LTI—Notitzbuch eines Philologen* (*LTI: Notebook of a Philologist*), published in East Germany in 1947. The acronym LTI was Klemperer's code word for *Lingua tertii imperii*, or "the language of the Third Reich." This brilliant study documented the corruption of the German language by the infiltration into it of an increasing number of Nazi terms and concepts. Klemperer demonstrated how Nazism penetrated the minds of Germans through single words, through the manner of speech and the construction of sentences, until even the opponents and the victims of the regime subconsciously adopted its modes of expression. In his diary he noted (as early as July 1941) that his study was intended to demonstrate how the "completely unchecked" leaders of Nazi Germany "seek to unscrupulously stupefy a silent mass . . . to turn the

---

[16] For a sketch of Klemperer's biography, see M. Chalmers, preface to *Witness*, 1:vii-xxii. See also Donahue.

[17] Donahue, 122–27, argues that the couple's relationship exemplified the German-Jewish symbiosis.

multitude of animated individuals into the mechanized collective, which they call the people and which is the mass. Out of this unscrupulousness arises the coarseness and extravagance of the rhetoric and the dominant position of rhetoric in LTI."[18]

I wondered who Klemperer was and what had become of him. Nobody could tell me much about him, and his book never received the attention it deserved. (It has only very recently been translated into English, following the success of the diaries).[19] Now I know that the fate of *LTI* mirrored Klemperer's own last years. At the war's end, he was determined to resume his academic career and complete the scholarly works that Nazism had interrupted. He kept his diaries and memoirs to himself. A liberal patriot before 1933, he joined the Communist Party in East Germany in 1945. He saw himself first and foremost as a German and a scholar; the recovery of his academic post at a German university spelled for him the final victory over Hitler.

After he died, his diaries were deposited in the state archive of Dresden, and they might have remained there to this day had they not been discovered, edited and transcribed for publication by a former student. Finding a publisher for these massive tomes—there are 1,600 pages in the original—was no easy matter. With so many memoirs of survivors already on the market, who would want to trouble themselves with this sprawling document? Finally the Berlin Aufbau-Verlag, which had published the original edition of *LTI*, decided to risk it. It has never regretted this decision: *I Will Bear Witness* became a best-seller in Germany, and has already had a major impact in the United States and Britain, too.

In Germany, Klemperer's diary has been cited by numerous commentators as providing conclusive proof that the Germans under Hitler were not all "willing executioners." Yet it would be a serious misunderstanding to consider Klemperer an apologist for "ordinary Germans" in the Third Reich. For Klemperer is not consistent (this is hardly surprisingly in his rapidly changing circumstances), and he is not free from contradictions and delusions. Nor is he always a cool and objective observer. Sometimes he is impassioned, angry, anxious. His vacillations make his book fascinating; but they also make his book

---

[18] Klemperer, *Witness*, 1: 404.

[19] V. Klemperer, *The Language of the Third Reich. LTI—Lingua Tertii Imperii: A Philologist's Notebook* (London, 2000).

useless for tendentious historians. Those in quest of "good Germans" will be as disappointed by Klemperer as those who believe in German "eliminationism." The diary reveals instead a gallery of individuals who act remarkably like ourselves under circumstances radically different from our own.[20]

The main focus of Klemperer's identity, throughout his life, was a powerful adherence to Germany. This does not mean that he was uncritical of the Germans. Quite the contrary. As the Nazi regime consolidated its rule over Germany, and as its propaganda was increasingly internalized by the population, Klemperer gradually came to see himself as the only true German left in the land. This was deeply ironic, and deeply tragic; for just as Klemperer was defined by the regime, and increasingly by his surroundings, as an undesirable foreign element to be isolated, marginalized, and finally done away with, he clung to his notion of true Germanness with ever more desperate tenacity.

Nor was this sense of identity unshaken by circumstances. Klemperer is seen as fighting a bitter battle with himself. He is filled with doubts, disappointments, and disillusionments. Still, he concludes in a tone of triumph. On May 30, 1942 he writes in his diary: "*I am German and am waiting for the Germans to come back; they have gone to ground somewhere*" (2:63). And on June 20, 1946, he writes his old friends, now living in New York: "I want to participate fully and willingly in draining the cesspool of Germany, so that something decent will once more become of this land."[21]

But this did not mean forgiveness for those who collaborated with the regime. Asked in 1946 by Hans Hirche, the son of an old friend and a former major in the General Staff of the Wehrmacht imprisoned by the British, to write a "warm-hearted testimony" (that is, a letter of good conduct) on his behalf, Klemperer vehemently refused to do so, although he had written many such letters over the previous months:

> What shocks me so much about your letter is the problem of guilt and non-guilt. You and so many like you say over and over again: we are guiltless, we didn't know about this. But did none of you ever read

[20] For an evaluation of Klemperer's perceptions of attitudes toward Jews by "ordinary Germans," see H. A. Turner, Jr., "Victor Klemperer's Holocaust," *GSR* 22 (October 1999): 385–95.

[21] Cited in W. Nowojski, "Nachwort," in Klemperer, *Zeugnis*, 2:876–77.

Hitler's "struggle" [*Mein Kampf*], where everything that had later been implemented was planned beforehand with shameless candor? And were then all these murders, all these crimes, in the face of which people similarly looked the other way, only obvious to us—by which I mean now by no means only the Jews, but all the persecuted? You write yourself: "every path led to Moabit" [the Gestapo prison in Berlin]; how can you say then in the same breath: my conscience is clear?[22]

Klemperer's wrath at the betrayal of his academic colleagues was even greater. His one-time friend, the historian Johannes Kühn, severed relations with him in 1935 and went on to support the Nazis and promote their cause. On August 16, 1936, Klemperer wrote in his diary

If one day the situation were reversed and the fate of the vanquished lay in my hands, then I would let all the ordinary folk go and even some of the leaders, who might perhaps after all have had honorable intentions and not known what they were doing. But I would have all the intellectuals strung up, and the professors three feet higher than the rest; they would be left hanging from the lampposts for as long as was compatible with hygiene. (1:184)

Yet such hopes for a purge of the intellectuals never materialized. Kühn greeted Klemperer in July 1945 as if nothing had happened in the intervening ten years, and he was soon reinstated to his profession, appointed first to a chair at Leipzig in 1946 and then at Heidelberg University in 1949.[23]

Klemperer clung to his Germanness despite his humiliation and near murder, but he was not unaware of the fact that so many of his victimizers had gone unpunished, and that the old elites, deeply complicit in the crimes of Nazism, proceeded to educate a new generation of Germans after the collapse of Hitler's Reich and all that it stood for.

THE UN-GERMAN NATION

Klemperer's painful trajectory, his path from his pre-Nazi allegiance to German identity to his renewed if transformed commitment to Germanness, cannot be grasped without at least a few pertinent citations from his diary. These excerpts will show also the extent to which his

[22] Ibid., 874.
[23] Chalmers, "Preface," in Klemperer, *Witness*, 1: xviii.

book reflects the magnitude of the catastrophe for German Jewry even before the killing began.

In March 1933, only three months after Hitler came to power, Klemperer asserts that Germany "will never wash off the ignominy of having fallen victim" to the Nazis, and exclaims that he "will never again have faith in Germany." Since he has "always felt German," he now professes a sense of "shame more than fear, shame for Germany." (1: 8–9) Following the boycott of Jewish businesses on April 1, Klemperer notes that "everything I considered un-German, brutality, injustice, hypocrisy, mass suggestion to the point of intoxication, all of it flourishes here," and he wonders whether "the current madness is indeed a typical German madness" (1:11, 15).

Still, as we read again and again in the diary, none of this will turn him against Germanness, which he increasingly formulates in cultural rather than nationalist terms. Klemperer's stubborn adherence to his German identity, along with his growing aversion to nationalism, is expressed in his vehement attacks on Zionism, which he perceives as a threat to his own analysis of the Jews as successfully integrated into European culture and society. Hence he argues, in July 1933, that "anyone who goes [to Palestine] exchanges nationalism and narrowness for nationalism and narrowness." He follows this with the fatalistic statement that he "must live here and die here." Yet he is not staying in Germany as a "foreign element": the fascist dictatorship, in his view, "is absolutely un-German and consequently will not have any kind of long-term duration," even if "for the moment it is organized with German thoroughness and therefore unlikely to be removed in the foreseeable future" (1:23–25).

The next few months persuade Klemperer that Nazism has taken hold of much of the population. In August, he can still detect "not a shred of politics, no anti-Semitism," and he "cannot believe that the mood of the masses is really still behind Hitler" (1:30). But a month later, in view of the Nuremberg rally and the fact that "the press worships Hitler like God and the prophets rolled into one," Klemperer concedes that his "hopes of a swift about-face are fading." That some of his Jewish friends declare "Hitler a genius," others see themselves as no longer "attached to Germanness," and others still "are beginning to submit inwardly and to regard the new ghetto situation as a legal condition which must be accepted," is "especially repugnant" to Klemperer who, like many other German Jews, trusted the German

Rechtsstaat (state based on law) in which Jewish emancipation was achieved and maintained. Precisely thanks to their deep attachment to German culture, he and his wife "suffer immensely because Germany violates all justice and all culture in such a manner" (1:33–35).

During the early years of Nazi rule, Klemperer continued to write his book on eighteenth-century France, a project that not only diverted his mind from the events around him, but also helped him to ponder the origin of Nazism in certain trends that he identified in the Enlightenment. His hero was Voltaire, his villain was Rousseau. (In his discussion of Rousseau's baleful impact on modern politics, he reminds one of scholars such as Jacob Talmon and Hannah Arendt.)[24] Reading Rousseau's *Encyclopédie* article on *"Economie politique,"* Klemperer remarks in July 1936 on the French philosopher's "flight from the present and from oneself in three divergent directions: to nature, to God, to the Spartan state, the prostitution of reason in the service of subjective feeling, Romantic longing . . . the obsession with virtue as antidote and self-deception" (1:180–81). In February 1937 he finds Hitler's speech the previous month "grist to my Rousseau mills: 'Sole bearer of sovereignty is the people'" (1:211). By July he finally concludes: "The posthumous unmasking of Rousseau is called Hitler" (1:230). (Talmon famously called this "totalitarian democracy.")

For Klemperer, Germanness was consistent with all that was best in European civilization. In early 1934 he writes his brother Georg that he is "a German through and through and intended to remain in Germany to the bitter end"; the following month he wonders whether Germany has "really become so completely and fundamentally different, has its soul changed so completely that this will endure?" (1:52–53) In April he asserts that his sister Grete, who says that she can no longer remain German, "has become un-German, inwardly degraded and quite resigned. *That* is no doubt how things stand with very many Jews" (1:63). And this only enhances his contempt for Jewish nationalism, bringing him to write in June that "in Zion the Aryan is exactly in the same position of the Jew here. . . . To me," he exclaims, "the Zionists . . . are just as offensive as the Nazis" (1:68–69). The assault on his German identity seems only to enhance Klemperer's increasingly virulent and irrational anti-Zionism.

That same day, however, Klemperer is confronted with a younger

[24] J. H. Talmon, *The Origins of Totalitarian Democracy* (London, 1952); H. Arendt, *The Origins of Totalitarianism* (New York, 1951).

colleague who makes "a wild, hysterical declaration for the 'Führer.'" Dismissing his objections, she says: "I have faith. We have come home—we have not been at home since 1918." The following day she severs their relationship by asserting that "everything must take second place to Fatherland and nation, the miraculous deed of the Führer, in which she believes" (1:69). Later that month his colleague Kühn describes the Nazi regime as "pure democracy," the German as "creative" and "at one with nature," and the Jew as "industrious, flexible, mobile, uncreative." As Klemperer realizes, his friend "professes himself an opponent of anti-Semitism and yet [is] fundamentally an anti-Semite" (1:72).

The faith in Hitler and anti-Jewish sentiments are accompanied by fears of communism. In April 1935 even one of his Jewish friends expresses worry that "if Hitler is overthrown," he might be followed by "an even worse Bolshevism"—a manner of thinking which, as Klemperer rightly notes, "keeps [Hitler] where he is again and again" (1:117). All this time, the regime's open antisemitism is displayed everywhere, with the Nazi rag "*Der Stürmer* . . . displayed at many street corners . . . special bulletin boards" with such slogans as "the Jews are our misfortune," and "whoever knows a Jew, knows the devil" (1:118).

As Klemperer reminisces about his father's "efforts on behalf of Germanness," which now appear to him as "nothing short of tragic," and again calls Zionism "betrayal and Hitlerism," he receives his dismissal notice from the university (1:118 -19). From this point on his isolation becomes almost complete, as hardly any of his colleagues bother about him. He compares his situation to an episode in World War I when, "running through machine-gun fire, I stumbled over a rail, fell, collected myself, reached cover after the others. A comrade looked up and said indifferently: 'So you're still here too? I thought, you were dead'" (1:121).

Throughout the summer the "Jew-baiting and the pogrom atmosphere grow day by day." Goebbels calls to "exterminate [the Jews] like fleas and bedbugs!" Anti-Jewish slogans, posters and notices appear on store windows, tram stop signs, and newspaper stands (1:128, 130). To those who try to persuade him to leave, however, Klemperer insists stubbornly that he is a "German forever, German 'nationalist.'" Indeed, "the Nazis are un-German": Klemperer protects his identity with willful and desperate definitions (1:129).

Still, he admits to himself that his "principles about Germany . . . are beginning to wobble like an old man's teeth" (1:129). And in September 1935, the Nuremberg laws on "German blood and German honor" finally define Klemperer himself as un-German. He now asks himself: "Where do I belong? To the 'Jewish nation' decrees Hitler." For Klemperer, however, "the Jewish nation . . . is a comedy," since he sees himself as "nothing but a German or German European" (1:134). Among the few gentiles who still do not shun his company, he confronts such views as those uttered by Frau Kühn, the historian's wife, who tells him that "even today one can still be a Nazi for idealistic reasons without being a criminal or an idiot"; or Martha Wiechmann who, in March 1936, admits that "nothing impressed me so much as rearmament and marching into the Rhineland," adding that upon hearing "a lecture about Russia" she realized that "we are much better off" (1:135, 156).

Klemperer is forced to the conclusion that he and his wife "are completely isolated," and that the regime no longer

> has enemies inside Germany. The majority of the people is content, a small group accepts Hitler as the lesser evil, no one really wants to be rid of him, all see in him the liberator in foreign affairs, fear Russian conditions . . . believe, insofar as they are not honestly carried away, that it is inopportune . . . to be outraged at such details as the suppression of civil liberties, the persecution of the Jews, the falsification of all scholarly truths, the systematic destruction of all morality. And all are afraid for their livelihood, their life, all are such terrible cowards. (1: 162, 165)

Aware that once the Olympics are over it will be "open season on the Jews," Klemperer still cannot bring himself to leave his homeland (1:175).

THE "NAZI CONTAGION" AND THE "JEWISH BUSINESS"

What is remarkable about Klemperer's diaries is that he has clearly understood the nature of the Nazi regime and the extent of the public's support for Hitler, but refuses to modify his view that those who brand him un-German are themselves un-German, even if their numbers appear to encompass a growing share of the population. He thus remains the only true German in a country that denies his right to exist there. What succors him are not the "good Germans" who increasingly abandon him, but his perception of himself as the guardian of a true Germanness that has been rejected by the political leadership, the intellectual elite, and the masses of his beloved homeland. In September 1936 he writes that the "NSDAP has assessed the popular mood quite accurately." Therefore "the Jewish dream of being German has been a dream after all. That is the most bitter truth for me." Still, even as he is denied access to the library reading room, even as his friends and relations keep leaving the country—often taking with them the Iron Crosses they earned at the front in World War I—he stubbornly asserts: "I am waiting . . . for my Fatherland, I have no other" (1:192, 195, 198).

Klemperer is also aware of the antisemitism of the more enlightened. His librarian friend Frau Roth, who is "vehemently opposed to the Nazis," says that had the Nazis merely "expelled the Eastern Jews or had excluded Jews from the bench, *that* at least would have been comprehensible" (1:199). (Thomas Mann, who was married to a Jewish woman and living in exile, wrote in his own diary that it was "no great misfortune" that "the Jewish presence in the judiciary has been ended.")[25] Hence Klemperer's conclusion that "the Nazi doctrine is in part not really alien to the people, in part is gradually polluting the healthy section of the population," not least in view of the fact that those he calls "the most humane among my former colleagues" are joining the Nazis and publishing racist articles in scholarly journals. By December 1936, as his telephone line is cut, his housekeeper is no longer allowed to work for him, and his friends are either in exile or with the Nazis, Klemperer acknowledges that he is "completely alone, absolutely alone" (1:201–2).

To be sure, there are fleeting flashes of light in the darkness. In June 1937, he is greeted on the street by a former colleague, now wearing a Party badge, who shakes his hand warmly (1:226). But what he finds most depressing is that even those opposed to the Nazis have internalized much of their rhetoric and prejudices. As early as March 1933 the Klemperers' foster child Johannes Thieme had "declared himself for the new regime with such fervent conviction and praise" (1:6), and by July 1937 their anti-Nazi neighbor speaks of the necessity of "the *Volksgemeinschaft*, of distinct races, of the identity of law and power, of the unquestionable superiority of the new German army against all attackers . . . of the need to fight off Communism. . . ." For Klemperer, this indicates that "Hitlerism is after all more deeply and firmly rooted

---

[25] T. Mann, *Tagebücher 1933–34*, ed. P. de Mendelssohn (Frankfurt/M., 1977), 46; cited in Kaplan, 26. Further in Friedländer, *Nazi Germany*, 13–14.

in the nation and corresponds more to the German nature than I would like to admit" (1:229).

Seeing a photograph of a seaside resort "prohibited for Jews" captioned by the *Stürmer* with the exclamation "How nice that it's just us now!" Klemperer is reminded of a similar statement made by his schoolteacher in the early 1900s, when the Jewish students did not attend class on Yom Kippur. "In my memory," he writes in August,

> these words took on a quite horrible significance: to me it confirms the claim of the NSDAP to express the true opinion of the German people. And I believe ever more strongly that Hitler really does embody the soul of the German people, that he really stands for "Germany" and that he will consequently maintain himself and justifiably maintain himself. Whereby I have not only outwardly lost my Fatherland. And even if the government should change one day: my inner sense of belonging is gone. (1: 233–34)

By now he notes that "everywhere on my way, I see the sign 'Jews Unwelcome!' . . . hatred of Jews is being whipped up again" (1:237).

By 1938 he has become so disillusioned with German conditions that he is even willing to contemplate a move to the United States. "The whole national ideology has quite gone to pieces" for him, and he will "never again be capable of trust, never have the same sense of belonging," since "too much of what, in the past, I took lightly, viewed as an embarrassing minor phenomenon, I now consider to be German and typical." His belief in progress has also been undermined, disturbed as he is by what he calls "the trite antithesis" between "such tremendous" creations as "radio, airplanes, sound film, and the most insane stupidity, primitiveness and bestiality . . . all invention results in murder and war" (1:248, 250).

His optometrist greets clients with "Heil Hitler!" and votes for Hitler even as he grumbles about the regime; the State Library attendant, who helps Klemperer borrow books, wears a Party badge; the villages and towns through which he drives with his wife are always gaily decorated with Nazi flags; academics write learned articles on "the *traits eternels* of Jews: cruelty, hatred, violent emotion, adaptability," their "ancient Asiatic hate," their "materialistic psychology," so unlike "the spirituality of the new theory"; *Der Stürmer* declares that "synagogues are dens of thieves"; insurance companies boast of "having uncovered a number of cases of 'racial shame.'" In August 1938, Klemperer loses another attribute of his identity: he is compelled to change his name to Victor-Israel (1:251–54, 258, 261–65).

Under these combined pressures Klemperer revises his notion of himself, but he does not surrender what he deems essential: "No one can take my Germanness away from me, but my nationalism and patriotism are gone forever. My thinking is now completely a Voltairean cosmopolitanism. Every national circumscription appears barbarous to me" (1:272). He takes refuge from the attack on universalism in universalism. From the Nazi perspective, he has finally been transformed into a cosmopolitan Jew.

The Kristallnacht pogrom of November 9, 1938, radically altered the condition of German Jewry. Klemperer experiences this when the police come to search for weapons in his house, and find his saber (but miss his bayonet). Thus his proud war record becomes a liability and almost leads to his arrest. Soon the news of concentration camps filters in. Klemperer's driver's license is taken away, people no longer acknowledge him on the street, and more and more Jews are reported to have committed suicide in desperation or to have been brutalized by mobs. Yet none of this will change Klemperer's opinion that calls for a Jewish state are nothing less than "pure Nazism," and that "whoever recognizes" the existence of a "German or West European Jewish question . . . only adopts or confirms the false thesis of the NSDAP and serves its cause." To his mind, "until 1933 . . . the German Jews were entirely German and nothing else," and the "anti-Semitism which was always present is not at all evidence to the contrary," since "the friction between Jews and Aryans was not half as great as that between Protestants and Catholics . . . employers and employees . . . East Prussians . . . and southern Bavarians" (1:291).

Still, in the face of the looming disaster, Klemperer makes a few half-hearted attempts to leave Germany, knowing all the while that he will eventually stay, despite taking note of Hitler's notorious speech of January 30, 1939, in which, as Klemperer writes, he "threatened the annihilation of the Jews in Europe if they were to bring about war against Germany" (1:293). Contrary to the historiographical convention that the Germans greeted the outbreak of war with much anxiety, Klemperer observes that "public opinion [is] absolutely certain of victory, ten thousand times more arrogant than in '14" (1:307). As his own "situation grows daily more catastrophic" due to "restricted access to bank account, surrender of all ready cash," and being "more strictly rationed than the general populace," Klemperer notes in late September that people are "intoxicated by the destruction of Poland" (1:312–13).

And yet he observes with contempt that "the Jewish community in Germany today are all extremely inclined to Zionism," exclaiming that he will "go along with that just as little as I do with National Socialism or with Bolshevism. Liberal and German *forever*" (1:319). Indeed, the war gives him hope that "National Socialism will collapse in the coming year. Perhaps we shall perish with it—but it will certainly end, and with it, one way or another, the terror." Yet this does not mean that he is unaware of the population's indifference to the fate of the Jews. He closes his diary for 1939 with the words: "I believe the pogroms of November '38 made less impression on the nation than cutting the bar of chocolate [ration] for Christmas" (1:323–24).

This perception of a largely indifferent (rather than rabidly anti-Jewish) public continues throughout 1940. In March, Klemperer writes: "I often ask myself where all the wild anti-Semitism is. For my part I encounter much sympathy, people help me out, but fearfully of course" (1:329–30). Simultaneously, however, the news keeps reaching him about mass deportations and a ghetto in Lublin, while the tremendous victories of the Wehrmacht in the West in May elicit universal jubilation and optimism in the non-Jewish population. Klemperer hears people asserting that "Hitler only wants what belongs to Germany, and besides he has always wanted to keep the peace" (1:337–38), just as he and his wife are forced to vacate their house and move into the "Jews' house," which from now on they share with other "mixed-couples" in cramped conditions and under the growing threats and intimidation by the authorities.

As fears of being sent to Lublin increase daily, Klemperer can only quip that their present situation amounts to a "superior concentration camp" (1:343). In July, they are given special ration cards stamped with a red *J*, for *Jude*; only Eva's "Aryan" card protects them from serious malnutrition. Following the fall of France, the inhabitants of the Jews' house discuss the possibility of being "packed off to Madagascar"—thereby revealing that Himmler's "secret" plans were well known to those who might have been affected by them, despite their isolation. Indeed, Klemperer hears reports in August that "a ghetto has been set

up in the Generalgouvernement Poland and the Jews have been ordered to wear Zion arm-bands; they are doing forced labor."[26]

Life in Dresden now consists of endless pestering and petty persecution accompanied by fear of imminent deportation. The Klemperers
are forced to pay for improvements in the house from which they have
been evicted; they are no longer allowed to use lending libraries; they
are subjected to exorbitant taxes and are in danger of running out of
money. In November, shortly after he hears of the brutal deportation
of the Jews of Württemberg to France, he experiences an air raid warn-
ing on Dresden as "some kind of revenge." That evening Klemperer
feels like "a hunted animal" as he almost fails to make it home before
the curfew for Jews while searching for food in the city, where the
"restaurants had been terribly crowded" (1:361).

By early 1941, he notes that "everyone is afraid of arousing the least
suspicion of being friendly to Jews." His sense of utter isolation is com-
pounded by the ominous news that "shootings were going on constantly" in Poland, and stories of atrocities in concentration camps
(1:374–75). All these events force Klemperer to examine their effect on
his identity, and for the first time he concedes that "once I would have
said: I do not judge as a Jew. . . . Now: Yes, I judge as a Jew, because as
such I am particularly affected by the Jewish business in Hitlerism, and
because it is central to the whole structure, to the whole character of
National Socialism and is uncharacteristic of everything else" (1:382).
And yet, in an argument with an elderly official of the Jewish community, whom he describes as "vehemently anti-German (with Iron
Cross from the World War) and Zionist," Klemperer "emphatically"
declares his "commitment to Germanness" (1:384–85).

Reality becomes more and more jarring. While Klemperer hears in
May about the "euthanasia" campaign and the mass killing in the Son-
nenstein mental asylum, he also witnesses "people talking with gen-

---

[26] Ibid., 347, 352. Other examples in Turner, "Klemperer's Holocaust." Turner argues, however, that "many ordinary Germans . . . very likely knew even less at the time
than he did about the full extent of the . . . Holocaust." Turner, "Klemperer's Holocaust," 394. This might have been more denial than ignorance, considering that even
after the war many Germans treated the extermination as a matter of opinion and not
fact. See H. Arendt, "The Aftermath of Nazi Rule: Report from Germany," *Commentary*
10 (1950): 342–53. On the "Nisko-Lublin Plan" and the "Madagascar Plan" see P. Longerich, *Politik der Vernichtung: Eine Gesamtdarstellung der nationalsozialistischen Judenverfolgung* (Munich, 1998), 256–78.

uine enthusiasm about Hitler and National Socialism," blaming the defeat of 1918 on the fact that then "the Jews were in charge," and saying that even now "our Adolf" must "be tougher" since "we're still being too decent" (1:385–86). The German invasion of the Soviet Union on June 22, 1941, writes Klemperer, "is a source of new pride for people," and "their grumbling of yesterday is forgotten" (1:391). But for him this is a terrible period, since on the following day he is jailed for eight days as punishment for neglecting to observe blackout regulations.

As he tries in vain to preserve his dignity, he must persuade himself that he is "not guilty of anything. . . . I am in prison as a Jew." Hence, he tells himself, "it is honorable to be imprisoned now, it will be advantageous to any future reference. Nothing can truly humiliate me, every humiliation only raises me up and secures my future." He recalls his visit to the Wilhelmplatz as a schoolboy, and his feeling that he, too, "was fighting . . . on the Prussian side" with Frederick the Great. Now all his "certainties with regard to Fatherland and nation . . . have collapsed . . . with the result that . . . I sometimes think this whole life's work a mistake. . . ." While he knows that his imprisonment cannot "be compared with what is experienced by thousands upon thousands in German prisons today," he admits that "for myself it was one of the most agonizing times of my life" (1:399, 408–9, 416).

Much worse is to come. The constant reduction of rations for "J-people," the refusal of restaurants to serve Jews, the confiscation of typewriters, the ban on smoking, and endless other limitations finally culminate with the most humiliating step of all: the introduction of the yellow star on September 19, 1941. As Klemperer admits, "I . . . feel shattered, cannot compose myself. . . . I only want to leave the house for a few minutes when it's dark" (1:429). Now even the Confessing Church will not admit converted Jews. Some people show sympathy to the Jews, but since the introduction of the star they can no longer "walk naturally on the street" (1:438). In October, the reports multiply of deportations of Jews from Germany to Poland: "They have to leave almost literally naked and penniless. Thousands from Berlin to Lodz ('Litzmannstadt')." That the isolated Jews in Dresden knew about these deportations reveals once more that none of this was unknown to Germans. Indeed, Klemperer asks: "Who among the 'Aryan' Germans is really untouched by National Socialism? The contagion rages in all of them, perhaps it is not a contagion, but basic German nature" (1:440–41).

In November, he is abused by some Hitler Youth in the street. As the deportations continue, the inhabitants of the Jews' house discuss suicide, escape, or encourage themselves by what Klemperer derisively calls "the eternal: 'He was very decent to me' (the policeman, some petty official or other, etc.)," a tactic of self-delusion which he now finds "appalling" (1:444). But in December he is shaken by a baptized Jewish friend's reference to the "Jewish nation," and asserts that "Hitler is the most important promoter of Zionism." Confronted by another Jew's accusation that he had gone "completely and doubly astray," being both "bourgeois and German," and that once he finds himself "sitting in a Polish or Russian ghetto," he too would be transformed into "a very poor and pitiable 'Yid,'" Klemperer reacts by describing his accuser as manifesting a "gruesome mixture of Communism and Zionism" (1:450–51).

For all his refusal to accept the realities of his situation, for all his doubts, his terrible loneliness, his terror and his delusions, Klemperer displays remarkable courage in the face of an inconceivable material and psychological catastrophe. He always keeps a cool, detached, critical eye on his surroundings. Still, his judgment of Jewish life and Zionism becomes horribly distorted by his stubborn adherence to a notion of "Germanness" that is by now entirely alien to the vast majority of Germans. As he writes on December 31, the last page of volume 1, the "heaviest blow" for him was "the Jew's star . . . Since then completely cut off." And still he will not give up. As the trains begin rolling to the execution sites and gas chambers, Klemperer writes the final entry for 1941: "Head held high for the difficult last five minutes!" (1:456)

THE LAST GERMAN

For those who have condemned the bombing of Dresden as a senseless act of retribution, Klemperer's perspective may be of some interest. Of the 1,256 Jews living in Dresden in late 1941, only 198 were left by early 1945. All of them had "Aryan" spouses. The rest had been deported to camps and ghettoes in the East, where the vast majority were murdered. On February 13, 1945, all Jews considered capable of work were ordered to report to deportation three days later. Klemperer considered this his death sentence; but that night the city was destroyed in a terrible fire-bombing. Miraculously, he and his wife survived this hell too. Finally Eva tore off his Jewish star and they fled to the West, where they were eventually liberated by the U.S. Army in Bavaria.

Klemperer's story is remarkable not only because it is about a Jew who survived twelve years of Nazi rule in Germany, but even more because it is told by a man who ends up perceiving himself as the only German to have withstood the assault of Nazism. This is not the way most Germans have read the book, and it is not why it has become a best-seller in Germany. Instead, the diary has been said to portray the Germans as having behaved with such decency that even a Jew persecuted by the regime chose to stay in their midst and persisted in thinking of himself as a patriotic (and anti-Zionist) German.

This is a misrepresentation. As far as Klemperer was concerned, the people around him had long ceased to be German. What enabled him to survive and retain his dignity was his tremendous confidence in *his* Germanness. Thus he came to describe the regime that denied him his German identity, and then the growing numbers of Nazified Germans around him, as un-German. One by one the Germans disappeared from view. These were not only fellow-travelers, opportunists, or devotees of the Nazis. Klemperer increasingly perceived the Germans as being Nazi, and thus un-German, by nature. He came to believe that Hitler had exposed some deep essence that made them susceptible to Nazi rhetoric and Nazi action. Only he was immune to this suggestion, since his very definition as a Jew by the regime prevented him from joining the multitude.

He thought that he was the last German. As the last German, Klemperer charged himself with the mission not simply to survive, nor, certainly, to ensure the continuation of Jewish existence in Europe, but rather to save Germanness, to seek out those Germans who had gone into hiding during the terrible twelve years in which he guarded the flame of true German identity. There was something deluded about all this, of course. For it was not the Germans who disappeared under Nazi rule, it was the Jews. The Germans for whom Klemperer was looking had been there all along, but they had changed into something that Klemperer refused to see as German; they had changed into active participants in, or indifferent observers of, the murder of the Jews. In those terrible years, indeed, many a Jew felt not that he was the last

German (or the last Pole, or the last Frenchman), but the last Jew.[27] Yet Klemperer did not bother himself with the perpetuation of Jewish identity. His cause was the reestablishment of that German culture into which the Jews had once integrated themselves with such love and devotion.

Klemperer's "disappearance" for so many years after the war was itself a consequence of the "disappearance" of the Germans. It took a long time for the Germans to come out of hiding, even as they rebuilt their country in broad daylight. For what remained hidden was their complicity in eradicating Jewish life from their midst. Several new generations had to be born so that Klemperer could reemerge, thirty years after his death, into a new, reunited, confident Germany, which had seemingly put the past behind it. And even then he was misread.

For Klemperer wanted the impossible. What he wanted was to bring back to Germany what had been lost forever under the Nazis. By now most of the professors who had turned their back on him under Hitler and then resumed their careers after 1945 (with letters of good conduct from such men as Klemperer) have disappeared from the scene; but the legacy of the betrayal casts a long shadow. What needed to be put to rest, then, was not Klemperer's ambivalence about his identity, but Germany's ambivalence about its past.

It was Klemperer who clung tenaciously to the idea of a different Germany, to a notion of Germanness rooted neither in exclusion nor in violence, but in humanity and hence culture; Klemperer, not Germany. His tale is not told from the perspective of the perpetrators, the bystanders, or the victims, but from the perspective of the men and the women who were deeply committed to a culture that has disappeared from a nation that has long refused to acknowledge its demise. Klemperer's story is the story of the other Germany.

There is a tremendous arrogance in Klemperer that can be respected only in those who, like him, did not flinch in the face of evil. It is an admirable arrogance: emanating not from power and violence, but from a firm confidence in the worth of a culture that had also produced evil, and in the fundamental dignity of the human soul. And so you might

---

[27] Simha Rotem, a survivor of the Warsaw Ghetto uprising, described to Claude Lanzmann how, upon climbing out of the sewer, "I didn't see a living soul. At one point I recall feeling a kind of peace, of serenity. I said to myself: 'I'm the last Jew. I'll wait for morning, and for the Germans.'" C. Lanzmann, *Shoah: An Oral History of the Holocaust* (New York, 1985), 200.

say that Klemperer timed his reemergence well. For the idea of a multi-cultural, multi-ethnic society is still considered anathema in many precincts of German society. This, too, is the undigested legacy of Nazism and its German (and European) precursors. It is a measure of the extent to which Germany has failed to come to terms with the profound cultural causes of the Holocaust, which included the refusal to accept Jews as no less German than Bavarian peasants and Prussian Junkers. This is what Klemperer comes to tell Germany today: that the Jews were Germans, perhaps the best Germans, may be even the last Germans, for they were the ones who were not Nazis.

Filled with contempt for the Germans around him and the regime that they support, Victor Klemperer prizes cosmopolitanism and Europeanism, and rejects any kind of mythical and biological nationalism. And all the while he dreams up the Germans who vanished, wishing them into existence in his own mind. Homeless in his fatherland, he conjures up a new world from the shattered hopes of his past allegiance. His dream may never come true; but it became a best-seller in Germany. And that, too, is a kind of justice.

8

Germans as Jews
REPRESENTATIONS OF ABSENCE
IN POSTWAR GERMANY

In 1987, during a conversation with a young German scholar, I remarked that, having spent a few months in Berlin, I had been struck by its distinctly provincial air as compared with other European capitals such as Paris and London. My friend sighed in agreement, adding that in the past Berlin, too, had of course been a much more vibrant and creative city but that, "seit die Juden weg sind" (since the Jews have been gone), it has lost its cosmopolitan atmosphere.

On the face of it this was a rather straightforward assertion, and at the time I gave it little thought, although I was slightly disturbed by my own instinctive agreement with it, which implied that I too believed that the Jews (as a distinctly different category from the Germans) had made city life more interesting. That, I conceded, was *my* prejudice. Subsequently, however, I realized that my friend's comment, perceived by him as a mere statement of fact, was anything but innocent of an ambiguous, multi-layered, and quite prevalent perception of Jewish presence and absence in German history. To be sure, this complex set of attitudes about the role of Jews, and the impact of their absence (as distinct from the mechanism whereby this absence was produced), is rarely acknowledged or even perceived by many Germans. Indeed, even German filmmakers and novelists, that is, those concerned with creating verbal and visual representations for public consumption, as well as German historians of precisely the period during which Jews were transformed from a presence to an absence— scholars, in other words, who are conventionally viewed as charged with constructing more "reliable" (if less popular) representations of the past—rarely seem to be aware of the implications that this German-Jewish (negative) symbiosis has on their own work, and on that past with which it is concerned.[1] And yet, perhaps precisely because of this lack of awareness, the representation of absence is arguably one of the most crucial tropes in German literary, cinematic, and scholarly representations of recent German history.

There is a major difference between the absence of representation and the representation of absence, although at the same time there may be close links between them.[2] In the case of postwar German representations of the past, and especially of the Nazi era and the period immediately preceding it, Jews were clearly underrepresented, except as opaque objects of Nazi ferocity.[3] Although one cannot speak of a complete absence of representation, the gap between the prominent role of Jews in German society, culture, and xenophobia, on the one hand, and the marginal place they were awarded in postwar representations of that past, on the other, is quite striking.

In view of the prevalent argument in the Weimar Republic and the early years of the Third Reich of Jewish *over-representation* in the professions, the media, and the intelligentsia, their postwar under-representation in representations of that past is only one of numerous ironies characteristic of recent German history and its various literary, cinematic, and scholarly reconstructions.[4] And whatever we may say about the portrayal of Jews (or the lack thereof) in postwar German discussions of the past, it is obvious that until quite recently, little attempt had been made to grapple with the problems of representing the Holocaust. Indeed, one is hard put to think of German films or works of fiction devoted to the Jewish experience of genocide,[5] while the much larger body of German scholarship on the subject has similarly concentrated almost exclusively on the German side, and especially on

[1] D. Diner, "Negative Symbiosis: Germans and Jews After Auschwitz," in *Reworking the Past: Hitler, the Holocaust, and the Historians' Debate*, ed. P. Baldwin (Boston, 1990), 251–61.

[2] E. Said, *Beginnings: Intention and Method* (New York, 1975), chap. 5; P. de Man, *Blindness and Insight: Essays in the Rhetoric of Contemporary Criticism*, 2d rev. ed. (Minneapolis, 1986), chaps. 7 and 9.

[3] R. G. Moeller, *War Stories: The Search for a Usable Past in the Federal Republic of Germany* (Berkeley, 2001); Z. Shavit, *A Past Without Shadow: The Construction of the Past Image in the German "Story" for Children* (Tel Aviv, 1999), in Hebrew.

[4] For an early fantasy of Jewish absence, see H. Bettauer, *Die Stadt ohne Juden* (1922; Frankfurt/M., 1988).

[5] Agnieszka Holland's film *Europa Europa* (1991) is neither wholly German nor about the typical Jewish experience of the Holocaust. Conversely, Jurek Becker's literary masterpiece, *Jacob the Liar* (1969), was written by a Jewish survivor.

either the technical and bureaucratic or the political and ideological facets of genocide. While not absent, the victims remained anonymous and faceless; the evil, whatever the causes attributed to it, was in the deed (and its effects on the perpetrators), not in its application to individual human beings. This is a type of representation not unrelated to the Nazis' own perception and representation of the victims as constituting targets for their actions totally lacking individual identity. Of course, the Nazis organized genocide, while postwar German representations deplored it, but in the latter the event itself assumed an abstract quality, bereft of precisely that empathy which has in the past, as well as much more recently, been seen as central to the recreation of a historical period and to the "pleasure of narration."[6]

In the years following German reunification this situation has begun gradually to change. This can be attributed to the growing distance from the past, a greater self-confidence in the newly reestablished German nation-state, as well as to the increasingly multi-cultural nature of German society, including a tripling of its Jewish population, notwithstanding the combination of right-wing xenophobia and conservative demands to maintain Germany's *"Leitkultur"* (that is, the predominance of *German* culture) that strive to pull society back to a murky past. As Berlin becomes ever more cosmopolitan and culturally vibrant, things Jewish are now quite the vogue in more progressive German circles, even as these very same circles express doubts about such attempts finally to provide concrete representations of Jewish life in Germany and of its destruction in the reunited capital. In what follows, however, I focus on the first postwar decades in West Germany rather than on this new if closely related manifestation of troubled philosemitism.[7]

---

[6] M. Broszat, "A Plea for the Historicization of National Socialism," in Baldwin, 78.

[7] For debates on the Holocaust Memorial and the Jewish Museum in Berlin, see C. Wiedmer, *The Claims of Memory: Representations of the Holocaust in Contemporary Germany and France* (Ithaca, 1999), 120–64. In 2000 the German television network ZDF produced a 270–minute documentary by Guido Knopp titled *Holokaust* that focuses on the event. Goldhagen's *Hitler's Willing Executioners* heightened awareness of the hiatus of German representations of the Jewish experience. See chap. 6, above. Conversely, Caroline Link's film, *Beyond Silence* (1998), in which a young woman raised by two deaf parents finds her liberation through a discovery of Jewish Klezmer music—about whose origins and destruction the film remains totally silent—retains the nostalgic echo of unspoken Jewish absence that haunted previous decades. Didi Danquart's film *Jew-Boy Levi* (1998), for its part, creates a stereotypically Jewish character so foreign to his German environment that one cannot be surprised by his exclusion

Not representing a phenomenon may have to do either with its per-ceived irrelevance to current preoccupations or with a sense of unease about its implications for the present. In other words, the absence of representation may be caused by two contradictory, though not nec-essarily mutually exclusive, factors: indifference and anxiety. They are contradictory, because we are rarely anxious about things to which we are indifferent, yet they are not necessarily mutually exclusive, be-cause our indifference may be superficial and assumed, rather than a true reflection of our consciousness. We may train ourselves to feel indifferent toward an object, a person, or an event that would other-wise cause us profound anxiety. To cite just one example, also related to the present discussion by a series of ironic links, it can be argued that attitudes toward the "Arab Problem" within the pre-state Jewish com-munity (*Yishuv*) of Palestine were characterized by that same absence of representation of Palestinian Arabs that could be seen in postwar Germany vis-à-vis the Jews. Having escaped the "Jewish Question" in Europe, the Zionists confronted what they called the "Arab Problem" by not confronting it at all. This was partly a conscious decision, mo-tivated by rational political arguments, according to which this "prob-lem" ought not to be dealt with before demographic equality or, even better, superiority had been achieved. But it was also rooted in a psy-chological reaction, whereby fear of Arab nationalism and a violent re-action to Jewish settlement in Palestine manufactured an assumed indifference to the issue, indeed, an argument that the problem that had caused this anxious reaction did not exist in the first place.[8]

Conversely, representations of absence may involve direct con-frontation with an acknowledged vacuum or void, perceived as either perpetual or as having been created by the disappearance of previ-ously existing objects and entities. Yet even in this case, by their own definition, such representations are not concerned with the creation of the vacuum (even if it is not an immanent condition) but with absence as such: with the void, not with the mechanism that had emptied a for-

---

from it once the Nazis arrive on the scene. See also S. L. Gilman, "Jewish Writers in Contemporary Germany: The Dead Author Speaks," in *Anti-Semitism in Times of Cri-sis*, ed. S. L. Gilman and S. Katz (New York, 1991), 311–42; S. L. Gilman, *Jews in Today's German Culture* (Bloomington 1995); J. Borneman and J. M. Peck, *Sojourners: The Return of German Jews and the Question of Identity* (Lincoln, Neb., 1995); Y. M. Bodemann, *Gedächtnistheater: Die jüdische Gemeinschaft und ihre deutsche Erfindung* (Hamburg, 1996).

[8] See A. Shapira, *Land and Power: The Zionist Resort to Force, 1881–1948* (New York, 1992).

merly occupied space. Now representing an absence, an emptiness, a no-thing, is almost a contradiction in terms, akin to representing silence or the ineffable or perfection—that is, the Absolute, which is by definition unrepresentable. And yet we know, of course, that such aesthetic and philosophical assertions notwithstanding, humanity has rarely accepted this judgment; has indeed felt itself challenged to try nevertheless to represent precisely that which had been deemed unrepresentable. The Jews, after all, have a long tradition of representing God, who both by decree and by definition is not amenable to representation.

Yet what concerns me here is not the representation of the Absolute, at least not in so far as absolute Evil is excluded from this definition. Moreover, I am not especially interested in the absence of representation of the Jews, and especially the Holocaust, in Germany. For one thing this was such an obvious phenomenon that recent signs of hesitant, ambivalent, yet nevertheless significant change, following four decades of silence, are hardly surprising, even if every two steps forward seem to engender a couple of steps back.[9] For another this does not mean that postwar Germany has refrained from preoccupation with the reality and direct consequences of Nazi crimes, that is, the physical murder of millions of human beings.

Indeed, anyone visiting Germany even for a relatively brief period will be struck by the amount of media attention given to Nazism, including very much the genocide of the Jews.[10] Rather, what interests me here is the representation of the absence itself, the representation of the ultimate result of Nazism's "success" in bringing about the "disappearance" of Jews from Germany (or Europe), and, by extension, the representation of the nature of postwar German society and culture as compared to prewar and pre-Nazi Germany, that Germany in which there had presumably been Jews who were "done away with," even if the information available about them is neither ample nor particularly

[9] For an analysis of these developments in historiography, see U. Herbert, ed., *National Socialist Extermination Policies: Contemporary German Perspectives and Controversies* (New York, 2000), 1–52.

[10] The alleged obsession of the Germans with the Holocaust culminated in the controversy over Martin Walser's speech of October 1988. See further in O. Bartov, *Mirrors of Destruction: War, Genocide, and Modern Identity* (New York, 2000), 214–16. While the recent fascination with Jews does not necessarily mean greater knowledge of their past existence, the establishment of new university chairs in Judaic studies indicates a more profound change.

accurate. Indeed, what appears to me most fascinating in this phenomenon is the manner in which postwar German representations of Jewish absence serve an apparently crucial need in German society and culture to identify, or to empathize, with its own immediate predecessors and to perceive itself as the inheritor of a tragic history of (its own) victimhood and suffering.[11]

In reality, of course, the Jews were never absent from postwar Germany, even if their numbers were even smaller than their meager share of the population of pre-1933, and their cultural and intellectual contribution was similarly diminished.[12] But in much of the German visual and literary representational universe they are seen as absent, to the extent that one may even find the Holocaust being described as "the end of European Jewry."[13] This, in itself, is a significant conception of reality, since it implies that, whoever the Jews currently residing in Germany may be, they have little to do with *those* Jews who had become absent and with *that* world of which they had been part.[14]

More important, however, is the implicit and wholly pervasive subtext of representations of absence in the German context. After all, everyone knows quite well (thanks not least to the media's preoccu-

[11] The two best books available in German on Jewish life under the Nazi regime were translated from English: S. Friedländer, *Nazi Germany and the Jews*, vol. 1 (New York, 1997); and M. Kaplan, *Between Dignity and Despair: Jewish Life in Nazi Germany* (New York, 1998). For an argument about the German inability to write on German suffering, see W. G. Sebald, *Luftkrieg und Literatur* (Frankfurt/M., 2001). Tragically killed in a car accident in December 2001, aged 57, Sebald is, however, also the author of the most extraordinary novels on the erasure of Jewish life, identity, and memory by a non-Jewish German writer. See W. G. Sebald, *The Emigrants* (New York, 1996) and *Austerlitz* (New York, 2001).

[12] Since German reunification the number of Jews living in Germany has grown substantially, mainly thanks to immigration from Russia, from 28,000 in 1989 to well over 70,000 and perhaps as many as 100,000 today. See M. Brenner, *After the Holocaust: Rebuilding Jewish Lives in Postwar Germany* (Princeton, 1997), 145; L. Rapaport, *Jews in Germany after the Holocaust: Memory, Identity, and Jewish-German Relations* (Cambridge, 1997). For Europe as a whole, see R. E. Gruber, *Virtually Jewish: Reinventing Jewish Culture in Europe* (Berkeley, 2002).

[13] A. Hillgruber, *Zweierlei Untergang: Die Zerschlagung des Deutschen Reiches und das Ende des europäischen Judentums* (Berlin, 1986).

[14] Strictly speaking, this is true. Most Jews who stayed in Germany after the war were not born there. On the early postwar period, see A. Grossmann, "Trauma, Memory, and Motherhood: Germans and Jewish Displaced Persons in Post-Nazi Germany, 1945–1949," *ASG* 38 (1998): 215–39. A fascinating view into the life and intellectual contribution of a Jew who decided to become part of the postwar German intelligentsia is M. Reich-Ranicki, *The Author of Himself* (Princeton, 2001).

pation with the issue) where the Jews "went" and what happened to them once they got "there." It is also acknowledged that Germans, or at least some Germans, had had a great deal to do with this "disappearance." Hence, the question is not at all what brought about this absence, or why novels and films find it difficult to represent the process whereby this absence "happened" and historians tend to concentrate on the mechanics rather than the human aspects of this "event." The question is, rather, what are the implications of German representations of the past from which the Jews are either absent or, in the rare cases in which they appear (just before they disappear), are represented as outsiders: as different, strange, indeed ephemeral beings, who are obviously about to disappear at any given moment precisely because they are not an inherent part of the reality reconstructed by the filmmaker, novelist, or historian. Moreover, it is necessary to inquire as to what are the ramifications of representations of Germany's destruction during the war and its suffering following the "capitulation," or "catastrophe," from which the Jews are once more almost entirely absent or, when they do appear, seem to have fared better than the average German during their long years of disappearance.

How does one deal with the question of absence? How does one come to terms with, or overcome, the absence of an object, an entity, a memory, that is known (if only perhaps vaguely and inaccurately) to have existed before, indeed, to have been seen by many as a far too pervasive presence? Does one lament the present condition (of absence), glorify past circumstances (of presence), and simultaneously decree that the process whereby the past was transformed into the present is a matter for a different, not unimportant, but nevertheless almost entirely unrelated discussion?

My friend, of course, knew a great deal about the Holocaust. Yet he was sorry that the Jews were "gone," since Berlin (of the 1980s) appeared much more boring compared to its glorious, if also tumultuous, past (say during the Weimar Republic). Is there an implicit blame here of the absentees themselves, those eternal "Weggeher" who for some reason left Germany in the lurch?[15] Is there a connection here between

---

[15] Edgar Reitz, maker of the film *Heimat*, wrote in 1984: "The Jews, since time immemorial 'people who go away' [*Weggeher*], fit well into this American culture" which, to his mind, is responsible for the fact that "With [the NBC television mini-series] *Holocaust*, the Americans have taken away our history." Cited in E. L. Santner, *Stranded Objects: Mourning, Memory, and Film in Postwar Germany* (Ithaca, 1990), 75, 80.

this sense of a past glory somehow diminished by the Jews' absence and the anger and frustration within the German public just before and after the end of the war that they were being punished for the crimes committed (by whom?) against the Jews?—that is, that the Jews (directly or by proxy) were destroying Germany?[16]

Absence, after all, has much to do with questions of guilt and innocence, justice and punishment, death and survival, just as it is related to the problem of distinguishing between fact and image, history and memory, the represented (object, person, event) and its representation. Absence, in this specific context, compels us to think about, and yet paradoxically also enables us to repress, the crucial distinction between perpetrators and victims, however much the boundaries between them are blurred and however great the overlap may sometimes be.

One of the greatest contributions of German thought and letters in the late eighteenth and nineteenth centuries was the introduction of the notion of empathy, or *Einfühlung,* both to representations of the individual and to the study of the past. While romanticism insisted on the need to "look into" one's innermost feelings and passions, historicism sought to "feel oneself into" the past. Both the social and the human sciences and the arts are profoundly indebted to the conceptualization of and experimentation with these ideas by German philosophers, historians, writers, and artists. Yet it should be stressed that empathy is, by definition, exclusive. Only God (at least under certain circumstances) can empathize with all His creatures. For human beings, however, empathy begins with the self and is therefore deeply rooted in a narcissistic view of the world. This may greatly enrich our understanding of human psychology and history, but it may just as much distort one's perception of others. And if, as Leopold von Ranke argued, "all nations are equal under God," they are not necessarily equal under the historian's gaze. Indeed, the very process of feeling oneself into history must establish clearly defined limits and boundaries in order not to degenerate into an impressionistic world history or a series of superficial platitudes, in which empathy replaces knowledge and understanding. Moreover, since all nations, periods, and individuals are necessarily burdened (and motivated) by their own

[16] H. Arendt, "The Aftermath of Nazi Rule: Report from Germany," *Commentary* 10 (1950); B. Engelmann, *In Hitler's Germany: Daily Life in the Third Reich* (New York, 1986), 331–33; O. Bartov, *Hitler's Army: Soldiers, Nazis, and War in the Third Reich* (New York, 1991), 169–70.

specific biases and prejudices, and since these biases and prejudices normally concern other nations, periods, and individuals, empathy must perforce also lead to antipathy, or at least to empathy with antipathy, without which understanding (*Verstehen*) would remain detached from the "reality" of the past.[17]

Now, considering this intellectual heritage, as well as the traumatic events of the first half of the twentieth century, and especially the manner in which this period came to a "catastrophic" end—from which, of course, it nevertheless continued to flow, as it surely must—it is not surprising that postwar Germany was so preoccupied with the recent past and that notions of empathy and understanding have been central to both historical scholarship and literary and visual representation. This context helps us understand why much of this body of creative work has been concerned with the relationship between the nation and the individual, on the one hand, and with history's anonymous forces of destruction and the limitless misery, suffering, pain, and sorrow they had brought in their wake, on the other.

The aura of tragedy that accompanies a great deal of postwar German fiction and film is rooted in a sense of betrayal and smashed hopes, unfulfilled aspirations and disillusionment from previously held beliefs, loyalty and falsehood, innocence and victimization.[18] Politics and ideologies do not fare well in such representations; individuals and the nation (the "true" nation, the presumed conglomerate of culturally and ethnically related individuals constituting a historical, perhaps even an organic, entity, not the nation created by doctrine and coercion) are at the center of our empathy. Finally, such strong empathies and such a tragic context must necessarily engender boundaries and distance, detachment and animosity. When one's own suffering is not only great but also perceived as tragic, it is difficult to feel, or even notice, the pain of others not clearly included in this community of misfortune. In other words, empathy necessitates absence; the

---

[17] G. G. Iggers, *The German Conception of History: The National Tradition of Historical Thought from Herder to the Present*, rev. ed. (Hanover, N.H., 1988), 63–89; A. L. Willson, ed., *German Romantic Criticism* (New York, 1982).

[18] A. Kaes, *From Hitler to Heimat. The Return of History as Film* (Cambridge, Mass., 1989); J. Ryan, *The Uncompleted Past: Postwar German Novels and the Third Reich* (Detroit, 1983); E. Schlant, *The Language of Silence: West German Literature and the Holocaust* (New York, 1999). But for a different preoccupation of early postwar German cinema with nostalgic memories of the *Heimat*, see H. Fehrenbach, *Cinema in Democratizing Germany: Reconstructing National Identity after Hitler* (Chapel Hill, 1995).

deeper our empathy, the more keenly felt is the pain; the more tragic the circumstances of our empathy, the more urgent is the need for absence.

Hence, empathy and absence are as closely related as pain and indifference. Now, under conditions of a clear-cut confrontation between friend and foe, empathy with the friend will "naturally" make for hostility toward his foe. But under such perceived tragic circumstances as those of postwar Germany, where the cause for which sacrifices had been made was largely discredited, the foe can no longer fulfill this need. Since this conventional dichotomy cannot be maintained, the foe is replaced by a gaping absence, which continues to function as that with which one cannot empathize, and yet is clearly separated from the enemy, who must now be acknowledged as the true destroyer of evil.

The issue under discussion, however, is even more complex, since it is not simply that the absent must take upon itself the role which the enemy can no longer fulfill; rather, the absent is *known* to have been the victim, the true, innocent, "ideal" victim, the victim with whom one precisely *should* empathize, had one not already chosen oneself as the preferred object of empathy. This is, one might argue, only natural. Furthermore this absent victim cannot be deprived of the status of victim, since that status is openly acknowledged, even if it does not evoke empathy. Indeed, this other's victimhood *must* be emphasized and reiterated, not least because, being so clearly and evidently immense, it becomes a kind of measuring rod for one's own victimhood, just as that other's tragedy becomes a measuring rod for one's own. And yet, in this skewed universe of competing victimhood in which the rationale for self-empathy is founded on suffering, can one concede first place to another? According to this logic, the absent must become ever more abstract, precisely because its presence is both a fundamental obstruction to self-empathy—which is perceived as crucial to individual and national existence—and its precondition.

A few examples from three different areas of representation— namely, literature, film, and scholarship—must suffice to demonstrate this process. Let me begin with three important young writers who emerged in the Federal Republic in the aftermath of World War II: Heinrich Böll, Günter Grass, and Siegfried Lenz. All three had lived as children and teenagers in the Third Reich, and all had served in the military. Born in 1917, Böll spent many years at the front, whereas

Grass and Lenz, born in 1927 and 1926, respectively, were conscripted only toward the end of the war, Lenz having actually deserted from his unit, a fact rarely mentioned in the dust-jacket blurbs of his works until quite recently.[19] There is little doubt that these writers were strongly preoccupied with German history and, in some of their best works, especially with the Nazi past. What interests me here in their oeuvres is not their literary merit, which I find to be considerable, but rather the manner in which they represented that past, what concerned them most about it, and what they chose to leave out. In other words, I am interested in presence and absence in their writing on Nazism and the connections between the two.

All three writers are strongly preoccupied with the fate of the unique, remarkable, or rebellious individual in the context of a violently conformist society. In this sense they are, of course, concerned with themselves but also, by way of extension, with the options and limitations of individual action, creation, and interaction. Thus, for instance, the protagonists of Böll's *Group Portrait with Lady* (*Gruppenbild mit Dame* [1971]), Grass's *The Tin Drum* (*Die Blechtrommel* [1959]), and Lenz's *The German Lesson* (*Deutschstunde* [1968]) are all extraordinary in one way or another; surrounded by a conventional, conformist environment, they are constantly threatened by another extraordinary minority of uniquely evil individuals. No less important, all these types, the individualistic, the indifferent, and the evil, are caught in the throes of something which is beyond their comprehension and capacities, an upheaval of universal proportions, against which individualistic action is all the more remarkable, because it is so utterly hopeless. Ultimately, all, or rather, all Germans, become victims of this anonymous force, and are either physically or mentally destroyed by it. The others, the non-Germans who arrive at the scene following the catastrophe, if represented at all, are obviously outsiders to the tragedy and wholly incapable of grasping it.

What is notable about these works is not merely the fact that all Germans end up in them as victims, but that there are no other victims but Germans. This is what I would call an absence of representation. Thus, for instance, in Böll's *The Train Was on Time* (*Der Zug war pünktlich*

[19] This information was given me by Lenz himself in a private conversation in 1981. But see now "Lebenslauf Siegried Lenz" (at www.der-weg-online.de, "Literatur und Kultur") for a brief and complete biographical note. For another discussion of German postwar works of fiction and film see the final section, "Aftermath," of chap. 1, above.

[1949]), the victim is the German soldier, the innocent, war-hating, music-loving, frightened young man who gets blown up by the Polish resistance. His is a tragic figure, because he is in the clutches of forces he cannot control and is destroyed by those with whom he in fact learns to sympathize, embodied in the figure of a Polish woman who is like him but works (with much greater conviction) for the other side.

But another aspect of these literary texts seems of greater significance, namely, their manner of representing absence. What I would like to suggest is that these exceptional protagonists could in fact be easily replaced by those most obviously absent, namely the Jews. From the point of view of the regime and its followers, as well as from that of many other Germans, whether antisemitic, philosemitic, or, most commonly, indifferent, the Jews were the example par excellence of all that was exceptional, different, bizarre, in other words, unlike the rest, for better or for worse. They too were surrounded by a multitude of conformists and were hunted down by a minority of exceptionally committed, or at least extraordinarily obedient, servants of a regime sworn to their destruction and willing to further the careers of those who carried out its wishes. Yet in these novels we hardly ever encounter Jews, while we do hear a great deal about exceptional Germans.[20] This is what I would call the representation of absence, since the absence of the Jews is represented by exceptional German protagonists, and the (fictional) existence of these protagonists makes possible the absence of the Jews. For, if we are to empathize with anyone during the Nazi period, and if we simultaneously insist that the focus of our empathies must be German (as defined by the Nazi regime, i.e., excluding former Jewish citizens), then it must be someone who has very similar qualities to those of the Jew (as perceived by German society).

This is not to say, of course, that such works are allegories of the fate of Jews in Nazi Germany, whatever else they may be allegories of (*The Tin Drum* is arguably a mixed metaphor of both Hitler's and Germany's fate). I do not think that any of these writers consciously gave their protagonists perceived Jewish characteristics; rather, all of the works have a strong autobiographical element and are imbued with the writers' own sense of victimhood and singularity, which combines

---

[20] On Grass's representation of a rare Jewish character in *The Tin Drum*, see Gilman, "Jewish Writers," 314–16.

the romantic notion of the artist with the specific details of their lives and times. Yet through this self-empathy, which in another way also makes possible empathy with the nation (in the sense of at least one righteous man in the city of Sodom), they need no longer empathize with their own, and their nation's, victims. Indeed, they thereby exclude those victims from the sphere of empathy altogether, since, as I have noted, empathy must by definition be exclusive rather than inclusive in order to have any meaning at all. Hence, the representation of absence acts as a crucial mechanism of empathic self-representation even under the most unlikely circumstances, such as those of persecution and genocide.

A later generation of German filmmakers was also greatly preoccupied with history.[21] Here I will also mention only three of the most prominent German directors of the 1970s and 1980s—Alexander Kluge, Edgar Reitz, and Rainer Werner Fassbinder—although many others come to mind, such as Hans-Jürgen Syberberg, Volker Schlöndorff, Helma Sanders-Brahms, Werner Herzog, and Wim Wenders. Here too I would like to focus only on one aspect of these filmmakers' work, that is, the interplay between presence and absence. Alexander Kluge's film *The Patriot* (*Die Patriotin* [1977–79]), about which I have written in greater detail elsewhere, is ostensibly about German history.[22] Not surprisingly, it is a tale of tragedy and folly, hopelessness and despair, destruction and mutilation (of people, of landscapes, of history, of the film itself). As a fragmented pastiche of images and words, it is a truly postmodern work, an attempt to confront both the conventions of filmmaking and of German history. It remains, however, part of a postwar German tradition of representation in that it presents the Germans as victims of history and its anonymous, evil forces and in that it is innocent of any preoccupation with other victims.

Considering the film's focus on World War II, the total absence of the Jews, whose own encounter with German history ended up in genocide, is especially blatant. Yet Kluge's insistence on digging up the past and revealing its hidden fragments is once more an exercise not merely in the absence of representation but also in the representation of ab-

---

[21] Kaes; Santner.

[22] O. Bartov, *Murder in Our Midst: The Holocaust, Industrial Killing, and Representation* (New York, 1996), chap. 7.

sence. For the heavy emphasis on the centrality of death and destruction in German history creates a consistent subtext that must perforce make the informed (and who is not informed on this?) viewer think of the Holocaust, an event never explicitly mentioned in the film. Once again we find ourselves empathizing with the victims of an inexplicable, omnipotent power and especially with the unique, eccentric schoolteacher who has taken upon herself the task of remaking history, not by telling it as "it really happened" but by changing it so as to be able to tell it "as I would like it to have been."

We can think of Kluge's protagonist as a survivor of the genocide who would greatly prefer *not* to tell the world what she had actually experienced—which she obviously cannot tell in any case, since no one can tell this tale without distorting it[23]—but, rather, to be able to change the past itself and thereby to transform it into a tale that *can* be told. I do not believe that this is the conscious subtext of Kluge's film; he truly empathizes with his heroic schoolteacher, as he does with the (German, not the Russian) victims of Stalingrad, a monumental battle with which he is so obviously obsessed. But this is nevertheless a representation of absence in the sense I have been developing here. Both Kluge and his viewers must, in the back of their minds, be constantly thinking about the genocide of the Jews. For as the camera eye winds its way through the piles of human and material wreckage which constitute Kluge's view of the (German) past, it is also traversing the very lands of (Jewish) ashes and obliterated memories that haunt the poetry of Paul Celan.[24]

Edgar Reitz's view of history, as presented in the film *Heimat* (1980–84), is far less fragmented and apocalyptic than Kluge's, despite, or perhaps precisely because of, the fact that he claims to be much more preoccupied with memory than with history. The German (rural) memory of the past, according to Reitz, is simple, modest, warm, and tightly knit; it is enclosed upon itself, and there is little room in it for outsiders. Indeed, the outside intrudes only in the shape of war, foreign countries, modernity, and Jews. The war is where the community must send its sons; foreign countries are where some other sons go and are unrecognizably transformed, not for the better; modernity is what finally destroys the harmony of village life, community, and the fam-

---

[23] P. Levi, *The Drowned and the Saved* (New York, 1988), 82–85.
[24] I refer here especially to Celan's poem "*Engführung.*"

ily; and the Jews are an ephemeral existence, appearing only to disappear rapidly as a somewhat disturbing, ambivalent presence, provoking hostility and fleetingly witnessing intimacy of which they have no part. Reitz's is a simpler work, and its symbolism is never very subtle. And, since it is about German *memory* rather than history, and because it represents that memory as wholly turned upon itself, it leaves no room for those whom the Germans would rather forget or repress, that is, their victims.

And yet Reitz's work too is dependent for its coherence not merely on an absence of representation, but also on a representation of absence. Conscious of a context of prejudice and genocide, evil and complicity, it must escape to the environment of a remote anachronistic village, finally connected to modernity only following World War II and the (apparently lamentable) Americanization of Germany. And yet, even in that distant location, the film cannot completely ignore a presence that its own realistic and traditional technique (so unlike Kluge's) must somehow acknowledge. Hence, Reitz feels obliged to make for a momentary appearance of the absent, if only in order to indicate that the absent remained absent for his protagonists, even while they were actually there. He must make the point that the Jews had no role in German (rural) memory, precisely because he knows that German memory is inseparably tied to visions of genocide. Indeed, the major motivation of *Heimat*, as Reitz himself argued, was to give back German history to the Germans, after it was taken away from them by the American film *Holocaust*—that is, taken away from them by the Jews, who are the main protagonists of both *Holocaust*, the mini-series, and the historical event of Nazi genocide.[25]

I suggest that the absence of the Jews is the fundamental subtext of *Heimat*, its motivation and the unspoken arbiter of its content. Without this absence, the film would have been nothing more than a sentimental, overlong tale of rural life in a God forsaken province. It is that absence that gives it meaning, providing it with the context it so emphatically rejects. In this sense *Heimat* is a film not about memory but about amnesia, that is, about the absence of memory and all that can be remembered and must nevertheless be erased.

Rainer Werner Fassbinder seems to have been more concerned with

---

[25] See note 15, above; see also E. Reitz, *Liebe zum Kino: Utopien und Gedanken zum Autorenfilm, 1962–1983* (Cologne, 1984), 102, 145–46.

representing Jews than any of his colleagues.[26] Perhaps the most accomplished director of the New German Cinema, he also gained a fair measure of notoriety. His films have enjoyed wide success in many countries, including Israel; yet his representations of Jews make the most blatant use of antisemitic stereotypes of any prominent German filmmaker. I would argue that Fassbinder, however, is not in fact concerned with Jews. His protagonists, like those of all these filmmakers and writers, are marginal yet exceptional individuals, simultaneously survivors and victims of a catastrophe. In *The Marriage of Maria Braun* (*Die Ehe der Maria Braun* [1978]), the main character, a truly heroic figure, survives all hardship and betrayal, only to be blown up in a gas explosion in her villa, which she had gained through hard work and determination. (One cannot avoid thinking of the implicit association made here with those other victims of gas never represented by the director).

In *Lili Marleen* (1980), yet another survivor of anonymous destruction (with whose well-known chiefs she had had a brief but glamorous association) fares much worse than the shadowy figures of Jews, who seem to be more capable of controlling the forces of evil, not least by their great fortunes. Indeed, as has been pointed out, the Jews appear to extract themselves from the Holocaust with little difficulty and to thrive once more, while the heroine, abandoned by her Jewish lover, is destroyed along with Hitler's empire.[27] We, the informed viewers, may of course be thinking of Auschwitz as we watch the stylized fighting at the front. But the absence of genocide makes room for the presence of money-grubbing Jews, and the misfortunes of the heroine are linked to the dubious accomplishments of the Jewish survivors (of an unmentioned Holocaust). Ultimately, it is the power of the Jews that is in the background of German suffering, and it is the absence of the Jewish genocide that serves as a crucial precondition for the representation of German victimhood.

Finally, I extend my argument to a few words about the historians. German scholarship has produced a remarkable volume of work on the Holocaust. In this sense there is no room to speak of an absence. Yet it is worthwhile to examine the nature of this scholarship and the

[26] G. Koch, *Die Einstellung ist die Einstellung: Visuelle Konstruktionen des Judentums* (Frankfurt/M., 1992), 246.

[27] Ibid., 254.

main focus of its concerns and lacunae. In this context I would like to mention three historians who have had a particularly strong influence on the historiography of the National Socialist regime in the two to three decades before reunification: Martin Broszat, Hans Mommsen, and Andreas Hillgruber. Broszat's well-known plea for a historicization of National Socialism provides a good starting point for this brief discussion, since it touches directly on some of the issues with which I am concerned.[28] Broszat argued that there was a need to reintroduce the notion of empathy to the study of Nazism and to eliminate the distancing techniques and rhetoric employed in such writing, whose impact had been to diminish greatly the pleasure of writing and reading such history. That is, Broszat quite clearly called for what I claim had been present all along in German cinematic and literary representation of the period: German empathy for their own history and its protagonists.

In his correspondence with Broszat, Saul Friedländer argued that it was still too early to approach Nazism in the same manner as one would, for instance, sixteenth-century France.[29] Yet, looking at this debate from the perspective of almost two decades, I am struck by the fact that Broszat's basic assumption—namely, that such empathy was lacking and, therefore, had to be reintroduced—was rather off the mark, since even among the historians empathy was never absent, even if it was wrapped in what he thought of as a kind of compulsory and unproductive detachment. To be sure, this empathy was expressed indirectly, in that German historians writing on Nazism, and even specifically on the Holocaust, had shown a complete inability to empathize with the victims, even while they did indeed distance themselves from the perpetrators (but not from the remaining, vast majority of Germans).

This is precisely what I would term a representation of absence, since the absence of empathy for the Jewish victims of Nazism left enough room for—indeed, made necessary—empathy with the German victims and survivors, who, from the perspective of the Jewish and other political and "racial" enemies of the Reich, were in fact the (often complicit) bystanders. Hence, the absence of representation (of

[28] Broszat, "Historicization."
[29] M. Broszat and S. Friedländer, "A Controversy about the Historicization of National Socialism," in Baldwin, 129–30.

Jewish victims as objects of empathy) is closely linked to a representation of absence, whereby the impossible empathy for the Jews is directed at the Germans, those large multitudes who were neither direct perpetrators nor active resisters but, instead, either complicit or resistant bystanders. The need for empathy has been rightly seen by Broszat as a crucial component of the historian's craft. But those who are the most obvious objects of empathy cannot be accorded that emotion, because, being as they are outside the frame of reference of identification and intimacy, empathy for them would block the option of empathy for oneself, creating thereby an unbearable psychological burden. This is what makes the mechanism of representing absence through enhanced empathy for one's own fate as individual, group, and nation all the more urgent.

Broszat's essay was important because it pointed to some of the fundamental problems of absence and representation (though I do not believe that he was aware of the implications of his argument as previously outlined). Hans Mommsen's contribution to the debate was of a more technical nature, insisting on the "functionalist" aspects of the "Final Solution" and the "cumulative radicalization" of policies during the Third Reich that led to genocide.[30] In one sense there is no empathy here at all, merely a detailed (and contested) interpretation of how a modern, bureaucratic, industrial state launches itself on the path to unprecedented mass murder. And yet here too absence and empathy constitute the fundamental subtext of the whole interpretive edifice. This could be gleaned momentarily from the expression of empathy made by Mommsen when writing on the "sober" mentality of German soldiers on the Eastern Front, which obviously also demonstrated sympathy for their fate.[31]

Most of the time, however, the subtext of the argument can be gathered only through the intense effort to understand the psychology of the middle-ranking perpetrators, on the one hand, and from Mommsen's complete lack of interest in their victims, who serve merely as the (somewhat opaque) object of the former's thoughts and actions, on the other. The absence of any empathy with the victims is not a simple function of Mommsen's focus on the perpetrators; rather, it is a pre-

[30] H. Mommsen, *From Weimar to Auschwitz* (Princeton, 1991), chaps. 7 and 11.

[31] H. Mommsen, "Kriegserfahrungen," in *Über Leben im Krieg: Kriegserfahrungen in einer Industrieregion 1939–1945*, ed. U. Borsdorf and M. Jamin (Reinbek bei Hamburg, 1989), 13.

condition for his interpretation, since any treatment of the victims as potential objects of empathy would strongly undermine the main thrust of the argument, which is, after all, based on the perpetrators' perception of reality. Having chosen that perspective, any discussion of reality from the perspective of the victims would seem a mere interference, an unnecessary complication, irrelevant to both the argument and its objects. Yet, of course, this too is a representation of absence, in that the only reason for our interest in the mentality and thought processes of such otherwise utterly uninteresting characters as Mommsen's functionaries is what they were actually doing. In other words, it is the absentees who are the raison d'être of the whole interpretive undertaking, even if they appear only as numbers and figures distorted through the Nazi prism.[32]

Andreas Hillgruber, my final example, expressed great interest in the objects of the historian's empathy and identification, though his approach was much less subtle than Broszat's relatively sophisticated (and ultimately far more influential) argument. As I have noted elsewhere, there is a clear link between Hillgruber's insistence that the historian (meaning, of course, the German historian) *must* identify with the fate of the Wehrmacht's soldiers in the eastern provinces of the Reich, his assertion that if there is any tragic element in World War II it is to be found in the carving up of Germany and the division of the world between the two flanking, non-European superpowers, and his cool and detached essay on the "end of European Jewry."[33]

Hillgruber feels, just like Broszat, that the historian must empathize with his protagonists, and he is similarly quite incapable of seeing the Jews as his protagonists, let alone empathizing with them. More radically than Broszat, he chooses to identify with the soldiers, the population, and even some of the Nazi party functionaries of the areas in the East under threat of invasion by the Red Army. While it is crucial to his argument, the genocide of the Jews is explicitly and intentionally absented from his empathic portrayal of the last months of the war in the East. It is crucial not only because it is constantly present both in the mind of the historian and in the minds of his protagonists, but also because it has to be removed so as to make empathy possible. It is

---

[32] This is of course the argument already made in H. Arendt's *Eichmann in Jerusalem: A Report on the Banality of Evil* (New York, 1963). See also now Eyal Sivan's film *The Specialist* (1999).

[33] Hillgruber, *Zweierlei;* Bartov, *Murder,* chap. 4.

there, but it is not there; it is relevant, but it is not relevant; it is a precondition for the events described, yet it is not discussed. And when, in the second essay of Hillgruber's volume, the focus is on the genocide of the Jews, the tone and style of writing undergo a radical transformation, adopting the bureaucratic language and detached rhetoric which both Hillgruber and Broszat have found so detrimental to good historical writing.[34] In this second essay, there is no case to be made of the absence of representation but very much of the representation of absence, since, while Hillgruber is explicitly concerned with the manner in which the physical absence of the Jews was achieved, the Jews as protagonists deserving the scholar's empathy are wholly absent from it, until their existence is systematically and totally "ended," in stark contradiction to the Germans, whose continued existence makes it possible for them to remain victims of a tragedy.

Tragedy is an important term in this context. It implies, we assume, an event or a circumstance in which the malicious forces of history had distorted the individual's or the nation's (heroic, in part even well-intentioned) actions into a self-destructive process, entrapping the individual in an inexplicable, and inescapable web of errors and horrors, disillusionment and despair. What is absent from such German representations of the past is the tragedy of others. Being the true precondition for Germany's own tragedy, that other tragedy must be represented as an absence, an unspoken, unexpressed, separate moment which is both known and unknown to have constituted the essential starting point of the one tale with which Germans can wholeheartedly empathize: their own history.

That other tragedy—which is, of course, radically different in that its objects were caught up not in the web of their own doings but in that of others—must serve as an unacknowledged model for comparison; one must constantly contend with the model and always avoid direct comparison. Even Ernst Nolte does not directly compare German and Jewish victimhood, preferring, much more conveniently, to use Stalin's victims for that purpose.[35] Hence, the representation of ab-

---

[34] Hillgruber, *Zweierlei*, 95–96; Bartov, *Murder*, 85–86.

[35] E. Nolte, "Between Historical Legend and Revisionism? The Third Reich in the Pe spective of 1980," and "The Past That Will Not Pass: A Speech That Could Be Written but Not Delivered," both in *Forever in the Shadow of Hitler? Original Documents of the Historikerstreit, the Controversy Concerning the Singularity of the Holocaust* (Atlantic Highlands, N.J., 1993), 13–14, 21–22, respectively.

sence is a basic, and yet never to be articulated, precondition of postwar German perceptions of the Nazi past. It is not confined to the sphere of literature, film, and scholarship. As my friend in Berlin had (quite unintentionally) shown me, it is an important element in many Germans' self-representation: the sense that something that had previously been there is gone and that, while this disappearance has had long-term cultural, political, and psychological consequences, it can nevertheless not be processed by way of empathy and understanding. The process whereby the Jews were made into an absence is therefore detached from the tragedy that this absence has meant for Germany, and that tragedy of Jewish absence is subsumed under the greater tragedy of German fate and history. In this case the Jews have played a double role in the tragic tales of modern German history—first by being there, and then by "going away."

Now that after the fall of the Berlin Wall the Jews have begun to "return," and as growing multiculturalism and globalization are accompanied by a new interest in Jewish culture and history among young Germans, this distorted postwar view of the past may be gradually changing. It is still difficult to say where this transformation will lead, and as recent fears over "foreigners" eroding Germany's cultural identity, resentment about monuments commemorating Germany's victims, and reluctance to compensate former Nazi slave laborers have shown, the past is still very much part of the German present and at times casts a dark shadow over contemporary issues. Nevertheless, there are signs of positive change. Precisely because Germany's war and the Holocaust were inextricably linked, perhaps the final end of the long postwar years will also herald the beginning of a post-Holocaust era of greater mutual understanding and more compassion for the multitudes discarded by the ferocity of the previous century.

Abbreviations

AHR	*American Historical Review*
ASG	*Archiv für Sozialgeschichte*
BA-MA	*Bundesarchiv-Militärarchiv, Freiburg im Breisgau*
BDIP	*Blätter für Deutsche und Internationale Politik*
BG	*Boston Globe*
BZ	*Berliner Zeitung*
CEH	*Central European History*
CHE	*Chronicle of Higher Education*
CI	*Critical Inquiry*
CoEH	*Contemporary European History*
CT	*Chicago Tribune*
DH	*Diplomatic History*
DNN	*Dresdner Neueste Nachrichten*
DPA	*Deutsche Presse-Agentur*
EHQ	*European History Quarterly*
FA	*Foreign Affairs*
FAZ	*Frankfurter Allgemeine Zeitung*
FR	*Frankfurter Rundschau*
FRT	*Historical Journal of Film, Radio and Television*
GH	*German History*
GPS	*German Politics and Society*
GSR	*German Studies Review*
H&M	*History & Memory*
HGS	*Holocaust and Genocide Studies*
HJ	*Historical Journal*
JGR	*Journal of Genocide Research*
JIDG	*Jahrbuch des Instituts für Deutsche Geschichte*
JMH	*Journal of Modern History*
JPS	*Journal of Palestine Studies*

JSS	*Journal of Strategic Studies*
KA	*Kameradschaft Aktiv*
LAT	*Los Angeles Times*
LF	*Lingua Franca*
LRB	*London Review of Books*
LT	*London Times*
LTM	*Les Temps Modernes*
MdL	*Le Monde des Livres*
MGFA	*Militärgeschichtliches Forschungsamt* (Military History Research Institute)
MH	*The Journal of Military History*
MiH	*Miami Herald*
NGC	*New German Critique*
NO	*Le Nouvel Observateur*
NYRB	*New York Review of Books*
NYT	*New York Times*
NYTBR	*New York Times Book Review*
NYTM	*New York Times Magazine*
NZZ	*Neue Zürcher Zeitung*
OPIA	*Occasional Papers in International Affairs*
P&P	*Past & Present*
POQ	*Public Opinion Quarterly*
PP	*Patterns of Prejudice*
PS	*Political Psychology*
SA	*Sturmabteilung* (Storm Troops of the Nazi Party)
SäZ	*Sächsische Zeitung*
SD	*Sicherheitsdienst* (Security Service of the SS)
SK	*Salzburger Krone*
SS	*Schutzstaffel* ("Defense Squad" of the Nazi Party)
ST	*Sunday Times*
StZ	*Stuttgarter Zeitung*
SZ	*Süddeutsche Zeitung*
TAJ	*Tel Aviver Jahrbuch für deutsche Geschichte*
TAZ	*Die Tageszeitung*
TB	*Teoria ve-Bikoret*
TLS	*Times Literary Supplement*
TNR	*The New Republic*
TNY	*The New Yorker*

VfZ	*Vierteljahrshefte für Zeitgeschichte*
VS	*Vigntième Siècle*
WP	*Washington Post*
WSJ	*Wall Street Journal*
WT	*Washington Times*

Acknowledgments

I would like to thank the following publishers, journals, and magazines for allowing me to use revised, updated, expanded, or abridged versions of book chapters, articles, and review essays in this book. Chapter 1 is composed of revised, updated, and somewhat abridged versions of the chapters: "Savage War," originally published in *Confronting the Nazi Past: New Debates in Modern German History*, ed. Michael Burleigh (London: Collins & Brown, 1996), 125–39; and "The Conduct of War: Soldiers and the Barbarization of Warfare," in *Resistance Against the Third Reich: 1933–1990*, ed. M. Geyer and J. W. Boyer (Chicago: University of Chicago Press, 1994), 39–52. Chapter 2 is composed of revised, updated, and in some places abridged versions of the chapters: "From *Blitzkrieg* to Total War: Controversial Links between Image and Reality," in *Stalinism and Nazism: Dictatorships in Comparison*, ed. Ian Kershaw and Moshe Lewin (Cambridge: Cambridge University Press, 1997), 158–84; and "Whose History Is It, Anyway? The Wehrmacht and German Historiography," in *War of Extermination: The German Military in World War II, 1941–1944*, ed. H. Heer and K. Naumann (New York: Berghahn Books, 2000), 400–416. Chapter 3 is a revised, updated, and expanded version of the essay "The Lost Cause," in *The New Republic* (October 4, 1999): 47–53. Chapter 4 is composed of revised, updated, and expanded versions of the essays: "The Penultimate Horror," in *The New Republic* (October 13, 1997): 48–53; and "The Devil in the Details: The Concentration Camp as Historical Construct," in *German Historical Institute London Bulletin* XXI/2 (November 1999): 33–41. Chapter 5 is a revised, updated, and expanded version of "Ordinary Monsters," *The New Republic* (April 29, 1996): 32–38. Chapter 6 is a revised and slightly abridged (in the footnote apparatus) version of "Reception and Perception: Goldhagen's Holocaust and the World," in *The "Goldhagen Effect": History, Memory, Nazism—Facing the German Past*, ed. Geoff Eley (Ann Arbor: University of Michigan Press, 2000),

33–87. Chapter 7 is a revised, updated, and expanded version of "The Last German," in *The New Republic* (December 28, 1998): 34–42. Chapter 8 is a revised, updated, and expanded version of "'Seit die Juden weg sind . . .': Germany, History, and Representations of Absence," in *A User's Guide to German Cultural Studies*, ed. Scott Denham, Irene Kacandes, and Jonathan Petropoulos (Ann Arbor: The University of Michigan Press, 1997), 209–26.

Index

Absence: empathy and, 223–25; historiography and, 231–36; of Holocaust from *GSWW*, 69–70, 73; of Jews from literature, 227–28; mechanisms of, 219–20, 222; memory and, 229–30; of representation, 217, 219, 226–28, 230, 232–33; tragedy and, 224–25, 227, 235
Almog, Shmuel, 123
Aly, Götz, xvii, 82–88, 128, 196
Antisemitism, xviii–xix, 204; absence of in postwar Germany, 146, 153; American view, 143–44; Christian/European tradition, 82, 123–24; in concentrationary universe, 115–16; German version, ix–x; of Hitler, 96–98; Israeli view, 179–80; Poland, 91, 120; as root of Holocaust, 125–26. *See also* Jews
Arab-Israeli war (1967), 56, 143
Arendt, Hannah, 123, 156, 183
Aronson, Shlomo, 179
Atrocities, 104–5
Auschwitz, 11, 195, 231

Barbarossa Decree, 5–6, 18
Behaviorism, xx, 140, 157, 181–91
Berlin, 216, 218, 223
Bitburg military cemetery, 12, 158
Black Book of Communism (Courtois), 166–68
Blitzkrieg, xvii, 33–35; airpower, 38–40; controversies and historiography, 43–52; criminal policies and, 43–44; economy and, 44–45; genocide and, 44, 48–52; images and representation, 39–40, 52–58; industrial and manpower constraints on, 37–38, 41–42; Marxist approaches, 47–48; as media spectacle, 57–58; realities and impressions, 35–43; Soviet Union and, 39–43; as tactical innovation, 47–48
Böll, Heinrich, 30–31, 225–26
Bolshevism, 5, 39, 49–50

Britain, 59, 62
Britain, Battle of, 36–37, 38
Brossat, Alain, 164
Broszat, Martin, 81, 88, 232–34
Browning, Christopher, 82, 87, 129–30, 144, 147, 156–57, 164, 181–82
Buchenwald, 110, 194
Bureaucrats, 82, 96, 98, 128–29, 234
Burrin, Philippe, 169

Camps, plural terminology, 165–66
Cat and Mouse (Grass), 31
Celan, Paul, 195, 229
Chaumont, Jean-Michel, 167
Churban, 126
Class issues, 27–29, 46–47, 189
Communism, 103–4, 106, 168, 199, 206
Community of suffering, 102–5
Competition of Victims, The (Chaumont), 167
Comradeship, 19–25
Conan, Éric, 169–70
Concentrationary universe, xvi, 81, 163, 168; antisemitism in, 115–16; autonomy of, xvii–xviii, 102–4, 108–9; hierarchy of, 103–4, 109, 112; as historical construct, 111–21; ideology, 105–10, 115; impact on twentieth century, 111, 120–21; as institution, 106, 109, 115–16; phases of, 117–18; sociological analysis, xvii–xviii, 99; structures and functions of, 102–3. *See also* Death camps
Consensual genocide, 93–98
Coquio, Catherine, 167
Course of German History, The (Taylor), 122–23
Courtois, Stéphane, 166–68
Criminal orders, 5–6, 8, 12–13, 17–18
Criminal policies, xi–xii, 64–65, 158; Blitzkrieg and, 43–44; normalization of, 166–68
Cumulative radicalization, 124, 154, 233